Intercultural Communication

Intercultural Communication

Everett M. Rogers
University of New Mexico

Thomas M. Steinfatt
University of Miami

WAVELAND PRESS, INC.

Prospect Heights, Illinois

For information about this book, write or call:
Waveland Press, Inc.
P.O. Box 400
Prospect Heights, Illinois 60070
(847) 634-0081

To

Corinne L. Shefner-Rogers
and
Cherie Berton Steinfatt

with love

Contents

Preface

Learning how others think about their lives and the world they live in is fascinating. Intercultural communication is the process through which we gain the insight provided by different perspectives and experiences. Few other topics can match the human interest inherent in intercultural communication. Students are naturally curious about how to develop personal relationships with individuals different from themselves in religion, socioeconomic status, gender, or sexual orientation.

This book seeks to build on the fascination that intercultural communication naturally holds for everyone. The United States is increasingly diverse in a cultural sense. We include numerous case illustrations of communication difficulties encountered because the participants in a communication situation did not share certain cultural assumptions. Many of us have experienced the difficulties of communicating effectively with an "unalike" other person, perhaps even a friend or a partner.

We think a historical approach to intercultural communication provides the foundation necessary to understand barriers to effective intercultural communication. We begin this book with a history of intercultural contact. We then explore the evolution of the field of intercultural communication from its sociological roots to its founding by the anthropologist Edward T. Hall and others at the Foreign Service Institute in the U.S. Department of State after World War II. The reader can better understand such important concepts as nonverbal communication, assimilation, ethnocentrism, prejudice, and individualism/collectivism by becoming familiar with the circumstances in which these concepts were created.

This book seeks to raise consciousness about cultural differences and to help students become more competent in intercultural communication. *Our own* way of eating, talking, gesturing, behaving, and thinking is not the *only* way, nor necessarily the *best* way (if such a thing exists). As you read this book, and discuss it with others, we hope you will learn to put yourself in the role of others who are unlike you and to see the world more through their eyes.

Competence in intercultural communication is important to success in meeting life goals. We hope that our book helps you to achieve this success.

Everett M. Rogers   Thomas M. Steinfatt
Albuquerque   Coral Gables

Acknowledgments

This book benefits from the inputs made by several intercultural communication scholars. We thank Professor Jack Condon, a distinguished scholar of intercultural communication at the University of New Mexico, for his advice and encouragement in writing this book. So also do we acknowledge the many useful inputs from Dr. Arvind Singhal, Associate Professor in the School of Interpersonal Communication at Ohio University. Dr. Brad Hall at the University of New Mexico served as a guide to us in planning and writing *Intercultural Communication*. Professor Young Yun Kim at the University of Oklahoma read and reacted to a near-final draft of this book. Bill Hart, at Old Dominion University, who is the ultimate information-seeker, also read earlier drafts of this book and made helpful suggestions. Kathyrn Sorrells and Sheena Malhotra, colleagues in intercultural communication at the University of New Mexico, called our attention to voices that we might not otherwise have heard. Yumiko Yokochi at the University of New Mexico advised us on our many examples involving Japanese culture. Kathyrn Sorrells and another colleague at the University of New Mexico, Professor Miguel Gandert, provided many of the photographs that illustrate the book. Dianne Millette, Gonzalo Soruco, and Edward Dreyer of the University of Miami offered valuable intercultural insights. We also thank the students in our intercultural communication classes at the University of New Mexico and the University of Miami who read and reacted to previous drafts of this volume.

Chapter 1

Context and Contact

> Culture [is] the total communication framework: words, actions, postures, gestures, tones of voice, facial expressions, the [handling of] time, space, and materials, and the way he[/she] works, plays, makes love, and defends himself [/herself]. All these things and more are complete communication systems with meanings that can be read correctly only if one is familiar with the behavior in its historical, social and cultural context.
>
> Edward T. Hall (1976)

This book focuses on the relationship of culture and communication and how these concepts are interwoven. In separating the strands we will discover concepts integral to understanding both ourselves and others. If you have never taken an anthropology course, you will learn the rudiments of the concept of culture. If you have never taken a communication course, you will learn the fundamentals of the communication process. If you have been exposed to both, you will have a head start in understanding the fascinating topic of *intercultural communication*, defined as the exchange of information between individuals who are unalike culturally.

Context is a key element in both communication and culture. In order to understand any culture, we must begin with the context that shaped the tools developed to survive in a particular environment, and the definitions of the symbols of verbal and nonverbal communication. The expectations individuals have for consequences of particular actions depend on the experiences of others woven into a particular cultural context and passed on to future generations. History chronicles the events that contour a society's character and determine the direction of its cultural flow.

1

How men and women think is not simply a function of what they have seen or felt in their own lives. Nor is their form of thought a genetic shadow cast by their parents or grandparents. People think within the intellectual and cultural currents that surround them—currents with histories, even if the sources cannot be seen from downstream. Even dissenters are soaked in the currents that they believe themselves to be swimming against. To paraphrase Marx, men and women think, but not in a language or concepts or even emotions utterly of their own making (Gitlin, 1995, p. 200).

The study of intercultural communication can help us step back from our habitual ways of viewing the world and open our eyes to the influences that have constructed our ways of thinking.

This chapter traces how intercultural communication became so important in our daily lives. Several centuries ago the world seemed small, and most people only communicated with others much like themselves. The typical villager in Medieval Europe seldom traveled as far as the nearby market town. There were no strangers in the village. Over the years, improved transportation brought wider travel; newer means of communication allowed information exchange over longer distances. Today, improved technologies of communication (like the Internet) and more rapid means of transportation (like the Concorde) have increased the likelihood of intercultural communication. Trade and travel brought strangers into face-to-face contact. So did invasion, warfare, and colonialization.

Why Study Intercultural Communication?

For many people, the sheer joy of learning about other cultures is sufficient reason to study intercultural communication. They are curious about how different worldviews affect communication and human understanding. People who consider their own culture as the only culture often feel that they do not need to study how others see the world. They presume that everyone sees the world pretty much as they do, or they are *ethnocentric*, judging other cultures as inferior to their own culture. A few people are even *xenophobic*, fearing that which is foreign, strange, and different. We will see some of the devastating effects of xenophobia and ethnocentrism later in this chapter.

Many of us perceive the world through the eyes of a single culture, surrounded by other people with similar views. In this chapter we attempt to move away from that monocultural viewpoint. The ability to see the world from different points of view is fundamental to the process of becoming intercultural. While students can study intercultural communication from their own single point of view, they will not learn or retain as much as students who are aware of multiple perspectives. This is not to say that the student's existing point of view is wrong and that another one is right. Rather, it is to suggest that there are different ways of thinking and that such differences must be recognized and respected.

Perhaps one of the most illuminating aspects of intercultural communication is that it opens our minds to the interplay of varied influences. In the West, we tend to categorize knowledge into clearly delineated segments—history, sociology, anthropology, communication. Different disciplines focus on different aspects of the same behavior or event. Before we discuss specific communication concepts, we borrow from several other disciplines to present an overview of how intercultural events can be perceived.

While in-depth history of even one culture is beyond the scope of this book, we want to introduce you to a sampling of historical influences. By looking at a few specific examples, we hope to convey the fact that culture is pervasive—and that it hides more than it reveals. Much of what you read may appear contradictory—a hint at the multiple interpretations possible of a single event. Looking back we can identify the consequences of the historical events that formed the backbone of future conceptions—constructions that define a people, their dignity, their status, and their connections.

Collective Cultural Consciousness

One of the concepts of cultural groups that acts as a message filter is *collective cultural consciousness*, defined as an embedded memory of historical events that are particularly significant to a given cultural group. These experiences are seen as so important that the culture in question *defines* itself at least in part by these events. The Holocaust is part of the collective cultural consciousness of Judaism. The behavior of Western merchants, missionaries, and soldiers during the opening of China to Western trade helped to define the concept of a Westerner in the Chinese collective consciousness. In the United States, the war for independence from Britain, the Westward expansion, and the role of defender of the free world during World War II are such events. When people from different cultures talk to each other or interpret world events, the meanings they assign to messages are automatically filtered through the collection of attitudes learned from their own cultures.

In order to understand the collective consciousness of a given culture, we must understand the most significant influences contributing to its *worldview*. In most cultures, religion is a primary component. It explains the unexplainable and is a foundation for many of the beliefs in a culture. We do not need to know all the historical events of the culture or all the tenets of its religions. Rather, we need to examine how members of the culture understand the outstanding features of their historical interaction with other cultures, features often told in narratives—whether stories read to children or the history taught in schools.

Our approach to intercultural communication involves perspective taking. Taking the role of the other (empathy) usually leads to important differences in the perception of a situation. Meanings are formed within people engaged in intercultural interactions based partly on their perceptions of the situation. When their belief systems include an understanding of the world from the perspective of the other, that is the necessary first step to improving communication across cultural boundaries.

We have selected historical events that provide an understanding of today's intercultural communication throughout the world. We write from a viewpoint that differs from the way these events are often understood in an effort to discover the effects of contact with outsiders. Everyone has some conception of history, and the specifics of that conception determine the background for interpreting current intercultural messages. There are certain events that have influenced collective cultural consciousness so strongly—and often in contradictory terms depending on the culture—that a solid understanding of intercultural communication is simply not possible without some knowledge of these defining events. Most importantly, these events teach us about the consequences of ignoring intercultural communication and rejecting attempts to understand others. The history of interactions among peoples of the world too often demonstrates the consequences of prejudice, discrimination, ethnocentrism, and xenophobia.

Increasing Intercultural Contact

There may have been a time when there was no intercultural communication, when human groups roamed in limited geographical areas populated only by themselves. Thousands of years ago, large numbers of small cultural groups lived in relatively isolated seclusion over much of the earth's surface. Intercultural communication occurred when groups encountered each other—in the form of trade, war and conflicts, romantic and sexual relations, and other human forms of interaction.

The beginnings of interactions between cultures separated by larger geographic distances may have begun through the desire for material objects to make life easier and to differentiate the rich from the poor. Incense, spices, and silk were such items. Incense was a commodity that could attract rather than repel dissimilar others, masking the body odors or cooking smells particular to one culture but repugnant to another. In an age before refrigeration, spices allowed for the preservation of certain foods. Silk, the strongest of all natural fibers, was traded as a very precious commodity. It was difficult to obtain and thus expensive. If you could obtain silk and move it, you could trade it for much more than you paid.

The best and finest silk came from worms which ate only the leaves of a variety of mulberry tree which grew in China. The Chinese began to use silk around 3000 B.C.E.[1] Its importance was so great that for many centuries only the Chinese nobility were allowed to wear it. Methods of silk production were highly secret, and its export was forbidden. The Han dynasty (206 B.C.E.– 220 C.E.) was the first to allow its exportation for trade. This decision opened the Silk Road, a series of caravan trade routes between what is today Northwest China and Western Iran, with other branches which dipped down into India. No traders walked all the way from Iran to China. They went as far as their funds and supplies would take them; they then traded what they had at intermediate points along the Silk Road.

Thus, most of the trade between East and West was conducted through a series of middleman transactions. This increased the cost of the goods with each exchange, lowered potential profits, and led to great inaccuracies in the transmission of knowledge of other cultures. The information gathered by a Persian trader on the Silk Road about the peoples far to the East would consist of rumor and tall tales intermixed with bits of accurate information. If one believed the reports that the skins of people to the East resembled a shade of yellow, then why not also believe the stories that their feet pointed backward? Was one more far-fetched than the other, based on the personal experiences of the listener?

The silk was brought through Iran or India and then exported to Mediterranean Europe, where the demand always exceeded the supply (Figure 1-1). In 553 C.E., two Persian monks living in China concealed silkworm eggs and mulberry seeds inside their hollow bamboo walking canes. They walked out of China, taking the raw materials to the emperor Justinian I, who used them to establish Constantinople as the center of a new silk production industry. Among some circles in China, Christianity and the West are still associated with the treachery of those monks. The secret reached Japan around 250 C.E., reportedly carried by four Chinese concubines, who similarly added another layer of interpretation to the reputation of their occupation.

The Silk Road allowed more than commerce between the East and the West. Christianity, Buddhism, and Islam spread along the routes of the Silk Road. At a minimum, the link between East and West brought vague, although distorted, knowledge that other cultures existed. However, stories that the strangers in far-off lands had the heads of wolves had ominous implications for attitudes about contact with them.

Indeed, when strangers came, the experience was often terrifying. Perhaps they came because they had nothing, and they wanted to take what you had. Armies were a special form of terror; they took whatever they wanted from the countryside. There was no way to resist. From Alexander the Great through the Roman Legions and Attila the Hun, few of the common people had reason to cheer the coming of another army which would attack, kill, and conquer. People who lived near you were known and shared many of the same attitudes, beliefs, and values. The stranger was from a distant, different place and was, for that reason, to be feared.

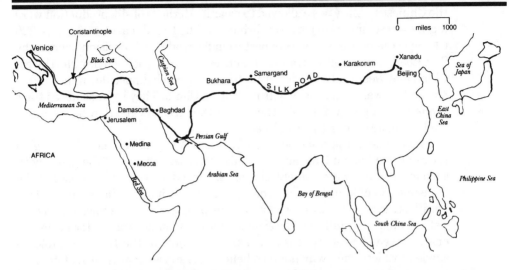

Figure 1-1. The Silk Road Linked Europe and China. The principal means of contact between Europe and China for many centuries was a series of camel caravan routes from northern China, through the vast deserts of Central Asia, across Iran, to eastern Mediterranean ports, from which silk and other valuable goods were shipped to Venice and Genoa. Each merchant typically traveled just one segment of the Silk Road, and then traded goods at a caravan *serai* (a safe haven) to other merchants, who then moved the goods over another segment of the Silk Road. The *serai* also were centers for the exchange of information and misinformation. Marco Polo traveled via the Silk Road to reach the court of Kublai Khan in Beijing.

Source: Drawn by Corinne L. Shefner-Rogers. Used by permission.

One outcome of the extensive military conquests of Alexander the Great was the introduction of the Greek language and culture to the East. In twelve years, he led his troops over 22,000 miles. He was accompanied by people who had been educated by Greek scholars; he himself had been tutored by Aristotle. The exchange of ideas had significant impact on future generations. However, the lives of most people at the time were marked by the scars of conquest; the benefits that derived from the violent contact were enjoyed by the privileged few.

European civilization had flourished for a thousand years during the Greek and Roman eras but almost disappeared during the several hundred years of the Dark Ages. Barbarian bands like the Visigoths, Huns, and Franks poured out of the steppes (vast, treeless, windswept plains of arid land) of what is now Russia into today's Europe. These strangers destroyed the Roman Empire around 400 C.E. The fall of Rome also ended much of the learning, commerce, music, and art that had flourished in the West.

The European continent during the Dark Ages was populated by people living in wretched poverty, with most working as serfs for an exploitive lord.

The only social institution seeking to continue Western civilization during the Dark Ages was the Catholic Church. One function of Catholic monasteries was to keep alive the inherited culture of Greece and Rome in the form of books and manuscripts. A copyist monk, by writing for one year, could reproduce two books. However, most of the books were lost in raids on Europe by the barbarian strangers.

The Spread of Islam

The man who would become the prophet of Islam was born in 571 C.E. in Mecca, Saudi Arabia. Mohammed married a wealthy widow and became the master of her caravans. Travelling the trade routes throughout the Middle East, Mohammed met Christian and Jewish traders and learned aspects of their religious beliefs. His years of travel provided time to meditate on the evils of society, including idol worship, prostitution, and abuse of women, children and debtors. In 610, he heard a voice in a cave near Mount Hira commanding him to cry. The voice of Allah, speaking through the angel Gabriel, then pronounced what would become the Koran to him. In order to be a Muslim, a follower of Islam, one must simply say and believe the *Shehada*: "There is no god but God and Mohammed is his prophet." *Ramadan* is the holy month of fasting that honors the revelation of the Koran to Mohammed.

Mohammed had been greatly admired for his honest and fair business transactions. He began to attract followers to his new religion. His life was threatened by those who opposed his teachings about a single god. Tribal leaders in Mecca, worshippers of multiple deities and idols, drove him out of Mecca to Medina in 622 C.E., the *Hegira*, which marks the start of the Muslim Calendar. Every Muslim is expected to make a *Haj*, a sacred pilgrimage to Mecca, to commemorate the *Hegira*.

In Medina, Mohammed built a body of followers which eventually overwhelmed Mecca. Islam spread throughout the Middle East, then east into today's Pakistan, India, and Bangladesh, and then to Malaysia, Indonesia, and the southern part of the Philippines. Arabic traders carried Islam with them via the overland trade routes of the Middle East, including the Silk Road to China, and then later via sea routes to the rest of Asia. Wherever the Muslims went, they constructed a hospital and a school, key institutions in the transmission of cultural values. Islam spread by the sword westward from Saudi Arabia to the gates of Vienna, across North Africa, through today's Spain and Portugal, and into southern France. There the Moors, Islamic warriors from Morocco, were finally defeated. Islam did not gain a foothold in Europe beyond Spain.

The Moors occupied Spain from approximately 800 to 1500; Arabic and European cultures mixed during these seven hundred years. Through Spanish, Arabic words and ideas spread into other European tongues. "Algebra," "azimuth," and "zoo" are of Arabic origin, as are many other English words that begin with "al" or that contain the letter "z." As words like algebra and azimuth might imply, advances in mathematics, astronomy, and other sciences were introduced from Damascus and other centers of Arabic learning into Europe through Spain. These skills were later applied to navigation and contributed to the Portuguese and Spanish success in exploration.

Many of the important manuscripts of Aristotle, Socrates, and other intellectual leaders of Greek civilization had been translated into Arabic. Islam served as the main repository of Western knowledge during the Middle Ages, through the library at Alexandria, Egypt. Without Islamic efforts, most writings of the Greek and Roman civilizations would have been destroyed in the barbarian attacks during the Dark Ages in Europe. This was one of many influences of Arabic culture on Western European civilization.

The Crusades

In the eleventh century, the Middle East was a meeting place for many diverse cultures and religions, due to its location between East Asia and Europe and due to the Silk Road. Jerusalem was one of the great cities of the Middle East, with Christians, Jews, Muslims, and other religious and cultural groups living together in relative harmony. Each group tended to live in different sections of the city. It had been this way for hundreds of years after the fall of the Roman Empire.

Jerusalem came under Muslim rule in the seventh century, about 200 years after the final decline of Roman authority. Christians had made pilgrimages to Jerusalem for centuries after the death of Christ. The new Muslim rulers were relatively tolerant of Christian pilgrims, some of whom chose to remain in Jerusalem. To the European of this time, Jerusalem was the center of the universe and was depicted as such on all European maps. The deepest common beliefs in the West came from Christianity. It united otherwise diverse peoples in a spiritual enterprise. It also allowed the dominant class to rationalize its predatory appetites and provided the opportunity to extend authority, marking the beginning of Western imperialism.

Infighting among the nobility in Europe had helped to create the knights, a class of warrior monks who swore vows of Christian chastity, poverty, and loyalty. Despite their vows, many knights were merely armed mercenary thugs, often from wealthy families, who wore armor and fought battles for whomever would pay them. Some were barbarian fighters who had converted to Christianity with little understanding of it beyond a change of allegiance. It was obvious to the nobility that the energies of the knights could easily be turned against the nobles. Running short of funds with which to pay the knights, many nobles decided that sending the knights on a long journey from which they were unlikely to return was a very desirable goal.

While Christians knew that Jerusalem was under control of "infidels," most Europeans were not familiar with exactly who those infidels were. They knew of the Moors in Spain but were unaware of the empire of Islam. They also did not know that in 1075 the Seljuk Turks had taken Jerusalem, slaughtering the Muslim Arab rulers. The only feasible land route between Europe and Palestine was through Turkey. With the rise of the Seljuk Turks, the passage of Christian pilgrims through Turkey to Jerusalem, which had been relatively peaceful, was threatened. The head of the Byzantine Empire and of the Eastern branch of the Christian Church, Emperor Alexius I of Constantinople, worried about the powerful Turks who had defeated his army in a major battle in 1071. Alexius was concerned about his ability to hold the territories around Constantinople. Hoping for reinforcements of trained fighters to assist his armies, he wrote a letter in 1095 to Pope Urban II in Rome requesting help. What he got was something else entirely.

The Pope was not particularly interested in aiding Alexis, who was his rival for power. Rather, the Pope wanted to bring the Eastern Church under his domination and to strengthen his position against the European kings and nobles by increasing the number of Christians loyal to him in Europe. He decided that an appeal based on saving fellow Christians would serve his purposes. In a public speech on November 27, 1095, Urban II launched the Crusades.

The speech was delivered at the Monastery of Cluny, the largest man-made enclosed space on the surface of the earth at that time. Thousands had heard the news that a truly important pronouncement was to be made by the Pope himself, and the grounds around the outside of the Cathedral were packed hundreds deep. Even the largest structure on earth could not hold them all, and the Pope delivered his address in the fields next to the church. The words of the Pope were relayed through shouts to the throngs.

Urban II spoke of the need to stop the desecration of the holy places by the infidel. He referred to Muslims as "an accursed race, utterly alienated from God" who had invaded the peaceful Christian land of the Middle East. He stressed the moral duty of every Christian to keep the "Peace of God," and to rescue Christians who had become "slaves for sale in their own land." While it was wrong to kill and to violate the Ten Commandments, the Pope promised forgiveness from God and indulgences for all sins committed in the freeing of the holy land. The revolutionary nature of these words was not lost upon the crowds. It was acceptable according to Urban's speech, in fact it was God's will, for Christians to commit the most grievous of sins in order to free the Christians enslaved by infidels in the holy land. It was only a sin to kill Christians, not the infidel.

While Urban II had hoped for a major impact from his speech, even he had to be surprised at the result. Think of the force of these words on an impoverished peasantry. For the common people of the Europe at this time, poverty and starvation were a constant worry. They made their living by farming small plots of land often owned and protected by the nobles. The leader of the church was promising God's forgiveness, in fact God's blessing, to take the lands and property of other peoples by force. Urban II may or may not have intended to put his blessing on pillage, looting, rape, and murder, but that was the way his words were interpreted.

Today we would regard Pope Urban's message as an example of hate speech. Intolerance of differences breeds hate and contempt. Giving voice to such hate legitimizes it and makes it acceptable. Once it is acceptable to hate, it is acceptable to crush and to destroy those whom one hates. Hate speech often has two effects. First, it creates the climate and rationale for one cultural group to attack another group. Second, the victims of the attack and their supporters assume that anyone associated with the attacking group is evil and deserves to be attacked in retaliation. While Pope Urban's message was contrary to the teachings of Christianity and many Christians disagreed with it, Christianity came to be seen as a bloodthirsty religion of murderers by the victims of the Crusades. This justified attacks on innocent Christians just because they were Christians. The hatred unleashed by the moral leader of Christian Europe brought an equal response of hatred toward Christians by the targeted group.

The common people of Europe—farmers, often with their wives, children, and parents—set out on foot with no planning, no training, and few provisions. They believed that they would attack the infidel and free Jerusalem for Christianity; their righteousness would bring them the wealth they could never obtain otherwise. The appeal was immense and the response astounding. With the cry *Deus vult!* (God wills it), 60,000 people began to move across the European countryside by early 1096. The word crusade comes from the Latin word *crux* meaning cross. Many Crusaders wore a red cloth cross sewn on their clothes to show that they had assumed the commitment to the cause and were indeed the soldiers of Christ. Anyone turning back and giving up the quest was to be excommunicated. This act would mean eternal damnation in hell.

One of the lasting influences of the Crusades is the necktie as a symbol of Christianity. Those leaving on the Crusades were often given a scarf as a remembrance by those left behind. When the Christians went into battle in the Holy Land, they knotted the scarves around their necks, enabling them to tell friend from foe. Over time, the Crusaders' scarves became today's neckties. Although most Christians are unaware of the historical significance of the necktie, many Muslims are. That is why the leaders of many Arabic nations wear open-necked shirts today.

Since anyone who did not believe in Christ as their savior was an infidel, the Pope's indulgences applied to the killing of Jews as far as the Crusaders were concerned. Why go all the way to the Holy Land before beginning God's work? Thousands of Jews were slaughtered in Worms, Cologne, and throughout the Rhine valley. While anti-Jewish prejudice had long existed, the Crusades institutionalized anti-Semitism in Europe. It became a permanent part of European culture.

The ragtag army of peasants on the first Crusade stole what they needed from those whose lands they passed through, leading to constant conflicts. They sacked and burned Belgrade, reaching Constantinople in the late summer of 1096, and then crossed into Asia. There they slaughtered the local residents across the Bosporus, most of whom happened to be Christian. Inflamed by the cause, no one took the time or had the skills and inclination to determine religious beliefs of peoples who looked different.

In 1097, the main army of the First Crusade—60,000 French and Norman knights and their supporters—arrived at Constantinople and crossed into Asia. The knights did not have the advantage they anticipated over the Muslim horsemen. Their heavy armor and large powerful horses made them slow. Hundreds died of thirst; many starved. The losses did not stop the butchery. The knights cut off the heads of the enemy dead and brought them back to camp on spears. Hatred and intolerance of others due to their differences led to unspeakable horrors. At Marat, it was recorded that the Crusaders roasted children on spits and ate them.

Fewer than 20,000 of the original 60,000 knights and soldiers were still alive. Two out of every three who had left Europe were now dead, in addition to the loss of all the Christian peasants before them. In June of 1099, the Crusaders finally reached Jerusalem (population 100,000), which had been taken by the Egyptians from the Turks in the years since the speech at Cluny. The religious tolerance that respected all religious groups in Jerusalem had been restored by the Egyptians.

However, the Crusaders had no interest in interaction that might have revealed similarities. They attacked and took the city on July 15, murdering everyone assumed to be infidels. The Jewish population gathered in the great synagogue for protection and prayer. The Crusaders sealed them in, set it afire, and burned them alive. Many Muslims fled into the main mosque; the Crusaders promised them safety and then slaughtered them the following day. Those clearly identifiable as Christian were spared, but much of the Christian population was also put to the sword. Martin Luther's famous hymn "Onward Christian Soldiers," written several centuries later, has a different connotation when sung in the light of the Crusades.

After sacking the city, the knights founded the Latin Kingdom of Jerusalem, which extended along the Eastern Mediterranean shore from the Gulf of Aquaba to Edessa. To defend their conquests, the knights used forced labor to construct more than one hundred great fortress castles. Krak des Chevaliers in northern Syria was the most impressive—and the one most despised by the Muslims. It was a symbol of the shocking confidence of the unwelcome small group, far outnumbered and far from home.

It took many years before the fragmented Muslims organized to confront the Latin Kingdom itself, but the Christian attacks became the inspiration to unite Islam under Saladin, who became the ruler of Egypt in 1169. Saladin called for a *jihad,* a holy war against the Christian Crusaders. This concept of *jihad* remains prominent in Islamic struggles for recognition and power to the present day. Jerusalem fell to Saladin and his troops in 1187 amidst savage fighting. Its loss seemed incomprehensible in Europe, and some claimed that the Pope died of shock on hearing of it.

The Crusades illustrate the role of prejudice in intercultural interaction. The Western image of the people from the Middle East as Muslim infidels has lasted for a thousand years. Within minutes of the 1995 bombing of the Federal Building in Oklahoma City, CNN was reporting that a man of Middle Eastern appearance was seen running from the area shortly before the bombing. Citizens of Middle Eastern origin were stopped, searched, and detained both in the United States and on their arrival in other countries, an example of collective cultural consciousness at work. To the people of the Middle East, the Crusaders represented the West and all of Christianity. In the Middle East, the cultural consciousness was of the Christian West as murderous barbarians who came to destroy religion and to slaughter indiscriminately. The Crusades moved Islam toward greater intolerance of those who did not believe in Allah and his Prophet. These contacts of the two cultures were devastatingly negative, creating a collective cultural memory for Christians and for Muslims about the evil lurking in the views of the other.

Genghis Khan and the Mongols

As Saladin was calling for the *jihad,* a baby was born thousands of miles away whose influence would stagger much of the world. Mongolia was inhabited at that time by several different cultures of nomadic peoples, including those called Huns and Tartars by Westerners. The term "Hun" was later applied by Westerners to their enemies, as in World War I propaganda which branded the Germans as "Huns." The culture experienced by the baby boy, Temujin, provides an example of what the cultures of many peoples in pre-history must have been like. What was the mindset of such peoples? How did they see the world?

The steppes of Mongolia were conducive only to travel and transport. The flat plains that could be traversed relatively easily were arid and had limited vegetation. Agriculture was not a viable option in this environment. The nomadic Mongol culture revolved around raising sheep and horses, constantly moving to new pastures when the old were depleted. Families lived in yurts, round tents made of felt. Mongols used no metal, wove no cloth, and their diets were limited to the animals they raised. The possibility of starvation was ever present; the greatest sin among the Mongols was to waste any food in any way. Entrails, afterbirth, and blood were all used by the Mongols; dried animal dung was a source of fuel. A consistent description of the Mongols by outsiders was that they wiped their hands, greasy with animal fat and blood, on their clothes.

The response to the challenge of the environment shapes the culture of a people. In the harsh, unforgiving environment of the steppes, the Mongols learned to be tenacious. They honed the skills necessary to survive and became masters at the logistics of moving large groups of people and animals in barren, inhospitable environments. The military skills of horseback riding and shooting bows and arrows were honored in Mongolian culture. They were ruthless militarily. When a conflict with another group arose, there was no time to understand or accept differences. The choice was to surrender or to resist. Unsuccessful resistance meant destruction.

When Temujin was only 10 years old, his father was poisoned. He swore vengeance on his father's killers and dedicated his life to becoming a great fighter. He joined with the fighters of a powerful Mongol leader and eventually became leader of that group. No one had ever succeeded in uniting all of the fierce Mongol clans in which blood feuds ran deep, but Temujin was determined, organized, and ruthless. He drilled his fighters in tactics and skills for months on end, forging them into a highly disciplined and coordinated unit. In 1204 when he was 37 years old, his forces won a decisive victory over all the clans in Mongolia. Temujin was then proclaimed *Genghis Khan*, meaning "universal ruler." He led the most formidable fighting force the world had ever seen. Nothing in Christian Europe, the Islamic Middle East, China, or India could compare with it.

In 1207, Genghis Khan led the Mongols east, on the first of several invasions of the Asian mainland. The Mongols went to war as a country. Families packed up everything and went along with the fighting men. The army was a giant dust cloud of horses, fighters, sheep, and the entire Mongolian nation gone to war, with about 40,000 to 50,000 men in arms. Genghis' goal was to raid kingdoms to take what he wanted and to remove the possibility of retaliatory raids. The Chinese were contemptuous of the Mongols, whom they saw as smelly, fighting barbarians who often did not cook their food. The Mongols were equally contemptuous of the Chinese, whom they saw as sissies who could not ride or fight like men—but had gold and silk and other treasures. By 1215, the Mongols controlled the territory of the Ch'in Kingdom (Northeast China including what is now Korea and Manchuria). They slaughtered most of the inhabitants and burned the cities.

Genghis Khan then turned to the Islamic Empire to the west. Two of its greatest cities were Bukhara and Samargand, both on the Silk Road and defended by an army of more than 300,000 men. The Khan's troops numbered half that. Leaving a portion of his army to engage the enemy on a river at the edge of the Shah's empire, Genghis Khan personally led the bulk of his army around the north flank and west through forbidding desert, with no known water holes and no landmarks. Months later in 1218, Genghis Khan emerged from the desert at the walls of Bukhara, defended by only a small garrison, which promptly fled. Once inside Bukhara, he rode his horses into a mosque, turned it into stables, and burned or threw out all copies of the Holy Koran, a grievous sin under Islamic Law. He gave a public lecture to the populace, proclaiming himself the wrath of God who had been sent against the people of Islam to punish them for their sins. He randomly gathered several thousand Muslims and killed them in front of the rest of the populace as an example. The women and children, along with the treasures of Bukhara, were sent off on a march to Mongolia to serve the Khan. The city was leveled and the remaining men were marched in front of the Khan's troops as a human shield in the attack on Samargand, which also surrendered.

As his armies advanced across Asia, each city was given the choice of surrender or slaughter. Those that surrendered were treated relatively well, with the local administration kept largely in place after swearing loyalty to the Khan. Those that did not were slaughtered, the walls pulled down, and all traces of their society essentially disappeared from the face of the earth.

When the Mongols razed a city, they left a few young men alive. Placed on horseback, the men were sent off in all directions to spread the message that resistance was useless. Populations of other cities in the path of the advancing hordes panicked in response to this early and highly effective form of intercultural communication as war propaganda. The choice of surrender or slaughter was not available to most of the rural peoples, who made up the vast bulk of any area's population. These people were mainly farmers, which was something the Khan had never experienced in his own culture. What was different was not understood. What was not understood was not liked. And what was not liked was destroyed. All the peasants were killed as a matter of course. The city residents then starved.

The Khan and his armies marveled at the sights of civilization. They transplanted engineers, artisans, poets, and mystics back to Mongolia. From one city alone, 100,000 artisans were deported. It was cultural mixing on a scale never seen before, one of the greatest forced mass migrations in the history of the world. At the time of his death in 1227, Genghis Kahn had conquered lands from the Black Sea to the Pacific Ocean. On his deathbed, after a fall from his horse, he told his sons that while he had conquered vast territories, his life had been too short to take the entire world; this was now their task—to fulfill Mongolian destiny as it had been ordained by the heavens. This was neither the first time nor the last that a culture was to define itself as a world conqueror, destined to be so by a higher power. His son Ogadai, the new Great Khan, set out to complete his father's work.

Ogadai Khan

Genghis Khan's attacks had been typical of the barbarian raiders who came before him. They were savage raids to take what was there, destroy what was left, and then leave. The Chinese had constructed portions of the Great Wall in response to such previous raids. Unlike his father and the Crusaders, Ogadai sought the advice of foreigners. He wanted to gain knowledge beyond his own background—that is, to engage in intercultural communication although from the distinct vantage point of power. A Ch'in official taken as a prisoner so impressed Ogadai with his knowledge and vision that he was elevated to the status of Prime Minister. The official convinced Ogadai to build a permanent city, Karakorum, as the capital of the Mongol Empire, a concept totally foreign to Mongol culture. The prime minister later persuaded Ogadai to spare the population (one million) of a conquered city, because people, not land, were the empire's greatest resource. This was another revolutionary idea. The Ch'in official also convinced Ogadai of the value of peasants. Farming produced food which was highly valued by the Mongols. The official used this Mongol cultural value to change Ogadai into valuing agriculture and peasants. This slowly produced "top down" change in Mongol culture toward a positive cultural value for agriculture.

Ogadai established the Yam, a communication system resembling an extensive pony express with thousands of small camps, thirty miles apart, stretching across the Asian countryside. The skilled horsemen manning the Yam would sleep in the saddle on their galloping horses to carry messages quickly to the far reaches of the growing empire. The teams of fast riders could cover 200 miles a day for 10 days, bringing communication anywhere within 2,000 miles of Karakorum. Communication this efficient was not established in the Western world for another six centuries. Yam riders were also expected to act as spies (another form of intercultural communication), who would report information observed on their trips beyond what they were told.

Ogadai's tendencies toward cultural exchange were not universally applied. General Subadai had commanded an expedition to the West for Genghis Kahn. Ogadai sent him on another mission. He marched 6,000 miles to Eastern Europe, slaughtering everyone who did not surrender. When the armies reached Russia, in the heart of Christianity, the Mongols leveled Kiev, which together with Rome and Constantinople formed the three greatest Christian cities on earth. Only a handful of monks survived, hidden in underground tunnels beneath the one church that was spared. The garrison at Krakow was slaughtered, and the population of Krakow fled in panic as the Mongols swept into the city. Visitors to Krakow can still hear the trumpeter reenact the call to arms each day, stopping at the same point in mid-note when the ancient trumpeter was killed. Krakow was leveled as were the other large Polish cities. In Hungary 40,000 troops died in the first European battle in which gunpowder was used. The Mongols had learned of it from the Chinese and used it in the same way, as fireworks to create fear and awe in the enemy. (The Europeans would later adopt this innovation, and use it to force their will on others.) The entire population of Europe was now in panic.

The search for some explanation for this frightful enemy could admit only one possibility: Europe was under attack from the forces of the Devil himself. Many Christians saw the "wrath of the Tartar" as God's punishment for an evil and disobedient world, and the Church did little to dispel this view. The Mongols were sent from Hell as divine punishment for the sins of humanity. The Pope in Rome led large masses in prayer against the invaders and called for still another Crusade (there had been six) to be mounted against the Mongols, but there were few takers. Only a few small scattered European forces remained alive. With their armies destroyed in previous battles, the people behind the city walls prayed for divine intervention, as the Mongols prepared for their final advance into Hungary and the heartland of Europe beyond.

One spring morning in May of 1242, the peoples west of the Danube awoke to look toward the Mongol encampment across the river, wondering if this would be the day of their death. But the mighty army had vanished in the dark of the night. The Mongols had disappeared, never to be seen again in that part of Europe. What were the people to make of these events? They had heard stories of how entire cities—groups of people who assumed the lives they led were part of the permanent order of the world—were eliminated from the face of the earth by alien strangers. Some had actually seen the encampment that would bring destruction. Now it was gone. What did it mean? How could it be explained? For some Christians this was clear proof of the existence of God, who had answered their prayers for deliverance. For others it was proof of the ultimate superiority of Western technology and culture over that of the East: the Mongols had become afraid and had run away. The real explanation was found in Mongol culture. Word had arrived that the great Khan Ogadai, whose illness had already delayed the order to attack for several months, had died. Mongol culture consisted of a rigidly prescribed hierarchy. Generals were fiercely loyal and would never advance, even to obvious victory, without the order from the great Khan. The duty of all Mongolians was to gather in Mongolia to determine the new great leader.

Europe had experienced an important intercultural lesson. Their presumed superiority over the "uncivilized" peoples of the rest of the world had been called into question. They had been brought perilously close to extinction. Yet many Europeans continued to believe in their cultural and technological superiority, as did the Mongols in theirs, each bolstered by their own cultural traditions of ethnocentrism: my way is the best way, and likely the only way. Some sought mystical explanations, but the near annihilation by the Mongols taught others a very practical lesson. They had flirted with disaster from a people about whom they knew nothing.

Eighteen years after the threat to Europe, 150,000 Mongols travelled to destroy all of Islam. Bagdad was a city of great wealth representing five centuries of Islamic culture; it resisted and was destroyed. As with the trumpeter in Krakow, the memory of this event surfaces in behavior today. In November, 1997, CNN broadcast video clips of Iraqi boys, ages 15 to 17, eating chunks of raw meat from a recently killed wolf. The clips were presented without explanation, hardening the dislike of Westerners for the Iraqis. However, the practice has a cultural context; it is sometimes used with army recruits to demonstrate that Iraqi soldiers are as fierce as the Mongols, who ate raw meat and destroyed Bagdad.

Persia and Iraq surrendered to the Mongols; and Damascus fell in seven days. The army moved toward Cairo, second in importance only to Bagdad in the Islamic world. In a remarkable parallel to the European experience, the new Khan died and the Mongols withdrew, leaving only a small army of 10,000 men in Syria. The Egyptian Muslims proposed an alliance with the remaining Crusaders, who now had a difficult choice. Many Crusaders wanted to align with the Mongols and crush Islam forever, but the Mongols were seen by the Christians as too treacherous. The Muslims were allowed to pass the Christian castles. The Muslims then attacked the small Mongol force left in Syria, inflicting the first loss on a Mongol army. The battle was fought in 1260 at Ayn-Jalut, where David is said to have fought Goliath.

Kublai Khan

Kublai Khan was installed as Great Khan in 1264. The contrasts between Kublai and his grandfather were quite amazing. Genghis grew up eating raw meat and learning to survive and fight on the steppe. Kublai was raised in a cultured life of privilege by Chinese servants, who taught him to read and write and to respect the peasants who worked the land. Their different experiences resulted in very different visions of the world they wanted to create. Where Genghis wanted to pillage and destroy, in that way securing peace and wealth for his own people, Kublai wanted to build and to integrate. Genghis wanted the world to mimic his own culture, while Kublai wanted to open the world to all cultures.

Rather than impose his own culture on the Chinese, Kublai Khan drew on the Confucianism of his youth. Kublai broke the constraints of a culture nurtured on the harshness of the barren environment of the steppes. He resisted the Mongol distrust of civilization. In essence, his life in China had changed him and the Mongols he ruled more than they had changed China. In part this was a question of numbers. The Mongols were a tiny minority ruling vast numbers of Chinese subjects. The culture of the majority was inevitably encroaching on the rulers. However, the Mongols were fearful of the effects of too much intermingling. The Chinese were forbidden to learn the Mongol language or to marry Mongols. Foreigners, including Marco Polo, were appointed to most administrative positions. Mongolian blood was necessary to reach the highest levels, and the lowest positions were given to the southern Chinese.

Kublai attempted invasions of Japan in 1275 and 1281. Both attempts failed when each armada was sunk by a typhoon, with 150,000 casualties in 1281 alone. These events strengthened the Shinto beliefs of the Japanese that the gods ruled their destiny. Shinto holds that the Japanese are the gods' chosen people. Thus, the gods sent a divine wind, a *Kamikaze*, to protect Japan. It was said to be proof that the gods would never allow Japan to be conquered by an invading army. These beliefs played a central role in the militarization of Japanese society and in the decisions to attack the countries of the Pacific Rim in 1941. When a divine wind did not protect Japan in the waning months of WWII, the Japanese created their own divine wind in the form of cheaply built planes designed as one-way bombs to attack the advancing Western fleets. The planes, and the pilots who flew them, were called the *Kamikaze*.

Kublai's failures paled in comparison to his accomplishments. He established the first central bank and a unified currency, with paper money based on a silver standard, for a nation of 50 million people. He built 1,000 new port stations on the Silk Road across the Asian continent, each with a hostel, a granary, stables, and fresh pack animals available for traders. He created employment by encouraging production of high-grade pottery, importing cobalt mined in Persia across his roads to produce the blue/white wares which would take on the name of the country itself, China. He built a great merchant fleet which sailed to India, the Persian Gulf, and the shores of Africa to trade in goods over 200 years before the Europeans sailed to African shores to trade in slaves. A convert from Chinese Confucianism and Taoism to Buddhism, Kublai fostered religious tolerance. Islam, Hinduism, Buddhism, and Christianity spread side by side along the Chinese coast. Again this was an instance of cultural change; previous Khans had sworn to destroy Islam, the Pope, and all of Christianity.

Kublai Khan established the Yuan dynasty, uniting all of China from Burma to Manchuria under a single ruler and extending the empire of the Mongols to its widest dimensions. In the *I Ching* of Taoism, Yuan means "the origins of the universe." Certainly Kublai's Yuan dynasty was the first successful attempt to create an intercultural universe of these dimensions. It was a time of great literary development and of art and painting, an Asian renaissance occurring well before the renaissance of Europe. Movable type was first used in Kublai Khan's China, centuries before that innovation reached the West. Kublai built the Great Canal of China; it extended for 150 miles, and took 3 million laborers over 10 years to build. Ships could now travel 100 miles inland on its waters. He moved the Mongol capital from Karakorum to Dadu, the city which he built at the canal's northern terminus. It remains the capital of China to this day, renamed Beijing. Despite these accomplishments, something in Kublai's heart retained the Mongol influence. Within Dadu, on a grassy field next to the great palace of the Imperial City which was built for him, Kublai Khan and his extended family lived in yurts. Over the centuries this Imperial City within Beijing that started as Kublai's tents would become the heart of the Forbidden City, the inner capital of the Ming and Ch'ing dynasties.

Kublai Khan opened China to the world and created a great intercultural society, taking the best from all cultures. The open society of the Yuan dynasty lasted for 75 years after Kublai's death in 1294. The Ming dynasty which replaced it completed the Great Wall of China, symbolizing a return to the old Chinese ways of xenophobia and suspicion of foreigners. China once again closed its doors, turning its back on the rest of the world for the next 500 years. The xenophoic Chinese cultural consciousness had survived 150 years of conquest and occupation by the Mongols.

While teaching at Bangkok University, one of the book's authors was invited to a Thai political function. He was seated next to an official of the Mongolian government. A discussion ensued about Genghis Khan, greatly admired as the father of Mongolia by the Mongolian people. In response to the author's question as to how the history of the Khans is taught in Mongolian schools, the official replied that Genghis Khan was the great unifier, seeking and bringing world peace by destroying warlike cities and supporting and protecting peaceful ones. The rule of the Mongol Khans was a time of great peace and tranquility. The warlike religions and rulers of the West naturally did not like to be subdued by a peacemaker, and so spread false rumors and created a false history about the greatest champion of world peace and instrument of the Heavens' justice the earth has ever known, Genghis Khan. While this perceived history was not quite the way the author taught it in class, it was a strong lesson in different intercultural perceptions.

Does the study of the Khans give you a better perspective on the experiences of Native Americans or African Americans? From one point of view, the Khans created a peaceful and prosperous society. The roads were safe for travel. There was trade, and there was work; people could feed their families. The later Khans created a cultured society of great wealth and sophistication. Conquered peoples throughout Asia benefited, although they were always treated as second-class citizens.

Would you accept that scenario if you were among the conquered? Imagine being forcibly thrust into a new society yet remembering the time of your ancestors. Would you trade the freedom of your original way of life for life as a second-class citizen in a great cultured society? Would you surrender or resist—the latter meaning the slaughter of all the people of your culture and the destruction of your language and your culture itself? Would you accept a reservation or ghetto of barren land, a government welfare check, and the opportunity to participate in a "greater" society?

Marco Polo

European merchants had traded in Chinese goods for years, purchasing them from middlemen. Kublai Khan had made the roads safer and easier to travel, and merchants could personally travel all the way to Eastern China. Niccolo and Maffeo Polo, two merchant brothers from Venice, were among the first Europeans to do so. On their second trip they took Niccolo's son, Marco, with them. In 1275 they reached Xanadu, the summer capital of Kublai Khan, and presented him with letters from the Pope. Marco entered the Khan's diplomatic service and served as his agent on missions to many parts of the empire. This gave him access to experiences no other European could have dreamed possible. Even in today's world, how many Westerners in their early twenties can say they met the ruler of China and traveled to many areas of China and Southeast Asia in his service? Marco Polo was given a truly amazing opportunity.

One of the missions that made a lasting impression on Marco was to Pagan, in what is now Burma. Many Pagans held to traditional beliefs in *shamanism* and *animism*, although organized religions such as Buddhism and Hinduism were also present. Marco's later reports of these beliefs led Christians to refer to those who have no religion as "pagans," since they did not recognize these belief systems as proper religion in the Western sense. The fact that Pagans had multiple wives, as was traditional in much of Asia, gave the term a hedonistic quality. Marco's service to the Khan was sufficiently impressive for Kublai to make him governor of the city of Yangzhou where Marco served for three years.

Seventeen years passed, and the Polos became increasingly anxious to return home. They finally persuaded the Khan to allow them to escort a Mongol princess traveling by sea to Persia in 1292. They reached Venice in 1295. Marco then obtained work as captain of a Venetian galley ship, which participated in a battle with Genoa in 1298. He was captured and imprisoned in Genoa. With little else to do in prison, he dictated a detailed account of his intercultural experiences to Rustichello, a fellow prisoner and well-known writer of the time. Released from prison a year later, Marco returned to Venice with the manuscript. He died in about 1324, and the manuscript was not published until the next century in France.

The illustrated edition of *The Travels of Marco Polo* had an enormous impact on the Western world. Some regarded it as fiction. It was met with astonishment and disbelief, but the systematic details of the accounts convinced others of its accuracy. Later explorations showed the book to be quite accurate in most of its descriptions. Marco's book became the primary source for the European image of the Far East until late in the nineteenth century. For many centuries it was the only source in Europe for information on the geography and culture of the Far East, and it formed the basis for the first accurate European maps of Asia. It was the most influential book on cultural differences in the history of the world. The book stimulated Western interest in Far Eastern trade and appears largely responsible for Christopher Columbus' interest in the Orient. Columbus always carried a well-worn copy of *The Travels* and constantly tried to identify locations on the east coast of the Americas with descriptions Marco had given of Asia. Marco had also suggested the all-sea route from Europe to the Far East around the Cape of Good Hope at the southern tip of Africa.

With the publication of *The Travels*, the Western conception of the total barbarianism of the East began to crumble, although it remained an underlying foundation upon which to build an expanded conception. Recall that Marco Polo came from Venice, the most sophisticated city of that time, yet he was astounded by what he found in China. Comparing China with the best the West had to offer, he described China as possessing cities of unparalleled magnificence, great public works which far surpassed those of Europe, efficient government with law and order, the existence of lavish wealth and luxury, and culture and refinement in manners and in dress. By comparison, the greatest cities of Europe were presented as minor backwaters of the world. The East was superior in all of the criteria used to measure cultural superiority. Whether or not it is right to make such judgments, people always have and always will make them. To ignore this tendency is to ignore a fundamental aspect of intercultural communication.

The narratives of unparalleled magnificence were tempered by another layer of the West's collective cultural consciousness of the East. In 1348 the Black Death (the bubonic plague) swept westward, a deadly remnant of one of the last Mongol attacks along the Black Sea. Within five years, the previously unknown disease had spread across Europe to Britain and Scandinavia, killing a third of the European population, more than all of the Europeans killed by all previous attacks of the Khans combined. Now, "the source of deadly diseases" was a permanent addition to the Western perception of Asia.

Colonialism

Europe was in an age of expansion following Marco Polo's book and Columbus' voyage to the New World. The extent to which the European powers both misunderstood world geography and overestimated their own importance in the world is illustrated by the Treaty of Tordesillas. Portugal and Spain both claimed ownership of the New World. The conflict grew so intense that the Pope was asked to settle the matter. The final agreement was reached in 1494 in the small Spanish town of Tordesillas. The Treaty of Tordesillas established a line with great intercultural consequences. All land east of approximately 50º west longitude would be Portuguese. All land west of the line would be Spanish. Spain and Portugal, with the blessings of the Church, divided up the Americas between themselves. Portugal got Brazil, which at that time had little wealth. Spain got the rest of North and South America and became a wealthy nation; its language spread throughout Central and South America.

Ethnocentrism was expressed, and reinforced, by the European colonizers in many ways. White-skinned colonists considered themselves more advanced than the colonials, who were people of color. European military force was stronger; their technology was more advanced; and their economies were richer. The subjugated peoples of Latin America, Africa, and Asia were made to feel inferior. They were told by the Christian invaders that their religion was pagan and that it had to be replaced by the European religion, which

---

Case Illustration:
Cortés and Montezuma

In 1519, the Spanish conquistador Hernán Cortés and 450 Spanish soldiers landed at what is now Vera Cruz and marched overland to Tenochtitlán, present-day Mexico City. The Spanish force had steel armor, horses, and firearms, which made up for their numerical inferiority. Cortés and his men captured the capital city and held Montezuma II, King of the Aztecs, as hostage.

Cortés and the Spanish were helped tremendously by La Malinche (also called Doña Marina), an Indian woman who served as a translator and interpreter for the invaders (Figure 1-2). She bore Cortés a son in 1522, the first Mestizo. La Malinche was the ultimate collaborator in betraying the indigenous peoples of the New World to the Spanish conquerors (Karttunen, 1994, pp. 1–23). In Mexico the word malinche means traitor.

Montezuma believed the Aztec myth that the god Quetzalcoatl would come from the east on April 22, 1519. This god was expected to have a white complexion and a beard. Cortés matched these expectations precisely. Thus the Aztecs treated Cortés and his Spanish troops as special guests, even when the invaders did not behave at all like guests. Cortés tried to convert Montezuma to Christianity, but the attempted conversion failed. Had Cortés succeeded, Montezuma might have rejected the Aztec myth about Quetzalcoatl and would have used his superior manpower to defeat Cortés. The Spanish conquistador did not understand that Montezuma treated him as a god, or he would not have worked so hard to persuade Montezuma to give up his "pagan" religious beliefs.

Another paradox in the relationship of Cortés and Montezuma was that while the Spanish held the king of the Aztecs under house arrest, they were in turn surrounded by half a million of Montezuma's loyal subjects. The Spanish were actually prisoners, and their lives depended upon the whim of Montezuma (Collis, 1978, p. 156; Thomas, 1993). The Spanish were in pursuit of the Aztec city of gold, Eldorado. They instructed Montezuma to direct them there. He could not do so; Eldorado existed only in myth. When the Spanish killed Montezuma, the Aztecs rose against them and drove them from Mexico City. Many of the soldiers were pushed or fell from the causeways that bridged the lake surrounding Mexico City and drowned because they had filled their uniforms with jewels and other loot. Eventually the Spanish forces recaptured Mexico City, and Mexico became a Spanish colony. The intercultural misunderstandings that marked this episode were repeated endlessly between the Spanish and the peoples whom they conquered throughout Latin America.

centered on worship of a deity symbolized by a white man. If local people resisted, they often were converted to Christianity by force. Many indigenous people in Latin America were baptized as adults, given Biblical names, and ordered to adopt Spanish or Portuguese culture. If they refused, they were killed. The Spanish displayed a colonizing zeal that surpassed most other European colonizers. They ruthlessly exploited native populations in their search for gold, spices, and converts (Gibney, 1992).

Figure 1-2. The young girl represents La Malinche (the guide for Hernán Cortés in his conquest of Mexico) in a ceremony held annually in the village of Tortugas, New Mexico.

Source: Photograph by Miguel Gandert. Used by permission.

The Slave Trade

While the interiors of Laos and Burma are perhaps the regions currently most isolated from the rest of the world, until the nineteenth century Africa held that position. Both European and Asian conquerors had seen the Euro-Asian landmass as more fertile ground for riches than Africa. The interior of Africa was difficult to access and was bypassed by the European powers for centuries. Sporadic intercultural contact had created some cultural exchange. The yam and the banana arrived in Africa from Southeast Asia with Indonesian sailors around 100 C.E. The camel came to Egypt from the Middle East through caravans around 1000 B.C.E.

In Africa, aside from the Mediterranean coastal areas such as Egypt, few large aggressive nation-states existed before the nineteenth century. Africans had developed civilizations quite different from Euro-Asian societies; they developed more slowly for a number of reasons. Africa had land, but relatively few people living on it compared with Europe and Asia. High population densities are needed to form large kingdoms. These population densities, and the existence of surpluses which can be taxed by kings and governments to form nations, did not exist in most of Africa. Poor soil for farming, unpredictable rainfall, and many crop-eating pests limited any surpluses that could be used to expand trade and extend economic and political domains.

Great nations also arise through development and technological progress, which often depend on conflict with others as a driving force and on the diffusion of innovations to assure success against the enemy. The dispersion of small groups of people over vast areas in Africa ensured that there would be little communication between them, lowering the chances for the knowledge of innovations to spread through the African interior. Conflicts with other groups in Africa could usually be resolved by moving to unoccupied areas (which were plentiful), rather than by creating a permanent warlike group to fight for rights to the land. This also reduced the creation of nations by reducing the need for armies. Peoples who live in peace and tranquility for long periods of time, with intermittent local conflicts but without major wars, do not need expensive standing armies. They and their cultures are consequently more vulnerable to outside influences and powerful military forces.

The histories of African societies are told quite differently than the histories of Europe and Asia. They are the histories of peoples' lives rather than of conquests. When asked about his people's history, an old man from the Herero people in southwest Africa responded: "Have not the Hereros been cattle breeders since god created them? As a cattle breeder does not one always live in the self-same way? That is the life of the Herero." The old man described the migrations for grazing of the herds, the search for water, and the occasional conflicts with other groups that these migrations produced. "That is the life my great-grandfather lived, and my father lived it too. When we all live in exactly the same way, there is not much to be told" (Vedder, 1932, p. 145). There is, of course, much to be told, but not of armies, conquests, and the rise of great nations. Rather, the histories told are of the people themselves and the events surrounding their everyday lives.

The importance of the difference in technology of Africa compared with that of the outside world cannot be overstated. The peoples of both the Muslim and Christian worlds based most of their contempt for the dark-skinned peoples of Africa on their "backwardness," that is, their lack of technological development. But with the exception of a few inventors, the majority of the lighter-skinned peoples of Europe and Asia had done nothing more to advance technological progress than had a traditional African cattle herder. Learning to fire a gun is not the intellectual equivalent of inventing one. Having lived in proximity to more advanced technology and having benefited by the diffusion of innovations, Europeans and Asians transferred the advantage gained by the accident of birth to an assumption of superiority. From there, it was a slippery slope to the conclusion that inferior creatures must have been intended by a creator to serve superior human beings. Enslavement is rationalized as the natural order and becomes morally acceptable.

The lack of a written tradition in much of African society means that we will never know the full richness of its cultures. In fact we know very little at all prior to the nineteenth century. One exception is the Muslim records of trade with Africa. Trade was recorded by Muslims with Ghana as early as 650 C.E. Slavery had existed throughout the world from its earliest times, usually through war captives serving the victors. Muslims traded with Kanem north of Lake Chad in West Africa at least 150 years before the time of the Crusades. The trade was mainly in slaves and secondarily in gold. Islam prohibits enslavement of another Muslim, but the Africans being enslaved were not Muslim. By around the year 1000 C.E., the merchants of the Sudan, and along the Indian Ocean and the Red Sea coasts, were dealing in slaves quite regularly. The market was not large and involved a small proportion of the African population at this time.

In 1419 Prince Henry of Portugal ("Henry the Navigator") began sending ships down the coast of Africa as European exploration expanded. By mid-century, Portugal had become the first Christian nation to enter the trade in African slaves. Initially the Portuguese slave trade was concentrated in West Africa. Early Portuguese traders would often kidnap a few unwary people who wandered near their ship, then sell them on return to Portugal for use as domestic servants. With the discovery of the Americas, the trade increased significantly. The Portuguese in Brazil required huge numbers of slaves; the British, French, and Dutch in the Caribbean and North America soon looked to the slave trade for laborers.

Slave traders were merchants who wanted to make money. They began dealing with local African chiefs and with middlemen as a more efficient way of obtaining slaves. Gift giving was a common practice in African societies, and one was expected to give gifts to the tribal leader. Sometimes the leader had enslaved captives from a previous fight with another tribe, and sometimes the slaves were given to him as tribute. The chiefs brought these slaves to the military command posts established by the Europeans, sometimes as gifts and sometimes in exchange for goods. The Europeans offered tobacco, alcohol, metalware, and bodily ornaments in exchange for slaves, but the most desired goods were firearms. Once a village chief had guns, he and his people became a formidable power in their area. Obtaining more people to sell as slaves was easier with guns. Rivals were then forced into the trade as well. There was no other way to obtain guns, and without guns they would be at the mercy of the armed group.

The traders moved the slaves from the interior through land areas to a point accessible by ship. Many slaves died from hardships between the military post and the port. This trek was termed the *initial passage*. Ships arrived in Africa with a cargo of guns and other items to trade for the slaves as well as money to pay the slave traders. In a letter to his father, Paul Isert (who served as the doctor on a Danish slave ship from 1783 to 1787) described the process before the people were placed on ships. "As the slaves were brought in by the tribal captors, they were sold on a barter basis . . . and then housed and guarded by their new owners in sheds or warehouses until the arrival of the slave ships." The Dutch and the British slaves "were set for branding with a hot iron on the breast or the shoulder with the identifying mark of the company" (I.P., 1987, pp. 11–12; Thomas, 1997).

The movement of the slaves from Africa to the Americas was termed the *middle passage*. Some captains preferred loose packing of slaves on their ships; more people would survive the trip with this method. The relatively cheap cost in Africa compared with the much greater value on arrival in the Americas made the temptation of more money through tight packing irresistible to some. "Try to imagine," said Dr. Isert, "the commotion aboard a slave ship, built originally to carry 200 people and now crammed with 452 slaves, kept in line by 36 Europeans" (I.P., 1987, p. 20). The death rate was as high as 43 percent in tight packing, and as low as 1 percent in loose packing.

The women were usually released from their chains and brought up on deck when the ship was at sea, to be used by the officers and crew as they wished. The crews were often composed of men who were social outcasts at home. The Danish ships brought all slaves on deck every few days while they attempted to clean the hold. The dead were thrown overboard each day. Dysentery and smallpox were the most dreaded diseases. The horror of the slave ships was starkly recreated in the movie *Amistad*, the story of the only successful revolt on board these ships.

Shortly before arrival in the Americas, slaves who survived the voyage were fed, washed, and oiled. When the ship landed, they were paraded past spectators. Dr. Isert described the auction:

> The sales day arrived. Our entire human cargo was transferred to a large auction-house. At a designated moment, a door was flung open. An army of planters stormed in and furiously grabbed Negroes and Negresses they had noticed and visually selected during the previous

days. The whole affair happened with such speed and fury that I was startled. One can imagine the fright of the Negroes.

After the *final passage*, from auction house to plantation, most of the slaves were sent to the fields; a few were selected for house positions. Slaves who were both docile and physically attractive were usually in the latter group. The hold was cleaned and a cargo of sugar and molasses or other colonial produce was loaded aboard for the trip back to the home country.

This three-legged process, Europe to Africa to the Americas and back, became known as *the triangle trade*. North American merchant ships also participated. One triangle route was to load the ship with rum from Bristol, Rhode Island, trading the rum in Guinea (on the West Coast of Africa) for slaves. The slaves were unloaded in the West Indies, often St. Thomas or St. Croix, and molasses was loaded aboard for the rum factories of Bristol . As European colonies increased in the Americas, the need for slaves kept pace. Historians estimate that for each slave arrival, another slave died on one of the passages. Some 30 million African people either died or were enslaved as a direct result of the slave trade in the 400 years between 1450 and 1850. The ratio of white Europeans who immigrated to the Americas between 1492 and 1820 compared to the Africans forced into slavery there was 1 to 5. For the next four decades the numbers were about equal. About 500,000 of the enslaved Africans arrived in the United States.

The Danish were among the first to end their trade in 1803, partially in response to Dr. Isert's urgings. Isert himself returned to Africa in 1788, setting up a plantation where he hoped to show that cooperation and paid labor would work better than slavery. He was murdered a year later by slave traders worried about his possible success. The slave trade was declared illegal by England and the United States in 1831, although the owning of slaves was still legal in the United States at that time. The British Navy, with assistance from the U.S. Navy, sought to combat the trade, stationing warships off the West African coast to seize the slave-trading vessels. The last slave ship docked in North America in 1859.

Partially over feelings of guilt at the wrongs of slavery, the political forces in England that had defeated the slave trade argued that these wrongs must somehow be made right. It was the "white man's burden" (from the title of a Rudyard Kipling poem), they argued, to uplift the less advanced to the level of Western civilization. This urge to "do good" to Africa soon served to justify an increasing interference in African affairs and so proved one of the main forces behind European imperialism" (Hallett, 1970, p. 170).

Christian missionaries were sent to "civilize" the African peoples in the late nineteenth century. Many of these peoples' ancestors had already been forcibly converted to Islam in a series of *jihads* or holy wars during the previous century and a half. The European nations changed from trading partners in slavery, to religious, military, and political overlords, as they colonized Africa in the name of liberalism and Christianity.

The Early Missionaries

The role of missionaries in history is of special interest since they represent direct attempts at intercultural communication. The entire purpose of a missionary is to change the beliefs of someone from another culture, someone with different religious views, through the process of intercultural communication. Early attempts to Christianize the East seemed to borrow the tactics of the Crusaders. Hindu temples were destroyed. The European armies worked with the missionaries to save the souls of the Hindus by torture and murder if necessary. Killing and burning in God's name created few loyal converts to the faith, and religious conversion by force began to decline. It gave way to a new emphasis on persuasion. St. Francis began the conversion of the Japanese to Christianity in 1549. His missions in western Japan laid the foundation for the most successful Christian proselyting in any country of the world. His success was partly responsible for the gradual change in the Church from force to persuasion as the means of spreading Christianity.

In 1622, Pope Gregory XV formed the *Congregation for Propagation of the Faith*. This was the origin of the word *propaganda*, originally a positive term. Propaganda in this sense was a form of intercultural communication to be used for converting people to Catholicism, in contrast with force and holy wars. Propaganda also retains this positive connotation in the Communist world, where it refers to the reasoned use of argument to influence the educated and the rational thinkers.

Knowing that the Chinese held learning in high esteem, the Church sent the Italian Jesuit scholar Matteo Ricci to China. He arrived in Beijing in 1601. Other Jesuit scholars followed and had great influence on the Chinese court. Their knowledge of mathematics, geography, and mechanical devices was highly prized. The Jesuit knowledge of astronomy was particularly valued, as it was used to predict crop cycles and to know when eclipses and other celestial events might occur. These were seen in China as omens of the potential fall of an emperor and other major political changes. The Jesuits were skillful practitioners of intercultural communication. They learned the Chinese language and enjoyed interacting with the citizenry.

The Dominicans and other orders followed the Jesuits to China. They forbade their followers from showing reverence to the tablets of their ancestors and to the tablets in Confucian temples. Christian converts to these orders were forced to cut themselves off not just from their religious heritage but from the customs of their culture as well. The Jesuits favored a more intercultural approach, allowing their followers to mix Chinese customs with Christianity. The disputes between competing Christian groups was bewildering to the Chinese. How could a religion with such intense conflicts within itself be the one true way? The various Catholic orders appealed to the Pope to settle the disputes, which was a mistake. The Chinese emperor was already suspicious of the political purposes of the Christians. The appeal to an outside political force, the Pope (who ruled against the Jesuits), confirmed his suspicions. All missionaries except for a few of the most scholarly Jesuits were expelled from China in the early 1700s.

A similar conflict between the Christian orders occurred in Japan, with deadlier results. Spanish priests arrived in Japan from the Philippines and conflicts ensued with the missions established by St. Francis. Suspecting political motives, as had the Chinese, the Japanese authorities expelled all Christian missionaries. Christianity was forbidden in Japan, and thousands of Japanese Christians were persecuted, tortured, and massacred on order of the Japanese authorities. The fear of political interference by the West in Japanese affairs, partially fueled by the example set by the directly observable actions of the Christian missionaries, was so great that Japan shut out the rest of the world, going into isolated seclusion for over 200 years. Political fear also turned the authorities against Buddhism as well, which had become the unofficial religion of Japan. Japan returned to its Shintoist roots, ultimately leading to the militaristic Japanese state which emerged in the 1930s and 1940s.

The Opium Wars

With very few exceptions China refused all intercultural interaction with the outside world between the mid-fourteenth and mid-nineteenth centuries. The British had become a world power by the eighteenth century and wanted to trade with the ports of China. For a century, they were allowed limited trade with thirteen merchants designated by the Chinese to engage in transactions in Canton. The restrictions strongly favored the Chinese, and the British wanted greater access. They succeeded in dispatching an emissary to Beijing, who carried a letter from George III (against whom the United States fought the War of Independence). The Chinese Emperor responded, and his reply is a classic example of the problems encountered in intercultural communication.

> If you assert that your reverence for our Celestial Dynasty fills you with a desire to acquire our civilization, [you should understand that] our ceremonies and code of laws differ so completely from your own that, even if your Envoy were able to acquire the rudiments of our civilization, you could not possibly transplant our manners and customs to your alien soil. Therefore however adept the Envoy might become, nothing would be gained thereby . . . [Ruling] the wide world, I have but one aim in view, namely, to maintain a perfect governance, and to fulfill the duties of the state; strange and costly objects do not interest me. I . . . have no use for your country's manufactures . . . Our Celestial Empire possesses all things in prolific abundance, and lacks no product within its own borders. There is therefore no need to import the manufactures of outside barbarians in exchange for our own produce (Peffer, 1958, p. 53).

From the British perspective the letter was absurd—"The Chinese Emperor sees us as *barbarians* and dares to refer to us that way?" From the Chinese perspective the letter was all that could be and needed to be said—"We rule the world, we have everything we need, you couldn't imitate us even if you tried, there is no point in attempting any change." Did the Chinese have the moral right to shut out the rest of the world? Intercultural communication is more than understanding the right words to say in intercultural situations. It often demands the ability to understand cross-cultural ethical questions as phrased from different cultural perspectives and to settle them in a way acceptable and reasonable to all.

The situation between the British and Chinese continued to deteriorate. By the 1830s, the Chinese viceroy in Canton refused even to receive a letter from the British trade commissioner. The viceroy returned it unopened to "the barbarian headman." There was more to the conflict than just the desire to trade, and both sides knew it. Both Catholic and Protestant churches wanted to regain access to China for their missionaries. The British treasury had been drained for decades by paying in silver for much of the porcelain, silk, spices, and tea from China. The British eventually arrived at a solution to their balance-of-payments problem with China.

Enterprising sailors had often traded some of their ship's medicine cabinet supply of opium (used for intestinal problems) for personal profit. Opium could not be taken in large quantities without producing internal disorders, but the Dutch had found a way of mixing opium with the tobacco exported from the Americas by the colonists. This allowed opium to be used in addictive quantities. The British decided to solve two problems with one addictive product. They had a problem in India—a large landmass with many people which made good profits for the East India Company (which also served as the government of India at the time), but not large profits. They had a problem with China—they were making money, but the Chinese were making far more.

The people of India were forced to plant and harvest poppies. The British had found a use for Indian labor. The opium was refined and placed on the company's ships, then traded in China for the goods wanted back home in England. The balance of payments began to reverse; Chinese merchants began to pay in silver for British opium grown in India.

By 1839, almost two million pounds of opium arrived in China each year. A large portion of the Chinese citizenry spent their days high, and the British grew fabulously rich. Current drug cartels from Colombia to Mexico are pikers compared to the extent of the British drug trade. The sale of opium had been forbidden in China since the eighteenth century. Each time the Chinese authorities created harsher penalties and stronger enforcement against the drug trade, the drug supply decreased, the price went up, and new drug suppliers were willing to enter the market at the higher price. In 1839, the Chinese authorities decided to target all foreign merchants to stop the flow. They also demanded that the British surrender a sailor accused of murdering a Chinese citizen. The British refused and retreated to a barren rock called Hong Kong. An armada of small Chinese junks followed them. After several warnings to stop the advance, the British blew the Chinese armada out of the water. This action began the First Opium War between the British and the Chinese. There was little loss of life, and in 1842 the Chinese surrendered without a major conflict.

By 1850, 5.2 million pounds of opium were arriving in China. A Second Opium War was fought from 1856 to 1860. As British and French forces advanced on Beijing, they sent out a small party to negotiate with the Chinese under a flag of truce. The party was taken captive, and 21 of its 39 members died. The Chinese Emperor fled to Mongolia, and the foreign forces walked into a lightly defended Beijing. Upon discovery of the fate of the negotiators, the British decided that the Chinese needed to be taught a lesson. Just outside Beijing was the beautiful summer palace, the Yuan Ming Yuan, which contained some of the greatest art treasures in all of China. The British burned it—deliberately leaving the ruins as a reminder for the Chinese. This intercultural strategy worked quite well. The ruins still stand, regarded as a visible symbol of the barbarism of the Western foreigner, especially the British. Chinese parents can sometimes be observed teaching this history to their children today, nodding in the direction of any white foreigners who might be present.

Another memory of the foreigner was deeply etched into the collective consciousness of China from the treaty ending the Second Opium War. Christian missionaries would be allowed to preach openly and to own property in China, and opium was to be legalized. The two provisions went hand in hand, intercultural symbols of what Western culture offered China.

> Opium and the Gospel: they were imposed together by a war that included the sacking of one of the world's most beautiful structures. . . . For the white man came to China bearing the Cross and the opium pipe, imposed them together at the mouth of a cannon, and has prided himself ever since on the high purposes and fine fruits of his civilizing mission (Peffer, 1958, p. 73).

Native Americans

When Columbus arrived on the shores of North America in 1492, he was searching for a westward passage to India and China. Given the skin color (Shoemaker, 1997) and dress of the original Americans he encountered, Columbus believed he must have found India and referred to the people as "Indians." Columbus' "discovery" came at least 30,000 years after the original people of the Americas crossed the land bridge then linking Siberia and Alaska. Hundreds of thousands of these Asian people discovered the Americas before Columbus. Their ancestors greeted Columbus on his arrival in the "new" world. Nor was Columbus the first European to "discover" this world. Some 400 years earlier the Vikings had sailed from Greenland to Newfoundland, Canada. Archeological remains of a Viking camp were found in Newfoundland in 1960, and it is known that the Vikings traveled farther south. The importance of Columbus' voyage was in terms of the diffusion of information about the existence of the American continents to Europe—and the beginnings of yet another episode in the history of intercultural contact marked by exploitation and power differentials.

There were 10 million Native Americans on the North American continent in 1492, according to the best estimates of historians. By 1800 only one million were left. On the islands where Columbus first landed and described the native peoples, none were left when later explorers returned to visit the islands. Diseases brought by the white man, together with slavery as a secondary cause, had decimated the original American peoples (Burns, 1995). Remember the symbolism of the Black Death as a scourge from the East—here was another instance with the victim now the villain.

The image of Native Americans as barbarians was firmly established in the immigrant collective consciousness well before the Revolutionary War. Early Massachusetts General Court documents refer to "the common Indian enemy" (1689), and to the "violation of their solemn treaties" (Phips, 1745). Phrases such as "the late cruel murders and ravages on our frontiers" and statements that the "Indians . . . have . . . fallen upon this province, and in a most cruel, savage and perfidious manner, killed and butchered great numbers of the inhabitants . . ." are common in the writings of the times.

The Cherokee of Tennessee, Georgia, and the Carolinas had signed treaty after treaty with the Europeans since the early 1700s, only to see each one broken by the white man with the result that tribal families were pushed farther away from their ancestral lands. Many Native Americans sided with the French against the British, and then with the British in 1776 against the European Colonists, hoping to stop the formation of an independent European homeland in North America. The Cherokee Nation, of what is now the southern United States, adopted a new strategy by 1800—they would integrate with the whites and adopt their ways. Technological and cultural innovations entered Cherokee society rapidly. The Cherokee began to weave cloth as the whites did, and many voluntarily converted to Christianity. They built log homes copied after those of the white settlers and gave up their traditional dwellings. They voluntarily sent their children to the colonists' schools to learn both English and Cherokee, and Cherokee was transcribed for the first time into a written form. They adopted European agricultural methods, and wealthy Cherokees even owned African slaves, so thorough was their pursuit of white culture (Meyers, 1994).

This entire transformation of a traditional culture to an "American" culture occurred in less than thirty years. It occurred as a concerted decision of the Cherokee people to preserve themselves and their language, if not their traditional cultural ways. "In 1827 the Cherokee Nation adopted a constitution based on that of the United States. The following year, a bilingual newspaper called *The Cherokee Phoenix* became the first Native American voice in U.S. journalism" (Carnes, 1995, p. 15–16).

Other Native American groups in the Southeast tried other strategies to deal with the massive immigration of whites in the early 1800s. The Creek, living their traditional peaceful life as farmers in Alabama, were not friendly to whites who wanted to take their land. They were attacked by the U.S. Army under Andrew Jackson of Tennessee, who was himself speculating in land at the time. Jackson was also sent against the Seminoles in Florida who put up great resistance. All attempts to cope with the white immigrants of the early 1800s, whether by integration or resistance, were in vain. The fate of all southeastern Native American groups was sealed by the election of Andrew Jackson as president in 1828. Whites wanted the remaining Cherokee land on the Alabama-Georgia border. They also wanted the remaining Creek lands south of the Cherokee, the Seminole lands in Florida, and the lands of the Choctaw and Chickasaw in Alabama and Mississippi. They not only wanted the land, they wanted the "Indian threat" removed. It is difficult to see how the term "threat" or even "Indian" could be applied to the Cherokee culture of 1830.

As president, Jackson decided to fulfill Thomas Jefferson's earlier proposal to move all Indians into *Permanent Indian Territory* west of the Mississippi. This proposal had been based on the belief that this territory would be sufficiently distant from white settlements that centuries would elapse before the U.S. government would have to face the "Indian Problem" again. Congress passed Jackson's *Indian Removal Act* in 1830, ending any pretence of peaceful co-existence with Native Americans in the eastern United States. The Cherokee Nation appealed this law to the United States Supreme Court, where they won their case. The Cherokee and their property rights had been recognized by the highest symbol of the white man's system, the United States Supreme Court. The legal victory did them no good, however. The president of the United States simply ignored the ruling. Jackson ordered federal agents to bribe a small group of the Cherokee, who then signed the New Echota treaty giving up the Cherokee lands. It was illegal and immoral but quite effective. Accepting the white man's ways was not sufficient, if you were not white. In May 1838, the U.S. Army under General Winfield Scott invaded the peaceful farms and towns of the Cherokee nation. "Across Cherokee country, men were ordered at gunpoint from their plows, women from their looms. Jubilant whites looted or burned or occupied the homes left behind" (Carnes, 1995, p. 18).

The forced march to Oklahoma at gunpoint by the Army came to be known as the Trail of Tears. Some groups of native peoples were forced to walk barefoot through the snow and were refused blankets by the Army escorting them. Babies and the elderly died first. Individual soldiers who tried to assist the people received dishonorable discharges (ordinarily a sanction for murder, sabotage, or espionage). Of the 100,000 Native Americans who were driven from their homes, over 25 percent died before reaching the West. When the Army would not allow them to stop long enough to bury their dead, a blanket stamped "U.S. Army" was placed over the body and the forced march went on (Williams, 1992; Meyers, 1994). A sacred fire still burns near Gore, Oklahoma, ignited from coals from the homelands near Lookout Mountain, Tennessee that Cherokee women carried with them. The Seminole today observe a tradition etched in the collective memory by the Trail of Tears: a new blanket is spread over the coffin of the dead at Seminole funerals.

In 1845, only 360,000 Native Americans in about fifty nations or tribes remained on the lands which would eventually become the original forty-eight states. The vast majority of these Native peoples now lived west of the Mississippi, in lands ceded in several treaties to Native American groups "in perpetuity" (forever) in exchange for their removal from the East (Burns, 1995). The current states of Kansas, Nebraska, Oklahoma, the Dakotas, and most territory west of the Mississippi to the Pacific Ocean were listed on official U.S. maps as the "Permanent Indian Territory." European immigrants had no more legal claim to this land than they had to the African or Asian continents. Only 20,000 European immigrants lived west of the Mississippi River, but all that was soon to change.

In 1843, a pass had been discovered through the Wyoming Rockies, low enough for an ordinary family to traverse in a horse-drawn wagon. Trains still cross the country through that pass today. In 1845, an editorial appeared in a New York newspaper calling for America to reach its *manifest destiny*. The idea had circulated for years. In 1811 John Quincy Adams declared:

> The whole continent of North America appears to be destined by Divine Providence to be peopled by one nation, speaking one language, professing one general system of religious and political principles, and accustomed to one general tenor of social usages and customs (Divine, 1960).

In other words, God had determined that the United States should extend from the Atlantic to the Pacific as one nation. Few responded to the call immediately, but the notion of manifest destiny was implanted in the collective consciousness of the nation.

In January 1848, gold was discovered by a mechanic checking on the mill wheel at Sutter's Sawmill in California's Sierra Nevada Mountains. Sutter pleaded in vain for his men not to let the news get out. Sutter himself did not covet the gold. He had a vision of California as a great agricultural paradise and did not want that vision ruined by men hungry for gold. The population of San Francisco early in the year of 1848 was 429 people. By 1849 it was 25,000. Not only was the gold rush on, but a massive population migration was beginning. The discovery of the Comstock lode (a vein of silver ore six miles long and lying close to veins of gold) in western Nevada in June of 1859 further increased the frenzied migration west. But it was the desire of the settlers for the land itself, to own it and possess it as theirs, that was the overall driving force. *The Homestead Act*, passed by Congress in 1862, gave anyone the rights to land that they actually settled on and worked. "Anyone" did not include Native Americans or slaves.

Intercultural communication and the behavior of peoples from diverse cultural backgrounds depends on the worldview embodied in their attitudes, beliefs, and values. Their religious beliefs are often paramount in bringing these concepts together into a coherent worldview. While there were many different Native American groups with quite different systems of beliefs, most Native Americans regarded the earth as their mother. It cannot be owned; it simply is. It is a spiritual part of oneself, and one is part of the land. People were to live in harmony with the plants, animals, and the earth itself, never taking so much from it that it would not replenish itself within a short time. Native Americans tended to see the world as having infinite space and infinite time that cycled through the seasons. The people moved with the seasons: to the north where it was cool in summer and to the south where it was warm in winter. Provisions were sometimes scarce, but the buffalo would normally provide both clothing and food to the Plains Indians.

Judeo-Christian origin legends were based on the story of Adam and Eve. The Garden of Eden was an idylic, heaven-like state where everything was available in abundance. When Adam and Eve forfeited the right to live in this paradise, they were forced to live out their lives on the *earth*, a foreboding place which was their enemy. The earth needed to be tamed and conquered; it had no value of its own other than providing the materials with which to build. The earth was not a place which needed to be cared for and nourished, to be replenished when stripped bare of its fruits, for the earth would be left behind and abandoned when people return to their heavenly paradise (Burns, 1995).

This contrast in beliefs about the earth represented a wide gulf in perceptions. One worldview saw the earth—the land—as the source of all sustenance, a continuous expanse to be treated with great respect, something which could not be owned but only occupied. The other view saw the land as ownable, divisible, and fenceable—a harsh enemy which throws hazards, trials, and tribulations against the people who occupy it. The earth must be attacked and made peaceful.

The completion of the railway across the North American continent in 1869 brought settlers from both coasts and linked the entire country. Covered wagons were replaced by an iron horse. The immigrants poured west in massive numbers. The views of many frontier newcomers on how to solve the "Indian Problem" were not far removed from those of the Nazis concerning the solution of the "Jewish Problem," or from some political policies in Israel concerning Arabs, or from the policies of extremist Muslims in Algeria. Native Americans were to be concentrated into camps called reservations. If there were problems or resistance, they were to be shot. In exchange, the native peoples would be protected from whites and would receive money, blankets, food, and the necessities of life from the white government. However, the white agents administering the government programs were often corrupt. The money seldom got through to the reservations; the food delivered to native peoples was often spoiled in addition to being foreign to their accustomed diet; and the land assigned to them was mostly barren. Neither hunting nor agriculture could produce food from it.

In June 1876, the last great meeting of the Native American Nations took place in Montana. Many wise chiefs were present including Crazy Horse and Sitting Bull. U.S. army troops, commanded by a cocky and incautious officer named Custer, attacked the assembled tribes near a branch of the Little Bighorn River. Custer's troops were wiped out. After the battle, Sitting Bull and the Lakota Sioux moved north into Canada for four years. The Army hunted Crazy Horse and the Oglala Sioux. Within a few years his people were starving, and Crazy Horse surrendered. He was bayoneted to death while his arms were held. His body was removed by his people and buried at a sacred site known only to the Oglala to this day.

When Sitting Bull returned from Canada, his people were also starving, reduced to less than 150 individuals, including women and children. The vast herds of buffalo (numbering 60 million in the mid-nineteenth century) that had roamed the plains of North America for centuries had been destroyed. In 1883 there were less than 200 buffalo alive throughout the entire American West (Burns, 1995). Buffalo Bill Cody and his fellow buffalo hunters had done their job quite thoroughly. Although the slaughter of the buffalo is sometimes portrayed as the result of trophy hunters looking for the thrill of the kill, it was much more than that. It was a deliberate and very effective policy to destroy the food supply of the native peoples. White men in the 1870s would sit atop mounds of buffalo skulls 30 feet high to have their pictures taken for posterity. Starving and dressed in rags, Sitting Bull gave up the fight in July 1881. He surrendered his rifle to his young son, not to the U.S. Army. The child handed the gun to the soldiers.

Policymakers in Washington now decided that since the Native Americans had been so badly treated, it was time to make it up to them. Without any understanding of intercultural communication that could reveal the attitudes and values of a people, or any ability to evaluate a situation without ethnocentric bias, the government simply dictated the course for "improvement." Native Americans were forbidden from practicing their "false" religions and conversion to Christianity was attempted. Many were also forbidden to speak their own language, and their children were sent away to school where they were forced to learn and speak only English. The first job after high school of one of this book's author's father was teaching in the local Indian School near Gowanda, New York. He explained to his son how he was told to instill in the Native children the concepts of thrift, Christianity, individuality, and personal property as valued ideals. Nothing of the Native culture was ever mentioned, much less taught.

The vast majority of the remaining lands of the Lakota and other tribes were opened to white homesteaders. A *Ghost Dance*, intended to communicate with and revive the dead, was a part of many Native American religions. For the starving Lakota of 1890 the Ghost Dance became a religion unto itself. The coming of the messiah—a Lakota holy man who could clothe the people so the bullets would not find them—was rumored. If the people joined hands in large concentric circles and believed and danced hard enough, all of their deceased relatives would arise again from the dead and join them in a great Lakota nation (Miller, 1959). The frenzy produced by the dance was perceived by the Indian agents as a threat, a war dance. The natives, it was said in messages to Washington, were becoming restless. In response, U.S. troops were dispatched to the Lakota reservation in December, 1890. Lakota policemen were sent to arrest Sitting Bull, still feared as a great leader by the whites. While they were arresting him, the old man was shot to death outside his cabin in front of his four wives (Brown, 1971; Burns, 1995).

Many Lakota fled, fearing a massacre. The Army tracked and surrounded a group of about 350. A shot, origin unknown, went off and the soldiers opened fire with cannons and smaller arms. Twenty soldiers and many Lakota fell in the first volleys, including most of the warriors. The others (mostly women and children) ran toward a nearby creek. Soldiers ran up both sides of the riverbank and began to shoot anything that moved. The firing against the remaining unarmed people continued for hours. Some of the bodies of the children attempting to escape were found with gunshot wounds in the back as far as three miles from the initial attack. Approximately 250 of the Lakota were dead, among them a Lakota brave named White American; another three dozen were badly wounded. The U.S. Army thus won the Battle of Wounded Knee (Axelrod, 1993; Brown, 1971).

By the early 1890s it was over. What had begun in the 1840s as a search for *manifest destiny* was now achieved, at the expense of peoples excluded from those goals. Native American culture was seen as nonexistent. Native Americans themselves were seen as evil, evidenced by the brutal phrase, "The only good Indian is a dead Indian." What explains the attitude that no one matters except for one's own group? When people are willing to define culturally different "others" as inferior, the stage is set for another intercultural tragedy.

Much current international communication involves accusations of violations of human rights and suppression of freedom, such as by China in Tibet and Indonesia in East Timor. Many Westerners find it difficult to understand the use of such violent methods in the suppression of native peoples. When the United States deplores the violation of human rights by other nations, we must remain mindful of the blood on our own hands. Other cultures look at the history of the United States and see settlers who stole the land of the Native Americans to create a country and enslaved the people of Africa to grow tobacco and cotton. Did the United States respect human rights when it was building its nation?

Summary

During the several centuries described in this chapter, the rate of intercultural contact increased rapidly with exploration, improvements in transportation and communication, and the rise of international trade. European culture became dominant throughout the world via colonialization, which often involved invasion and warfare. The European colonizers, and the missionaries who accompanied them, were *ethnocentric*, defined as the degree to which other cultures are judged as inferior to one's own culture. The Europeans believed they were superior to the indigenous cultures they encountered in the Americas, Africa, and Asia.

Notice, however, the many influences on European culture from other parts of the world. Crusaders returned from the Middle East with new foods and cloth. Marco Polo introduced the readers of his travel book to art, technologies, and other ideas from China. Arabic intellectual and scientific influences came into European civilization via the seven hundred years that the Moors occupied Spain. So European civilization borrowed heavily from other cultures with whom Europeans came in contact. European migrants to the United States brought this amalgamation with them, where it mixed with still other cultural elements to form a "100 percent American culture."

The cultural diversity of modern life is a strength of today's society, but it also poses a basic difficulty for many attempts at human communication. An understanding of the importance of communication between cultures is essential to promote the benefits of shared experience rather than the tragic consequences of imposed beliefs. Intercultural understanding and sensitivity cannot change the past, but they can offer hope for the future. We can build a better world if we understand the principles of intercultural communication.

Note

[1] C.E. is an abbreviation for "of the Common Era" and, along with B.C.E. (Before the Common Era"), is used in this book rather than B.C. (before Christ) and A.D. (*anno Domini*, "in the year of the Lord"). Other era designations include A.H. (*anno Hegirae*, "in the year of [Muhammed's] Hegira") or A.H. (*anno Hebraico* (in the Hebrew year). As the last two entries demonstrate, systems of chronology are context-specific. One must know the meaning of the symbols to the particular culture using the designation. A.H. in one system uses the equivalent of A.D. 622 to begin counting and A.H. in the other system refers to the equivalent of 3760 B.C. as the starting point. Still another designation is A.U.C. (*ab urbe condita* "from the founding of the city" [Rome, in 753]. T.C. refers to the Thai Calendar based on the birth of the Buddha in 543 B.C.E. The year of publication of this book is 2542 T.C. Any date can be used as the foundation of a system—as long as the parties communicating agree on the definition.

Chapter 2

The Study of Intercultural Communication

66 Communication constitutes the core of culture and indeed of life itself.

Edward T. Hall (1966)

The story of intercultural communication begins at the Foreign Service Institute.

Wendy Leeds-Hurwitz (1990) 99

Intercultural communication as a field of study began in earnest after World War II. At that time, the United States was the leading world power, but its diplomats were ineffectual. They seldom knew the language of the nation to which they were assigned and had no understanding of its culture. The U.S. Department of State established the Foreign Service Institute (FSI) in order to retrain its diplomats. In this chapter, we trace the roots of intercultural communication from the beginnings of social science around the turn of the century to the contributions of Edward Hall and his colleagues at the FSI to the formation of a scholarly paradigm for intercultural communication.

The Roots of Intercultural Communication

The first department of sociology in the United States was formed at the University of Chicago in 1892. Intercultural communication scholars owe an intellectual debt to the Chicago School, as the department was known, for pioneering empirical investigations based on the theories of Georg Simmel, a German sociologist (Rogers, 1994). From 1915 to 1935, the dominance of the Chicago School in the field of sociology was established through studies of social problems like prostitution, poverty, crime, and racial conflict in low-income areas.

The two most influential members of the Chicago School, George Herbert Mead and Robert E. Park, pursued graduate study at the University of Berlin and enrolled in courses taught by Simmel. Albion Small, founder and chair of the sociology department at Chicago, translated 15 of Simmel's writings and published them as articles in the *American Journal of Sociology*, which he edited. Small had been a fellow student with Simmel at the University of Berlin. Simmel's stranger (*"Der Fremde"* in German) and its intellectual descendants—social distance, marginal man, cosmopoliteness, and homophily/heterophily—are key concepts in both sociology and intercultural communication, which we discuss below.

Georg Simmel earned his doctorate at the University of Berlin in 1881. He taught there for twenty-nine years before moving to the University of Strassburg. Simmel's lectures were very well-attended (in fact, they were held in the largest lecture hall at the University of Berlin). The topics of Simmel's lectures, and of the books and articles that he wrote, varied widely: from the sociology of money (*The Philosophy of Money*, 1900), to the nature of urban life, to communication networks (*The Web of Group-Affiliations*, 1922).

The topics that Simmel chose to analyze were related to his personal life experiences. Simmel was the son of Jewish parents who converted to Christianity; he experienced anti-Semitism in Germany. The model for his concept of the stranger was the Jewish trader: "Throughout the history of economics the stranger everywhere appears as the trader, or the trader as stranger . . . the classical example is the history of European Jews" (Simmel, 1950, p. 403).

Simmel thought of himself as a stranger. His circle of friends included artists and intellectuals, rather than other professors, government officials, or businesspeople. Many of his non-establishment friends were alienated observers of society. They were social strangers who shared with Simmel the stigma of the outsider (Coser, 1977, p. 195).

What Is a Stranger?

The stranger, as defined by Simmel (1950, p. 402), is an individual who is a member of a system but who is not strongly attached to that system.[1] The essence of Simmel's definition of the stranger was that the stranger was not completely accepted by other members of a system. The stranger was unlike others in the system in certain important ways. A *stranger* is an individual who is different from oneself (Sorrells, 1997). People who are culturally heterophilous are strangers to each other. An individual's communication relationship with a stranger is at the heart of intercultural communication. The stranger is often viewed with suspicion because of the uncertainty and unpredictability of the stranger's behavior. Extreme cases of suspicion result in xenophobia, fear of strangers.

Figure 2-1.   The German Scholar Georg Simmel (1858–1918).
Simmel himself was a stranger, which he defined as someone who is a
member of a system but who is not strongly attached to it.

Source: Drawing by Corinne L. Shefner-Rogers. Used by permission.

Simmel's insights on the role of the stranger were part of his general concern with the relationships between individuals. For Simmel, exchange was
the primary form of social life: "Interaction between individuals is the starting point of all social formation" (Simmel, 1900/1978). He was also concerned
with the relationship of the individual to the larger system: "The socialized
individual always remains in dual relation toward society: he is incorporated
within it and yet stands against it" (Coser, 1965). Society exists wherever a
number of individuals enter into reciprocal relationships. The process of
actions and reactions between individuals determines the forms and functions of society, which in turn influence the interaction of individuals.

The dual relationship is a theme in Simmel's work. He viewed members
of society as both a product of society yet operating from a personal, conscious
intent. Although he described modern society as a web whose delicate threads
are woven between one person and others (Frisby, 1985), he believed that

analysis of social structures alone (the type of analysis pursued by sociologists in that era) was not sufficient to understand modern society. His examination of reciprocal interactions at the individual level within a larger social context inspired much of the research at the Chicago School.

When individuals enter into a group, they essentially choose to relinquish some of their individuality and to align themselves with the generality of the group. Having done so, group members no longer look at each other in purely objective terms but rather through the lens of the group that has become part of their consciousness. The shared interests and experiences shape the framework from which future interactions take place. Simmel (1922/1955, p. 140) stated: "The groups with which the individual is affiliated constitute a system of coordinates, as it were, such that each new group with which he becomes affiliated circumscribes him more exactly and more ambiguously."

With each group membership, the individual becomes both more and less than an individual personality—both part of that society and something else. This ambiguity is particularly noticeable with the person who is shut out from the group—the stranger. The very definition of who is—and who is not—admitted means the stranger is partly formed by the group. The role of member is assigned to some and the role of stranger to others.

The stranger provides the unique advantages of a distanced perspective (Simmel, 1950, p. 402). The stranger sees the system in a different light than do others. Perhaps the stranger is a recent migrant to the system, who retains the freedom of coming and going. The stranger is free of the network links in the original system and not yet bound by the new system. Therefore, strangers are relatively unconstrained and can more easily depart from social norms. They can move across boundaries and live on the margin between different groups. For example, a multicultural individual can more easily look at the behavior in an interaction from the perspective of the other. Rather than immediately categorizing the meaning of a gesture as having universal significance, the stranger has the experience to know there are multiple possible meanings. The distanced perspective allows an individual to recognize the form of a symbol without immediately linking that form with a specific content. In short, the stranger has an intercultural perspective on communication.

The arrival of a stranger in a system is often the foundation upon which a work of fiction is built (McLemore, 1970). A stranger may be perceived as exciting, alluring, and attractive (Sorrells, 1997). For example, a new student in high school can be very popular. Although strangers can be perceived as threatening because there is less certainty about predicting behavior, that same uncertainty can be enticing. The balance between the need for security (expectations fulfilled) and the need for novelty varies depending on the context of the interaction. The school context has a number of factors that satisfy security needs while other situations involving strangers would not.

Simmel distinguished between form and content. He analyzed conversation as an example. People use conversation as a tool to communicate specific content or to reach an agreement about action to be taken. They also use conversation simply as an art—at a party for example. Rather than communicating particular content, the form itself is elevated. Conversation requires two people and establishes a relationship in which the form of the interaction is as important as the content (Martindale, 1981).

Simmel viewed conflict as an integral part of the human tendency toward association. He believed an element of community weaves itself into every hostility. For him, competition was a formal relation of tension; it determined the form of the group, the members' reciprocal positions, and the social distance of the elements.

Simmel's perspective on communication can be summarized as follows (Levine & others, 1976):

1. Society consists of communication among individuals.

2. All human communication consists of information-exchange that has reciprocal effects on the individuals involved.

3. Communication occurs among individuals who are at varying degrees of social distance from one another.[2]

4. Communication satisfies certain basic human needs, such as for companionship.

5. Certain types of communication become relatively stable over time, and thus represent culture and social structure.

The Stranger and Scientific Objectivity

The key scholar in translating and applying Simmel's concept of the stranger was Robert E. Park, a former newspaper reporter who earned his Ph.D. degree in Germany. In 1900 Park took Simmel's course in sociology at the University of Berlin. It gave him the fundamental perspective on communication and society for which he had been searching and on which he based his doctoral dissertation.

For the next decade, Park was employed as a press agent by the Congo Reform Association, established to protest the harsh colonial rule of the Congo by Belgium. Park worked for Booker T. Washington, an important African-American leader of the day, on the staff of the Tuskeegee Institute in Alabama. Out of this decade of experience of working with and studying African Americans in the South, Park developed his concept of the marginal man (Hughes, 1980, p. 69).

In 1915, at the age of 50, Park began teaching sociology at the University of Chicago. He soon was regarded as the intellectual leader of the Chicago School of sociology and the most influential figure in determining the direction of North American sociology. Park was particularly instrumental in changing the new field of sociology to a more objective science (Hughes, 1980, p. 73). Chicago was a city of immigrants from European villages living in urban slum conditions. While the empirical studies by Park and his doctoral students were intended to provide understanding of these social problems, Park insisted that such investigation must be objective. This meant that the researchers could not also be what Park termed "damn do-gooders." The proper role of the social researcher, Park felt, was to study and report research results—not to engage in ameliorating the social problems that were studied. The danger of combining the two roles was that the investigator might then view a problem of study in a judgmental way, and bias might result.

Park drew a model for scientific objectivity from Simmel's concept of the stranger. As discussed earlier, the distanced perspective of a stranger has distinct advantages. Objectivity is advanced by a perspective from outside of the system, which is less biased than an insider's view that accepts the assumptions of the system (Sorrells, 1997). For example, a Chicago sociologist might investigate prostitution, but the scholar's personal opinions about this profession should not affect how the research was conducted or the interpretation of the findings (Rogers, 1994, p. 187). A social researcher should mentally stand outside of the system of study in order to see it more clearly. Park (1922) described Chicago sociology as "A logical scheme for a disinterested investigation of the origin and function of social institutions as they everywhere existed."

The Concept of Social Distance

Inspired by Simmel's notion of the stranger and his related idea of interpersonal closeness versus distance, Park developed the concept of *social distance*. He defined this concept as the degree to which an individual perceives a lack of intimacy with individuals different in ethnicity, race, religion, occupation, or other variables (Park, 1924; Park, 1950, pp. 256–60). Park's doctoral student, Emory S. Bogardus, developed a social distance scale which measured whether a respondent felt closer to, for instance, Chinese or Mexicans. A respondent was asked, "Would you marry someone who is Chinese? Would you have Chinese people as regular friends? As speaking acquaintances?" (Bogardus, 1933). Then the respondent was asked the same series of questions for Mexicans, and others. Essentially, the Bogardus social distance scale quantified the perceived intimacy versus distance of an individual's relationships with various others.

Culture specifies how intimate or socially distant two individuals should be in a given situation. For instance, North Americans often use first names with someone they have just met. This is very puzzling to most Europeans, who are much more formal in their relationships. They only use first names (and the intimate personal pronoun "*tu*" or "*du*") with very close friends and family. When one of the authors taught in a German university, he was addressed by students and other faculty as "Professor Doctor Rogers." He became friendly with his host, a German faculty member. The two talked every day and enjoyed meals together. But they still used formal titles when they chatted. After a month or so, the German professor told Rogers that he could call him by his first name, which was symbolic of their lessened social distance.

The Concept of Marginal Man

The concept of the stranger also influenced Park (1928) to conceptualize what he called the *marginal man*, an individual who lives in two different worlds—and is a stranger in both (Levine & others, 1976). Park studied the first-generation children of European immigrant parents in the United States. These marginal individuals typically rejected the European culture and language of their parents but did not consider themselves to be true North Americans either. Their freedom from the norms of both systems led to a relatively higher crime rate. Park (1928) stated that the marginal man is "a cultural hybrid, an individual on the margin of two cultures which never completely fused." Park (1928) thought that the marginal man represented a special way to understand social change: "It is in the mind of the marginal man—where the changes and fusions of culture are going on—that we can best study the processes of civilization and of progress."

In addition to immigrants, other instances of marginal individuals are children from cross-cultural marriages or cultural hybrids like Christian converts in Asia. One of Park's doctoral students, Everett V. Stonequist, described many examples in his book, *The Marginal Man* (Stonequist, 1937). Park's concept of the marginal man was later extended to the *sojourner*, an individual who visits another culture for a period of time but who retains his/her original culture (Siu, 1952). The experience of sojourning often gives individuals a unique perspective for viewing both the host and home cultures. The sojourner later became a favorite topic of study for intercultural communication scholars; it led to such concepts as the U-curve of adjustment, culture shock, and reverse cultural shock (see Chapter 7).

The Concept of Heterophily

Another intellectual descendant of Simmel's stranger, related to the Park/Bogardus concept of social distance, is *heterophily*, the degree to which two or more individuals who communicate are unalike. The opposite concept, *homophily*, is the degree to which two or more individuals who communicate are alike (Rogers, 1995).[3] The concepts of homophily/heterophily (and their synonyms) have been utilized in research on communication in organizations, small groups, communities, publics, and other systems.

Homophily and heterophily have been measured (1) at the subjective level, as the degree to which an individual perceives himself/herself as similar to, or dissimilar from, another person, or (2) at the objective level, as the degree to which two or more individuals are observed to be similar or dissimilar

(Rogers & Bhowmik, 1970). When both subjective and objective homophily are measured for the same individuals, the results indicate that they are positively, although not always strongly, related. Further, subjective homophily is more closely related (than is objective homophily) to other variables like frequency of communication and interpersonal attraction between two or more individuals (Rokeach, 1968, p. 63).

Generalizations about the concepts of homophily/heterophily were derived by Rogers and Bhowmik (1970) from various communication research studies:

1. **Most communication occurs between homophilous individuals.** People find it easier to talk with someone like themselves.
2. **Homophilous communication is more effective than heterophilous communication.** When two participants in a communication situation do not share a common perspective, the meanings obtained from the information-exchange by the receiver are unlikely to be those intended by the source.
3. **Effective communication between individuals leads to their greater homophily in knowledge, attitudes, and overt behavior.**
4. **Maximally effective communication occurs between individuals who are homophilous on certain variables and heterophilous on other variables that are relevant to the communication situation.**
5. **A heterophilous source/channel is perceived by a communication receiver as having *expertness* credibility (on the basis of the source's formal education and technical expertise), while a homophilous source/channel is perceived as being *trustworthy*.**

Cosmopoliteness

The fourth concept drawn from Simmel's notion of the stranger is *cosmopoliteness*. Communication scholars define this concept as the degree to which an individual has a relatively high degree of communication outside of the person's own system (Rogers, 1995). Cosmopolites provide a system with *openness*—the degree to which a system exchanges information with its environment (Rogers & Agarwala-Rogers, 1976, p. 140). The concept of cosmopoliteness[4] was developed by Robert K. Merton (1949, pp. 441–74) from his study of influential people in Dover, New Jersey. He found two quite different orientations among the people in that city: localites and cosmopolites. Localites identified strongly with the community, were well-known by other residents, and mainly read local newspapers. In contrast, cosmopolites were more mobile, more highly educated, traveled widely, and had friendship networks with individuals outside of the community. Cosmopolites read either *The New York Times* or the *New York Herald Tribune*, or both; they also read *Time* magazine. Localites read none of these media.

The concept of cosmopoliteness has been widely applied in organizational research, where individuals high in cosmopoliteness are called boundary-spanners (Thompson, 1967; Janowitz & Delany, 1957). Cosmopolites are concentrated at the top and at the bottom of many organizations. Top executives travel widely and have contact with other organizations in the environment. Operational-level employees at the bottom deal directly with clients and customers and with incoming materials and information (Rogers & Agarwala-Rogers, 1976, p. 67).

Research on the diffusion of innovations has also made extensive use of the concept of cosmopoliteness (Rogers, 1995). For example, an investigation of the spread of hybrid seed corn among Iowa farmers found that farmers who were more innovative in adopting the new seed traveled more often to cities like Des Moines (Ryan & Gross, 1943). A similar relationship between innovativeness (the degree to which an individual is relatively earlier than others in adopting new ideas) and cosmopoliteness was found in a study of the diffusion of a new medical drug among doctors (Coleman & others, 1966). The most innovative physicians traveled more often to out-of-town medical specialty meetings. Because innovators are oriented outside of their system, they are relatively more free to deviate from system norms in adopting a new idea. However, this orientation also means that other members of a system do not view innovators with much respect. As a result, innovators usually do not persuade others to follow their lead. The next category of individuals likely to adopt a new idea (called early adopters) are relatively higher in opinion leadership. After the early adopters begin using a new idea, the rate of adoption in a system speeds up and forms an S-shaped curve.

Simmel's original concept of the stranger, and the concepts later derived from it, all deal with the interpersonal relationship of the individual to other individuals and/or to the system of which the individual is a part. Implied in the concepts of the stranger, social distance, marginal man, heterophily, and cosmopoliteness is the notion that the individual does not have a high degree of cohesion with the larger system of which he or she is a part. Simmel's theoretical perspective recognized the benefits of distant relationships: greater objectivity, innovativeness, and creativity. As you encounter other concepts in this text, you will detect the influence of Simmel's thinking as it applies to the study of intercultural communication (Figure 2-2).

Critical Concepts in Intercultural Communication

When European theories like Simmel's were brought to the United States, they were applied in research bearing on social problems. Empirical studies by sociologists, social psychologists, and anthropologists began about a century ago. These studies produced the concepts, empirically-based theories, and generalizations about human behavior that form the heart of intercul-

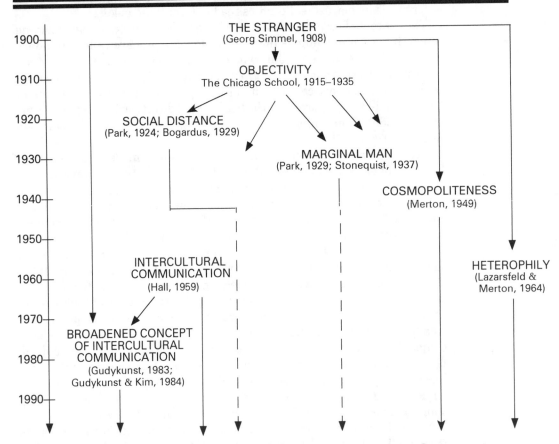

Figure 2-2.   Intellectual Descendants of Simmel's Concept of the Stranger. Georg Simmel defined the stranger in terms of intimacy versus social distance in interpersonal communication relationships, a dimension fundamental to the study of intercultural communication. Simmel's concept led to a family of four concepts (social distance, marginal man, cosmopoliteness, objective scholarly research) and to a broader conception of intercultural communication as interaction between any type of unalike individuals.

tural communication. About the same time that Georg Simmel was writing about the stranger in Germany, William Graham Sumner wrote *Folkways* (1906), in which he discussed three important concepts: ingroup, outgroup and ethnocentrism. These analytical tools are used by scholars of intercultural communication today. Sumner's concepts, as well as cultural relativism, prejudice, discrimination, stereotypes, and the authoritarian personality resurface throughtout the text.

Ingroups and Outgroups

Sumner (1906/1940, pp. 12–13) described how individuals in a population affiliate with various groups. These groups become differentiated as they struggle for existence with each other. The individuals within any given group have peaceful relationships, but they are hostile to other groups. An *ingroup* is a collectivity with which an individual identifies. An *outgroup* is a collectivity with which an individual does not identify. Individuals in an ingroup may refer to persons in outgroups as "pig-eaters," "uncircumcised," or "jabberers." Koreans refer to the Japanese as "dwarfs"; the Japanese call Koreans "garlic-eaters." An ingroup exalts itself by boasting about its own ways and looks with contempt on outsiders. Without thinking, an individual takes the values of the ingroup as an ideal and automatically uses them to judge other, less familiar values and behaviors.

To what ingroups do you belong? Perhaps your nationality is one ingroup. Other ingroups could be: left-handers; people who are disabled; individuals with a particular lifestyle, such as joggers, mountain-climbers, or gourmets. Each ingroup to which an individual belongs automatically defines certain outgroups. For instance, left-handers often feel that their special needs are overlooked by the rest of the world. This perception creates a certain degree of resentment against the right-handed world.

Case Illustration:
The Left-Handed Ingroup

What do Bill Gates, Albert Einstein, Aristotle, Leonardo da Vinci, Bill Clinton, and Whoopi Goldberg have in common? They are all left-handers, along with 11 percent of the total population. These individuals are penalized by having to live in a right-handed world that has been designed by, and for, right-handers: computer keyboards in which the most-used keys are placed conveniently for the 89 percent majority, right-handed scissors, and classroom desk-chairs that are extremely uncomfortable for left-handers. Consider the indignity implied by such expressions as "a left-handed compliment" and "out in left field." Even the word for "left" in most languages carries a negative connotation. For example, the French word for left is gauche, which also means clumsy or maladroit in both French and English.

Understandably, left-handers tend to band together as an ingroup and to resent "other-handers." Lefties share information with each other about how to cope with a right-handed world. For instance, a home page on the Internet provides information to port-siders about stores specializing in left-handed tools, golf clubs, guitars, and computer keyboards.

In striving for equality, women and men may constitute an out-group/ingroup. A century ago, women in the United States began to obtain more formal education and to become vocal about voting and other rights. In the early 1900s the women's suffrage movement led to women gaining the right to vote. During World War II, women increasingly entered the workforce outside of the home. In the 1960s the women's movement worked to achieve economic and political power. Struggles continue today on such issues as: equal pay for equal work, the "mommy track," sexual harassment in the work-place, men-only clubs, etc.

Ethnocentrism

Ethnocentrism is the degree to which individuals judge other cultures as inferior to their own culture. The concept of ethnocentrism comes from two Greek words (*ethos*, people or nation, and *ketron*, center) which mean being centered on one's cultural group (and thus judging other cultures by one's cultural values). No one is born with ethnocentrism. It has to be taught. Everyone learns to be ethnocentric, at least to a certain degree. Sumner divided the concept of ethnocentrism into two parts: the belief in the superiority of one's own group and the consequent belief that other groups are inferior. It is quite natural to feel that one's own group is the best, whether a country, a culture, or a college sports team. The problems arise not from feeling pride in one's own culture but from drawing the unnecessary conclusion that other cultures are inferior. Ethnocentrism is a block to effective intercultural communication because it prevents understanding unalike others.

Ethnocentrism is not just an intellectual matter of making comparisons with another culture; emotions are involved (LeVine & Campbell, 1972, p. 1). The symbols of one's ethnicity, religion, or national ingroup become objects of pride and veneration, while the symbols of an outgroup (a flag, for example) become objects of contempt and hatred. Outgroup members are perceived as inferior and perhaps immoral. For example, European colonialists often perceived the native peoples that they conquered in Latin America, Africa, and Asia as subhuman (see Chapter 1). Extreme ethnocentrism may lead to conflict and even to warfare with an outgroup. A threat from an outgroup leads to greater cohesion among the members of the ingroup.

Many languages inherently convey a certain degree of ethnocentrism. For instance, the word for the language of the Navajo people, *Diné*, means "the people." So all non-Diné are, by implication, non-people. An ethnocentric parallel exists in many other languages. For example, *La Raza* (Spanish for "The Race") implies exclusivity for Latinos in the United States. The word for foreigner in most languages is negative, implying something that is undesirable. An example is the expression "a foreign object in my eye." In Hindi, the word for foreigner is *ferengi*. This word is not a compliment in India. The Chinese refer to their own country as "the Middle Kingdom," implying that it is the center of the world. Similarly, people living in the United States refer to themselves as "Americans," forgetting that everyone who lives in North America, South America, and Central America are also Americans.

Outcroppings of ethnocentrism can be observed in maps of the world. All maps suffer from the basic difficulty of expressing a three-dimensional world in a two-dimensional plane (a piece of paper). The way in which such projections are made often displays the ethnocentrism of the mapmaker. For example, the commonly used Mercator projection (Figure 2-3) has a Eurocentric perspective, with the prime meridian of longitude running through Greenwich, near London. This arbitrary arrangement of the map was understandable in the 1500s. Europeans thought of themselves as located in the center of the civilized world. At that time, they were major seagoing and colonizing powers (Wood, 1992).

A Westerner is usually surprised by Japanese maps of the world, which are centered on the 180th meridian of longitude. Asia appears in the center of the map; the United States and Europe are on the edges (Figure 2-4).

The Mercator projection grossly distorts land areas. It exaggerates size at the higher latitudes and arbitrarily and artificially shrinks the land-mass of countries in the southern part of the world. Europe with its 9.7 million square kilometers appears larger than South America with 17.8 million square kilometers. In fact, South America is actually twice the size of Europe. On the Mercator map, the United States is 68 percent larger than its real size, while Africa is 15 percent smaller. North America (19 million square kilometers) appears larger than Africa (30 million square kilometers). Arno Peters (1990), a German historian, created an equal-area projection, which shows the continents and oceans drawn in proportion to their actual area (Figure 2-5).

The usual convention in mapmaking is to locate north at the top of a map. This too is an arbitrary matter and one that is resented by many Australians, who may not like being told that they live "down under." An Australian scholar named McArthur produced what he calls a universal corrective map of the world (Figure 2-6), in which *south* is up, and the map is centered on a meridian running through Wellington, New Zealand.

Do you think maps convey power? If you lived in a nation that is placed on the edge or at the bottom of most maps would your national self-image be affected? What about living in a nation arbitrarily drawn as small-sized? Can you imagine a map that avoids all types of ethnocentrism?

The Ethnocentrism Scale (Adorno & others, 1950) was the first attempt to measure ethnocentrism. It measured attitudes of North Americans toward Jews and other ethnic groups. Its items are outdated for use today. Almost no research on ethnocentrism has used a standardized and validated scale for measurement. Neuliep and McCroskey (1998) developed a modern version of the Ethnocentrism Scale, the fifteen-item Generalized Ethnocentrism Scale (GENE) for use in cross-cultural research (Table 2-1).

Figure 2-3.   Mercator Projection. This map, developed in the 1500s, exaggerates the size of continents in the north and is centered on Europe.

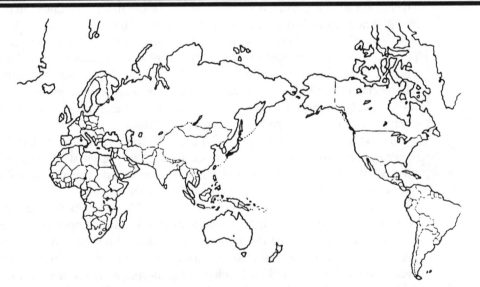

Figure 2-4.   A Japanese Map of the World. This map is centered on the 180th meridian rather than the prime meridian.

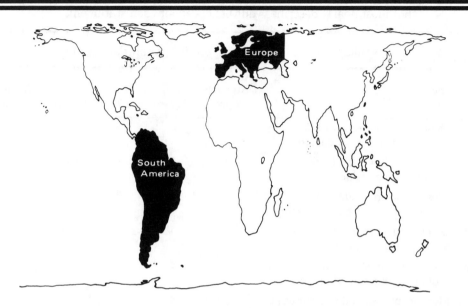

Figure 2-5.   The Peters' Projection. In this map by Arno Peters (1990), continents and oceans are shown in correct proportion to their actual size.

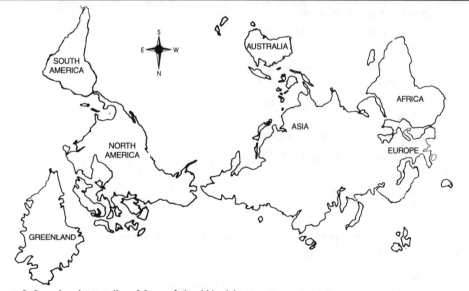

Figure 2-6.   An Australian Map of the World.   South is at the top of the map.

Can you accurately predict your level of ethnocentrism? Circle the number that most nearly describes your beliefs about each statement.

Table 2-1.   The Neuliep-McCroskey Generalized Ethnocentrism Scale

Scale Item	Strongly Agree	Agree	?	Disagree	Strongly Disagree
1. Most other cultures are backward compared to my culture.	5	4	3	2	1
2. My culture should be the role model for other cultures.	5	4	3	2	1
* 3. Lifestyles in other cultures are just as valid as those in my culture.	5	4	3	2	1
4. Other cultures should try to be more like my culture.	5	4	3	2	1
* 5. People in my culture could learn a lot from people in other cultures.	5	4	3	2	1
6. Most people from other cultures just don't know what's good for them.	5	4	3	2	1
7. I have little respect for the values and customs of other cultures.	5	4	3	2	1
8. Most people would be happier if they lived like people in my culture.	5	4	3	2	1
9. People in my culture have just about the best lifestyles of anywhere.	5	4	3	2	1
10. Lifestyles in other cultures are not as valid as those in my culture.	5	4	3	2	1
* 11. I respect the values and customs of other cultures.	5	4	3	2	1
12. I do not cooperate with people who are different.	5	4	3	2	1
13. I do not trust people who are different.	5	4	3	2	1
14. I dislike interacting with people from different cultures.	5	4	3	2	1
15. Other cultures are smart to look up to my culture.	5	4	3	2	1

Source: Neuliep & McCroskey (1998).

*Reversed items.
Scores range from a low of 15 to a high of 75. Scores below 38 indicate relatively low ethnocentrism, while scores above 52 indicate relatively high ethnocentrism.

Cultural Relativism

The degree to which an individual judges another culture by its context is *cultural relativism* (Herskovits, 1973). Stated another way, cultural relativism evaluates the actions in a culture by the premises of that culture—by *its* assumptions about society, the environment, technology, religion, and science. The ideas and purposes of the actors—not the spectators—guide the understanding. A fundamental notion of cultural relativism is that cultures tend to be internally consistent. That is, one element of a culture, which by itself may seem strange to an observer from another culture, generally makes sense when considered in light of the other elements of that culture. For example, the Old Order Amish in the United States refuse to allow their children to attend public schools. Instead the Amish provide their own schools, with the instruction taught in the German dialect spoken by the Amish. These schools are intended to maintain Amish cultural values and to prevent the assimilation of the Amish into the melting pot of U.S. society. State laws require that parochial schools provide a comparable education to that of public schools, and school officials often rule that Amish schools are inferior. Amish parents are then ordered to send their children to public schools. When the parents refuse to do so, they are jailed for breaking the law.

If school officials viewed this situation in terms of cultural relativity, they might understand that the Amish schools are functional in preparing Amish youth to be farmers, carpenters, housewives, and for the other manual occupations available to them. The Amish strongly value their religion, the German dialect they speak, and their pastoral way of life. The Amish resist efforts like mandated public schooling, which they feel are intended to assimilate them into U.S. society.

Ethnocentrism tends to be strongest concerning outgroups that are most socially distant and most unlike the ingroup. An outgroup perceived as highly similar to the ingroup will be treated more like the ingroup than are outgroups that are perceived as dissimilar (LeVine & Campbell, 1972, p. 219). At least some degree of ethnocentrism is almost always involved in intercultural communication and is a barrier to communication effectiveness. An individual who despises a particular outgroup because he/she perceives that outgroup ethnocentrically will not be able to exchange meaningful information with that outgroup.

Prejudice and Discrimination

Prejudice is an unfounded attitude toward an outgroup based on a comparison with one's ingroup. Prejudice is prejudging, without knowledge or examination of the available information. It often consists of judgments made about an individual based on assumptions about the outgroups that individual is presumed to represent. Some prejudices consist of the irrational suspicion or hatred of a particular group or religion. For instance, a prejudiced individual might say, "African Americans aren't as smart as other Americans." Or, "Asian Americans study all of the time, and always get the highest grades in my classes." These are prejudices. They can create avoidance and interpersonal conflict—and prevent effective communication between culturally different individuals.

When a negative attitude toward an outgroup is translated into action, the resulting behavior is called *discrimination*, defined as the process of treating individuals unequally on the basis of their ethnicity, gender, age, sexual orientation, or other characteristics. Prejudice is an *attitude*, while discrimination is overt *behavior*. An admissions officer at a university may be prejudiced in favor of Asian students because she believes they work harder, but she will not act on the prejudice in granting admission because that type of discrimination is illegal. Civil rights legislation made many types of discrimination illegal in the United States, but by no means has discrimination been eliminated.

As a result of past discrimination, particularly discrimination against African Americans, affirmative action programs were established. Affirmative action is a policy or a program that seeks to compensate for past discrimination through active measures to ensure equal opportunity, particularly in education and employment. Affirmative action gives preference to individuals or groups that have experienced discrimination in order to correct for this discrimination. For example, there were no African-American firefighters in Miami Beach, Florida, before 1968. Affirmative action policies required the city government to give preference to hiring African-American firefighters over other equally qualified firefighters until the proportion of African Americans in the city's fire department matched the general population.

Affirmative action is a very controversial policy. Critics charge that the method that created the problem is now used to solve it; they believe affirmative action is *reverse discrimination*. In 1977, Allan Bakke, a White male, was refused admission to the University of California law school. He sued, claiming that he was rejected while less qualified African-American applicants were admitted. Bakke won the case and was admitted. In 1997, affirmative action was ended in California universities. The result was a 32 percent reduction in Latino admissions at the University of California law school and an 80 percent decrease in African-American admissions.

Racism categorizes individuals on the basis of their external physical traits, such as skin color, hair, facial structure, and eye shape, leading to prejudice and discrimination. Race is a social construction—an attempt to give social meaning to physical differences. Race is biologically meaningless because biological variations blend from one racial category to another. Assigning people to arbitrary categories based on subjective interpretation of physical characteristics is perhaps the most telling example of prejudice as a preconceived opinion.

Richard LaPiere, a Stanford University sociologist, conducted a much-cited study of prejudice and discrimination in the early 1930s. He traveled

10,000 miles by car with a young Chinese couple, stopping at 250 hotels and restaurants. At that time, many North Americans had a high degree of prejudice against Asians. They were refused service only once, by the proprietor of a motel in a California town who exclaimed: "No, I don't take Japs!" (LaPiere, 1934). As a follow-up LaPiere wrote to the 250 hotels and restaurants to ask "Will you accept members of the Chinese race as guests in your establishment?" Ninety percent replied that they would refuse to serve the Chinese. LaPiere's findings were interpreted as evidence of the difference between an *attitude* (defined as a relatively enduring belief by an individual that predisposes action) and overt behavior, like discrimination.

LaPiere's study was later replicated by Kutner, Wilkins, and Yarrow (1952) who arranged for an African-American woman, accompanied by two European American friends, to request service at eleven restaurants. All admitted the interracial party of three, but all later refused to make reservations in response to a letter (six restaurants also refused to make reservations over the telephone).

How might one explain the greater degree of prejudice than discrimination? The simple explanation is that it is more difficult to refuse people service face-to-face than by letter or telephone (Brislin, 1981, p. 141). Further, the Chinese couple was well dressed (as was the African-American woman) and accompanied by one or more European Americans. As LaPiere (1934) noted, the hotel clerks were likely to have judged the Chinese couple by the quality of their clothing and their baggage, and assumed they were of high socioeconomic status. These nonverbal characteristics were not involved when the communication channel was by letter or telephone. Thus the communication context of the face-to-face visit was unlike that of the letter or telephone request.

A telephone conversation with one of the eleven restaurants in the Kutner, Wilkins, and Yarrow (1952) study illustrates behavior that falls between the two outcomes discussed above: "Are you colored?" "Yes." "I like everyone. My kitchen help are colored and they are wonderful people. But we have a certain clientele here. . . . This place is my bread and butter. Frankly I'd rather you not come." This restaurant proprietor then recanted, and made a reservation for the African-American woman. Although the telephone is not a face-to-face means of communication, it does involve interaction, which a letter does not.

The individual answering the mail or the telephone at a restaurant or hotel might not have been the same individual who was at the establishment six months previously. Thus, another possible explanation for the difference between attitudes and overt behavior is that these studies measured one person's attitudes and another person's overt behavior (Steinfatt, 1977).

Kurt Lewin, a famous social psychologist, pioneered research on prejudice. Prior to the 1930s, Lewin was a well-known psychologist at the University of Berlin. When Hitler came to power, Lewin decided to immigrate to the United States in order to escape anti-Semiticism. With the shouts of "*Juden heraus!*

Juden heraus!" ("Jews out! Jews out!") on the streets of Berlin ringing in his memory, one of Lewin's scholarly interests in the United States became prejudice (Rogers, 1994, p. 324). One measure of Lewin's lasting intellectual influence is that the study of prejudice is still a favorite topic among social psychologists today. Prejudice is also an important concept in intercultural communication.

Stereotypes

Gordon Allport, a Harvard University psychologist, was another pioneering scholar in research on prejudice who showed that *stereotypes*—generalizations about some group of people that oversimplify reality—lead to prejudice. Allport's (1954/1979) book, *The Nature of Prejudice*, discussed how human cognitive activities like categorization and generalization can lead to prejudiced attitudes. Prejudiced individuals often think in stereotypes. The generalizations prevent accurate perception of the qualities of unalike others.

Allport suggested the "contact" theory of prejudice. ***Individuals who lack close interpersonal communication with a particular culture are more prejudiced toward individuals with that culture***. With personal contact, an individual may become less prejudiced. Allport's original contact theory dealt with face-to-face communication, but scholars later extended Allport's theory to mass media contact. If a particular ethnic group in the United States, for example, seldom appears on prime-time television, people will be more prejudiced against this ethnic group (see Chapter 8).

The Authoritarian Personality

Another important investigation of prejudice, stereotypes, and ethnocentrism was conducted after World War II. Scholars sought explanations for the inhumane acts committed by Germans under Hitler's fascist leadership. *The Authoritarian Personality* (Adorno & others, 1950/1982) reported the data gathered from several thousand people in the United States—including prison inmates in San Quentin, students at the University of California at Berkeley, Lions and Rotary Club members, psychiatric patients, and others. Scales were developed to measure prejudice and ethnocentrism.

Various types of prejudice were found to be highly interrelated. If an individual was prejudiced against Jews, he/she was also prejudiced against African Americans, Asian Americans, and other individuals perceived as outgroups. Further, individuals scoring high on the ethnocentrism (E) scale also scored high on the F (fascism) scale of prejudice. A typical item in the E scale was: "One trouble with Jewish businessmen is that they stick together and prevent other people from having a fair chance in competition." The F scale included items like the following: "Obedience and respect for authority are the most important virtues children should learn." Individuals who highly agreed with these two scale items were high on ethnocentrism and fascism, respectively. Most respondents who strongly agreed with one scale item also strongly agreed with the other; conversely, if they strongly disagreed with one, they disagreed with both.

The highly prejudiced and ethnocentric individuals had an "authoritarian personality." The authoritarians perceived the world as a competitive struggle in which they were relatively weak and dependent. They sought to maintain law and order by enforcing a punitive morality (that is, they insisted that criminals should be strongly punished). The authoritarian thinks in stereotypes and is strongly prejudiced against outgroups of all kinds. An underlying self-image of weakness and self-contempt leads the authoritarian to an embittered struggle to prove that he/she belongs to the strong and good (Rogers, 1994, p. 120). Archie Bunker, the lead character in the popular television series of the 1970s, *All in the Family*, portrayed an authoritarian personality who used such derogatory terms as "jungle bunnies," "wops," and "greasers." Archie also displayed sexism toward his wife Edith. The storyline of *All in the Family* continually punished Archie Bunker for his prejudices, ethnocentrism, and stereotyping by making him the butt of ridicule and laughter.

Rokeach (1960) both built upon and criticized the work in *The Authoritarian Personality*. Rokeach argued that the F-scale of authoritarianism produced high scores if the person in question was either authoritarian or was right wing, or both. He devised the Dogmatism Scale to measure authoritarianism independently of political beliefs, arguing that it was just as possible to have an authoritarian communist as an authoritarian fascist.[5] In Chapter 8 we consider some of Rokeach's suggestions for overcoming prejudice and discrimination.

Intercultural Communication after World War II

The study of intercultural communication did not come together as a scholarly field until the period after World War II. The war ended in 1945, with the United States firmly positioned as the most powerful nation in the world: economically, politically, militarily, and scientifically. Despite having entered the war relatively late and only very reluctantly, after the war U.S. citizens felt a world responsibility (1) for maintaining peace and (2) for the socioeconomic development of poorer nations. Unfortunately, the United States was ill-prepared for the world leadership role that was suddenly thrust upon it.

Initially, the United States looked across the Atlantic to its European allies and former enemies, where the Marshall Plan helped England, France, Italy, Germany, and other nations rebuild their bombed-out cities and factories. A U.S. military government under General McArthur ruled Japan, seeking to install a democratic form of government. Both Japan and the European nations had been well on their way to industrialization, a process temporarily interrupted by the war. Post-war recovery in those countries, with the aid of the U.S. Marshall Plan, occurred rapidly, leading to the overly optimistic con-clusion that the development of the poorer nations of Latin America, Africa, and Asia would be equally easy.

Development Assistance

The United States next moved to provide technical assistance in the development of the newer nations of Latin America, Africa, and Asia. This development program was called Point IV (today this program is called the U.S. Agency for International Development, or AID). Organizationally, it was placed in the U.S. Department of State, linking it with foreign policy. The underlying motivation for aiding development was the increasingly hostile cold war between the United States and the Soviet Union. In order to halt Soviet expansion, the United States formed regional strategic alliances with Third World nations. One aspect of these agreements was for the United States to provide funding, technology, and technicians to teach adult literacy, improve health, raise agricultural productivity, and build hydroelectric dams and steel mills. It was assumed that if these poor nations advanced socioeco-nomically, they would also move toward a government characterized by par-ticipatory democracy.

Many well-intentioned development programs failed. Development turned out to be a much more difficult process in the Third World than the post-war Marshall Plan experience in Europe had suggested. Some develop-ment programs were poorly planned or improperly implemented. For exam-ple, an expensive bridge was built over a major river in Bangladesh, using funds provided by the World Bank. But then the river's watercourse shifted, and the bridge no longer spanned the water flow. In Thailand, where obtain-ing pure water was identified as the highest-priority problem, a Texas well-driller sunk shafts for handpump wells in hundreds of villages. Within six months, most of the pumps were broken (Niehoff, 1964). A huge steel mill was built at Ranchi, India, but it never operated at more than 10 percent capacity. A much-needed hospital was built with U.S. funds in Bogotá, Colom-bia. Graft, bribes, and kickbacks contributed to improper construction, and one wing collapsed. Millions of participants in adult literacy programs in Bra-zil soon reverted to an inability to use their new skills because there was little material for them to read. Western chickens were introduced in Nigeria in order to add needed meat and eggs to people's diets. The driving force behind this development program was Dr. "Chicken" Davis, an American poultry expert. The chickens were profitable, and chicken-growing spread rapidly to villagers throughout the nation. But soon after "Chicken" Davis returned to the United States, a local virus killed all of the Western chickens (Rogers, 1995, pp. 341–42). These development programs failed for reasons that had little to do with the technology that was introduced—and everything to do with *how* it was implemented.

An important lesson learned from these costly and frustrating failures was that the development process was much more difficult than originally thought. The failures of the 1950s and 1960s taught that analysis of the prior situation was crucial before launching a development project. Cultural factors had to be weighed, along with economic, political, and technical dimensions. For example, an investigation of the broken water pumps in Thailand showed that the main problem was the lack of someone responsible for their maintenance. Whenever, by accident, a well had been dug on Buddhist temple grounds, the monks looked after the pump, repaired it if it broke, and often built a concrete base around the pump to prevent mud from polluting the water (Niehoff, 1964). These wells, unfortunately few in number, were sustainable. The AID officials who planned the well-drilling project believed that religion should be separated from a government development program, as would be appropriate in the United States. This separation of church and state would have led to complete failure of the pump project in Thailand. The ideal development project should be *sustainable*, that is, able to continue to be effective after the original development effort ends. Too often, when an observer would return to visit the site of a development project a few years later, nothing remained (see Chapter 9).

The Ugly American

The failure of many development projects in Third World nations led to public disappointment with development efforts. A kind of development weariness set in. This dismay was fanned by a best-selling book, *The Ugly American* (Lederer & Burdick, 1958), which became a marker for the U.S. view of the world in the 1960s.

Development failures were blamed on inept, culturally insensitive technicians, working in Third World nations whose language and culture they did not understand.[6] Edward Hall (1959b, p. 371) summarized the problem by asking, what if the United States were an underdeveloped nation?

> What . . . would [it] be like if we had, say, ten thousand foreigners, all of the same nationality, living in our midst, none of whom learned our language, and who kept themselves isolated from us? Who, furthermore, gave parties, imported their own goods, drove their own brand of automobiles, . . . mispronounced our names, couldn't tell us apart, and then made rude and tactless remarks?

Lederer and Burdick (1958, p. 268) recommended that all U.S. development workers speak the national language of the country in which they were assigned; that housing should be modest, no more luxurious than workers could afford back home; commissaries should be closed and development workers should consume local foods and drink; no private automobiles should be imported. Thus the social distance between the workers and their local counterparts would be greatly reduced. People would be attracted by the challenge of development work, rather than by the appeal of an improved level of living. U.S. technical assistance workers should understand intercultural communication, as well as the agriculture, health, and other technologies that they sought to introduce. A variety of intercultural communication training programs were launched in order to better prepare U.S. development workers.

The Foreign Service Institute

If U.S. development workers were relatively ineffective, U.S. diplomats were even more inept. Most members of the diplomatic corps had earned a bachelor's degree in liberal arts from elite Ivy League universities. They passed the Foreign Service Examination, which mainly measured their grasp of U.S. and world history and politics. Diplomats seldom bothered to learn the language or culture of the country to which they were assigned by the U.S. Department of State. In defense of this linguistic and cultural weakness, one spokesman for the status quo claimed: "Selecting, training and promoting Foreign Service officers on the basis of foreign language skill is a little like picking chorus girls on the basis of moles and dimples. From the balcony it doesn't matter" (Bradford, 1960).

U.S. diplomats usually lived and worked in a small circle of English-speaking individuals, seldom venturing outside of the country's capital city. Often the U.S. diplomats were ethnocentric in their view of the local people, an attitude that they displayed in various ways and which their national hosts resented. The U.S. diplomats were indeed "ugly Americans." In a cultural sense, they were flying blind. The diplomats of other nations, such as those from Europe (with a tradition of colonial experience in Third World nations), were adept in language and culture. The United States gained a reputation of having the world's least effective diplomats.

At the time that Lederer and Burdick (1958, p. 273) wrote *The Ugly American*, U.S. ambassadors to France, Italy, Germany, Belgium, the Netherlands, Norway, Turkey, Japan, Korea, Thailand, Vietnam, and Indonesia did not know the national language of the country to which they were assigned. They could only speak and be spoken to by interpreters (although the U.S. ambassador to Paris could speak German, and the ambassador to Germany could speak French). In contrast, 90 percent of all Russian diplomatic staff, including officials, secretaries, and chauffeurs, spoke the local language *before* they arrived at their foreign post.

In 1946, the U.S. Congress passed the Foreign Service Act, which established the Foreign Service Institute (FSI) in the U.S. Department of State to provide pre-service and in-service training throughout the careers of Foreign Service officers (and others, including development technicians). The FSI was staffed mainly with linguists and anthropologists, as it was thought that the problems of ineffective diplomats stemmed mainly from the need to be educated in the language and culture of the host country.

Many of the linguists came from a U.S. Army language training program in Washington, D.C., that had developed highly effective methods of training soldiers to learn French, German, Japanese, and other languages during World War II. The language trainers were native speakers of the language of study; students could therefore absorb the correct pronunciation of the words they were studying. The native speakers taught a good deal about the cultural context of the people speaking a language, as well as the nonverbal communication (such as hand gestures) that accompanied the language. Language teaching at the FSI was quite successful.

The anthropological side of the FSI training was another story; everything seemed to go wrong. It was not the fault of the anthropologists who taught the FSI courses dealing with cultural understanding. They were excellently prepared and highly experienced in working in various cultures.

To the surprise of the anthropologists at FSI, the content of the courses they taught was not what the student-diplomats wanted to know! The anthropologists taught the FSI participants the macro-level aspects of a culture that anthropologists study, such as kinship structure and economic exchange. The participants "wanted concrete information about how to interact with persons in the specific culture to which they were being sent" (Leeds-Hurwitz, 1990). In essence, what the FSI participants wanted to learn was the cultural aspects of intercultural communication. They wanted to know how to communicate with individuals in a specific culture.

One of the leading anthropologists at the Foreign Service Institute, Edward Hall, decided that a radical change was needed. First, he noted that "There seemed to be no 'practical' value attached to either what the anthropologist did or what he made of his discoveries" (Hall, 1959a, p. 32). Hall tossed out the macro-level material about kinship structures and focussed on micro-level cultural aspects of vocal tone, gestures, time, and spatial relationships (many of the main elements of what we today call nonverbal communication). Hall taught the participants how to exchange information *across cultures*, that is, communication between individuals who were culturally unalike. He labelled what he was teaching "intercultural communication"—the first usage of that designation. Until Hall, anthropologists had not paid very much attention to human communication. While teaching at the FSI, Hall (1959a, p. 217) realized that "Culture is communication and communication is culture."

Edward Hall, Founder

Edward Hall, an anthropologist who had extensive intercultural experience, led the training courses at FSI. While there, he coined the expression "intercultural communication," began the analysis of nonverbal communication, and wrote his famous book, *The Silent Language* (Hall, 1959). What path led Edward Hall to the FSI? He was born in St. Louis but grew up in New Mexico. As a young man, he built dams and roads for the U.S. Indian Service,

Figure 2-7.   Edward T. Hall is seated ninth from either side of the table in this photograph of a training class for diplomats at the Foreign Service Institute in 1951.

Source: Box 5, Folder 6 of the E. T. Hall papers, Special Collections, University of Arizona Library. Used with permission.

working with construction crews of Navajos and Hopis (Hall, 1992). In later life, he credited this close contact with culturally unalike people as one inspiration for his interest in intercultural communication (intercultural contact of some kind is a common experience for many intercultural communication scholars).

Eventually, Hall's fascination with culture took him to Columbia University for a Ph.D. in anthropology, a degree that he received in 1942. He was especially influenced by Ruth Benedict, Margaret Mead, and Ralph Linton (his professor), all of whom were leading anthropologists in the United States. During World War II, Hall was assigned as an officer to an all-black regiment. After the war, Hall investigated the U.S. government's administration of the South Pacific island of Truk, which had just been freed from Japanese occupation (Hall, 1950). He joined the teaching staff of the Foreign Service Institute in 1951. Hall directed the training of 2,000 technicians over the next five years for the State Department's Technical Assistance Program. Although his main responsibility was to train U.S. development workers for assignments in Third World countries, he actually trained both development workers and diplomatic staff. In essence, he headed the anthropology division of the FSI.

At the Foreign Service Institute, Hall collaborated closely with Dr. George L. Trager, a protegé of the linguist Edward Sapir, who with Benjamin Lee Whorf formed the theory of linguistic relativity (see Chapter 5). As Hall (1992, p. 203) said, his background as an anthropologist "meshed perfectly" with that of the linguists at FSI. "I saw language as an expression of culture; they saw language as reflecting culture." Trager and Hall spent several hours every workday in discussions about culture and communication. Here they worked out the basic formulation of intercultural communication over the period from 1951 to 1955.

Hall also acknowledged Benjamin Lee Whorf (1940; 1940/1956) as a dominant force on his thinking about intercultural communication. He credits Whorf as "One of the first to speak technically about the implications of differences which influence the way in which man experiences the universe" (1959a, p. 121). Hall learned to look beyond verbal communication for the meaning of behavior. He took Sapir and Whorf's linguistic relativity theory and applied it to nonverbal communication.

The other intellectual influence on the conception of intercultural communication that Hall and his colleagues formulated at the FSI was Freudian psychoanalytic theory. The unconscious level of communication had not been given much attention previously, but Hall found that a good deal of intercultural communication, particularly nonverbal communication, was out-of-consciousness. During the early 1950s Hall worked closely with psychoanalysts at the Washington School of Psychiatry, often inviting psychoanalysts to observe his training sessions at the FSI.

Hall was invited by the editor of *Scientific American* to write an article about the paradigm for intercultural communication that he was teaching at the Foreign Service Institute. "The Anthropology of Manners" (Hall, 1955) caught the interest of many readers. Hall gradually refined his ideas about intercultural communication over the next several years. He credits his collaboration with Trager as the source of many of the ideas that appeared in *The Silent Language* (Hall, 1959a). He also acknowledged his application of the principles proposed by Benjamin Lee Whorf for linguistics to other aspects of human behavior (Leeds-Hurwitz, 1990). His book, *The Silent Language*, became extremely popular, selling over half a million copies in its first ten years of publication. This slim volume was the core founding document for the new field of intercultural communication. *The Silent Language* made Edward Hall famous, disseminating his ideas to a wide audience of scholars and to the public.

After publication of *The Silent Language* in 1959, Hall moved from the FSI to a variety of research and teaching positions, spending fairly lengthy periods at the Illinois Institute of Technology and at Northwestern University. Hall taught in departments of anthropology and considered himself an anthropologist rather than a communication scholar, although he continued to advance the field of intercultural communication. During the later part of his career, Hall published a series of books about intercultural communication, expanding upon his original ideas (Hall, 1966, 1976, and 1983). He formulated important conceptual tools that are widely utilized in intercultural communication today. One example is the classification of high-context versus low-context cultures (Hall, 1976), which will be discussed in Chapter 3.

Edward Hall lives today in retirement in Santa Fe, New Mexico, occasionally offering a graduate course at the University of New Mexico. Recognized by anthropologists, his work is also the foundation for scholars of intercultural and nonverbal communication. Mitch Hamer of American University, who earned his Ph.D. in intercultural communication in the 1970s, recalls that *"The Silent Language* was our Bible."

Figure 2-8.   Edward T. Hall, founder of the field of intercultural communication, shown here on the campus of the University of New Mexico, where he was teaching in 1997.

Source: Photograph by Kathryn Sorrells. Used by permission.

Time Talks and Space Speaks

The training staff at the FSI sought to convey an understanding of nonverbal communication and of other aspects of intercultural communication to U.S. diplomats and technicians. They assumed that if this training were successful, U.S. diplomats would be able to communicate more effectively with their foreign counterparts. The end result should be improved diplomacy and development.

Hall and the other trainers at the Foreign Service Institute in the 1950s were extremely creative in formulating the new field of intercultural communication. They brought to bear the useful aspects of their anthropological and linguistic training and discarded the conventional approaches to teaching culture. The FSI staff created new concepts where none existed. For example, Hall coined the term *proxemics*, which he defined as nonverbal communication that involves space. Hall realized that proxemics and other out-of-consciousness types of communication were specific parts of a broader entity, which he eventually decided to call *nonverbal communication*, defined as all types of communication that do not involve the exchange of words.

Whether an individual was late for an appointment, how closely two people stood while talking, and other aspects of nonverbal communication often determined the effectiveness of intercultural communication, even if both parties were perfectly fluent in the language. The participants in a conversation are themselves usually unconscious of their own nonverbal communication. As mentioned earlier, Sigmund Freud's psychoanalytic theory provided a basis for Hall to conceptualize this subconscious level of human communication. Hall described much nonverbal communication as being out-of-awareness. He warned that "We must never assume that we are fully aware of what we communicate to someone else" (1959a, p. 38).

The significance of the warning is readily apparent if we think about the nonverbal communication involved when playing poker, on a first date, or when making a speech. Participants in these situations are often not fully aware of what they are "saying" nonverbally. The mysterious nature of nonverbal communication is one reason why individuals are so eager to better understand it. Many people who have had intercultural experience read Ed Hall's (1959a) famous phrases "Time talks" and "Space speaks" and immediately identify with those insights.

North Americans sometimes feel vaguely uncomfortable when conversing with an Arab or a Latin American. They sometimes perceive the other person as pushy or aggressive and back away. In turn, their conversation partner might have found them aloof, a *"Yanqui frio."* In the presence of such disturbing nonverbal currents, the verbal exchange between two individuals is unlikely to be effective. Each person carries around an invisible bubble of space, which can expand or contract depending on the situation. Northern Europeans and most European Americans carry rather large bubbles. They do not stand very close to each other while speaking. Southern Europeans,

Latin Americans, and Arabic people have smaller bubbles; they converse in a much more intimate space. To these people, touching is an important part of interpersonal communication.

Time is another important dimension of nonverbal communication. Pity the novice U.S. diplomat in a Latin American nation who is invited to a party at 8:00 P.M. and arrives at his host's home promptly, only to find the host still taking a shower. No one else arrives at the party until 10:00 P.M. Obviously, time has different meanings in various cultures, and not only in the sense of promptness (Hall, 1983). Hall taught his FSI trainees not to rush Arabs or Japanese in making a business agreement. These people want to get to know their collaborator as a person before putting ink to paper. If someone from the United States pursues a decision in what is culturally perceived to be a rush by his/her counterparts, the result is likely to be no decision. The FSI participants were taught how to avoid insulting or misreading others by failing to learn their norms for time.

The work of Edward Hall at the Foreign Service Institute in a five-year period after World War II left a lasting impact on the field of intercultural communication in at least five important ways.

1. **Intercultural communication began as an applied type of training, intended to ameliorate the inept behavior of U.S. diplomats and technical assistance workers**. The emphasis in intercultural communication today is still on useful applications, although (1) the applications are much different than the earlier purpose of the FSI, and (2) the field is now mainly in the hands of university scholars of communication who conduct research and teach students.

2. **Intercultural communication grew out of efforts to improve international communication between U.S. diplomats and technicians and their host country counterparts**. The conception of intercultural communication that later emerged from the Foreign Service Institute, however, dealt with any type of intercultural communication, whether involving national cultures or other kinds of person-person differences. International communication is one component in the broader field of intercultural communication.

3. **While the intellectual roots of intercultural communication were in anthropology and linguistics (and psychiatry), it became recognized as a specialty field in communication study**. Edward Hall's book, *The Silent Language*, was the key document in this transfer.

4. **From the start, nonverbal communication was a crucial part of intercultural communication, a fact widely recognized today**. Nonverbal communication is less intentional and self-conscious than verbal communication. Consequently, knowledge about the various components of nonverbal communication is essential to avoid misunderstandings between culturally unalike people.

5. **Experiential learning is a key component in intercultural communication.** Lectures, reading, and discussion were inadequate at the FSI to convey the skills and understandings (as opposed to knowledge) necessary for intercultural communication. One should do more than just *talk* (or read) about this topic. One must *experience* intercultural communication if one is really going to understand it. The experiential aspects of intercultural communication have continued in recent decades at the Summer Institute in Intercultural Communication, held near Portland, Oregon, for some nine hundred participants each year from about thirty countries. The institute's workshop courses stress games, simulation exercises, and other types of participatory learning.

One of the reasons for the disjunction between the progress made at the FSI in teaching intercultural communication and the failures of diplomats and development workers discussed earlier in the chapter was the lack of support given to the FSI by the State Department. Simmel's discussion of the constraints placed on interaction by the system applies here. One part of the system—FSI—worked to achieve particular goals while the attitude of those higher in the system constrained and limited such successes.

Top administrators at the U.S. State Department often did not appreciate the contributions being made by Edward Hall and his staff at the Foreign Service Institute. The State Department hierarchy tended to view U.S. diplomacy as a "twist their arm, gun to the head" process. Conversely, the FSI taught diplomats to communicate more effectively by putting themselves into the roles of their culturally unalike counterparts. The FSI perspective "was that enforced programs based on European philosophies, degree of economic development, and good intentions, while balm to American souls, were highly unreliable, frequently irrelevant, and certain to be misunderstood by the people we were dealing with at the cultural interface" (Hall, 1992, p. 202). Hall remembers that "My message was frequently misunderstood and actively resisted by most of the administrators as well as the members of the Foreign Service" (Hall, 1992, p. 202).

Increasing resistance to the FSI built up in the U.S. State Department. Administrators asked themselves, "How do I explain the presence of anthropologists who study old bones and South Sea Islanders to Senator Joseph McCarthy?" (who made headlines alleging the State Department had been infiltrated by communists in the mid-1950s). "FSI's standing in the State Department was so lacking in power as to be laughable" (Hall, 1992, p. 206). Eventually, the State Department decided to "clean out the anthropologists" from the Foreign Service Institute (Hall, 1992, p. 250). Edward Hall left the FSI, and with his departure the window of academic creativity that had flourished there from 1951 to 1955 closed. The intellectual center of intercultural communication moved elsewhere.

Forming a Paradigm of Intercultural Communication

A *paradigm* is a conceptualization that provides explanations and ways of seeing to a community of individuals. Here is an example of contrasting paradigms. Which of the following additions are correct?

1. $1 + 1 = 2$
2. $2 + 3 = 5$
3. $10 + 9 = 7$
4. $2 + 6 = 8$
5. $9 + 7 = 4$
6. $4 + 9 = 1$

All of these additions are correct according to one paradigm of numbering. According to the base-10 mathematical system, only additions #1, #2, and #4 (above) are correct. According to a base-12 mathematical system, additions #3, #5, and #6 are also correct. (Base-12 is used in keeping time.) Now imagine two individuals, one with a base-10 paradigm and the other with a base-12 paradigm, who are trying to communicate with each other about addition. Disagreement and conflict will result; appointments will be missed. Each individual will have a different perspective, depending on his/her different assumptions.

A *scientific paradigm* is a conceptualization that provides exemplary problems and methods of research to a community of scholars (Hart, 1996a). The concept of a scientific paradigm was created by Thomas Kuhn in order to understand how scientists in a discipline decide what research questions to pursue in their investigations. In his book, *The Structure of Scientific Revolutions* (1962/1970), Kuhn points out that scientific progress often occurs suddenly, through the acceptance of a new scientific paradigm, rather than slowly by means of the incremental testing of hypotheses.

Examples of scientific paradigms that revolutionized thinking are the sun-centered conception of the universe by Copernicus and Galileo, Einstein's theory of relativity, and the structure of DNA by James Watson and Francis Crick. Many other scientific paradigms were much less earthshaking than these famous examples but nevertheless reshaped thinking. Scholars later realized that everyone, not just scientists, learns paradigms that guide their perceptions and influence their decisions.

What is the paradigm for intercultural communication and where did it come from? Previously in this chapter, we traced the early history of the field of intercultural communication. Here we order this background into the stages that usually describe the evolution of a new scientific paradigm.

1. *Preparadigmatic research*: At this first stage, the new scientific paradigm has not yet been proposed, and so the research studies conducted in what is to become a scientific field are sporadic and may not add up

to advancing a theory. In the field of intercultural communication, this preparadigmatic era occurred in the decades preceding publication of *The Silent Language* by Edward Hall (1959). Various components of the paradigm had been published in the preparadigmatic period such as William Graham Sumner's (1906) concept of ethnocentrism, Georg Simmel's (1908) concept of the stranger, and Kurt Lewin's and Gordon Allport's work on prejudice. What was missing, until publication of *The Silent Language*, was a name for the new field, recognition of nonverbal communication as one key part of intercultural communication, and the identification of communication between people of different cultures as the distinguishing mark of the new field (Figure 2-9). These three crucial aspects of the new paradigm came together at the Foreign Service Institute in a brief intellectual Camelot from 1951 to 1955, with the work of Edward Hall and his colleagues in anthropology and linguistics.

Earlier, we reviewed the four main intellectual influences on Hall in setting forth the paradigm: (1) George L. Trager, his linguistic colleague at the Foreign Service Institute, (2) Edward Sapir, Trager's doctoral dissertation advisor, (3) Benjamin Lee Whorf, who, with Sapir, formulated the theory of linguistic relativity (see Figure 2-9), and (4) Sigmund Freud's psychoanalytic theory, which influenced Hall to explore subconscious levels of human communication (Rogers & Hart, 1998).

2. *Appearance of the new paradigm*: This stage in the process of scientific advance began in 1959 with publication of Hall's *The Silent Language*. A new scholarly field began to take shape around the intellectual ideas worked out at the Foreign Service Institute for the training of U.S. diplomats and technical assistance workers. The field of intercultural communication was conceptualized, but it still lacked an academic home in universities, textbooks and journals, and professional associations to coordinate the activities of intercultural communication scholars. These elements were essential for the growth of the new field and for its institutionalization. This academic infrastructure began to fall in place around 1970.

3. *Normal science*: During the normal science stage, consensus develops about the new field's central concerns, its main concepts and theories, and the directions of its research. At this stage an *invisible college* (a network of scholars in a field who share a scientific paradigm) forms. Its members are attracted by the excitement generated by the new paradigm. Other scholars oppose the new conceptualization, and conduct research in order to disprove it. Thomas Kuhn calls this stage "normal science" because the revolutionary new paradigm is gradually being accepted and a scholarly field is beginning to grow. Signs of this establishment of the new field of intercultural communication were:

1860

Charles Darwin, *FACIAL EXPRESSIONS*, 1872.

1880

1900

William Graham Sumner, *ETHNOCENTRISM*, 1905.
Georg Simmel, *THE STRANGER*, 1908.

1920

Edward Sapir & Benjamin Lee Whorf, *LINGUISTIC RELATIVITY,* 1920s.

1940   Kurt Lewin, *PREJUDICE,* 1940s.

Theodor Adorno & others, *AUTHORITARIAN PERSONALITY*, 1950.
Gordon Allport, *PREJUDICE,* 1954.
Edward Hall, *INTERCULTURAL COMMUNICATION*, 1959.
1960   Edward Hall, *PROXEMICS,* 1963.
Ray Birdwhistell, *KINESICS,* 1970.
Charles Berger & Richard Calabrese, *UNCERTAINTY REDUCTION,* 1975.
Edward Hall, *LOW-CONTEXT/HIGH-CONTEXT CULTURES*, 1976.
1980

Harry Triandis, *INDIVIDUALISM/COLLECTIVISM,* 1985.

2000

Figure 2-9. A Road Map of Key Contributions to the Field of Intercultural
Communication. Although many important concepts in understanding intercultural
communication were developed previously, the paradigm for this field was formulated by
Edward Hall at the Foreign Service Institute (FSI) after World War II. The founding document for
the new field was Hall's (1959a) book, *The Silent Language*.

(a) The first university courses in intercultural communication were
offered at the University of Pittsburgh, Michigan State University,
and at other universities after the mid-1960s. The AID (Agency for
International Development) seminars run by the Department of

Communication at Michigan State University in the 1960s and 1970s provided another impetus for studying intercultural communication. Between 1975 and 1985, the Department of Speech Communication at the University of Minnesota surged to the forefront of intercultural communication, led by Professor William Howell. Ph.D. degrees were awarded to scholars specializing in this field. Other universities began making significant contributions to the field.

(b) Textbooks in intercultural communication began to appear that expressed the core elements of the new paradigm. Smith (1966) edited a reader on communication and culture. Larry Samovar and Richard Porter (1972) edited an influential book, *Intercultural Communication: A Reader*, which helped shape the field. John Condon and Fathi Yousef (1975) authored an early textbook, *An Introduction to Intercultural Communication*. Professor David Hoopes, an early intercultural communication scholar at the University of Pittsburgh, established the Intercultural Press, which has published many important books in the field. William B. Gudykunst and Young Yun Kim wrote *Communicating with Strangers: An Approach to Intercultural Communication*, which centered on Simmel's concept (Gudykunst & Kim, 1984/1992/1997). They stated that strangers, conceived of as people who are unknown and unfamiliar to us, pose special problems to effective communication. "An African American student in a mainly European American school, a Mexican student studying at a university in the United States, a groom meeting the bride's family for the first time, and a manager from the United States working in Thailand are all examples of strangers" (Gudykunst & Kim, 1997, p. 49). Gudykunst and Kim utilized the concept of the stranger as a unifying theoretical theme for the study of intercultural communication. They broadened the scope of intercultural communication from its origins in international communication at FSI to communication between any type of unalike individuals (see Figure 2-2).

(c) An important journal in the intercultural communication field, the *International Journal of Intercultural Relations*, began publication in 1977.

(d) In 1970, the International Communication Association (ICA) established an Intercultural Communication Division (which later became the Intercultural and Development Communication Division). In 1975, the National Communication Association (NCA) established an Intercultural Division. The annual conventions of ICA and NCA became important meeting places for intercultural communication scholars.

(e) Training in intercultural communication expanded to include, for example, Peace Corps volunteers or business executives who were to sojourn overseas. A professional association, SIETAR (the Society for Intercultural Education, Training, and Research) was formed in 1974 to advance the new field. In 1976, the Summer Institute in Intercultural Communication began at Stanford University, and, in 1986, moved to Portland, Oregon. This summer institute is a mecca for students and teachers of intercultural communication.

4. *Anomaly*: This stage occurs when the research evidence illuminates failures in the paradigm, which eventually lead to a decline in scholarly interest. At this stage, most of the important research questions have already been investigated. This fourth stage in the growth of a scientific field has not yet occurred for intercultural communication.

5. *Exhaustion*: At this stage scholarly interest in the scientific paradigm has waned, and it may be replaced by a new paradigm.

Today the field of intercultural communication is well-established in the United States and in a number of other nations. Further, a healthy industry stands behind this academic specialty, represented by private companies that provide intercultural communication training to people who wish to improve their skills of communicating with culturally dissimilar individuals. University training is provided in intercultural communication for undergraduate students and at the graduate level. Scholars conduct research on all aspects of intercultural communication.

Non-Western Perspectives on Intercultural Communication

Much of the scholarly research on intercultural communication cited in this book was conducted by European Americans. Most theoretical concepts like individualism-collectivism, low-context versus high-context cultures, stereotypes, and ethnocentrism were explicated by White Euro-American scholars. Does the preponderance of Western scholars inject a bias in our understanding of intercultural communication? Perhaps. The cultural values of the scholars who study intercultural communication affect what they investigate, with what methods, what they find, and how they interpret their findings. In recent years, this potential bias has been recognized and several attempts have been made to do something about it.

Molefi Kete Asante (1987), a communication scholar at Temple University, argued that so-called "Western civilization" actually had certain roots in Africa. We know that Roman civilization was a dominant influence on Western civilization and that the Romans were, in turn, directly influenced by the Greeks. Greek civilization was historically influenced by Egyptian civilization, which drew upon various African cultures. Asante's perspective is an example of Afrocentricity, placing African cultural values at the center of an analysis of African culture and behavior (Asante, 1987).

Other scholars (Kincaid, 1987) have raised interesting questions about whether human communication would look different if viewed from various Eastern perspectives. For example, would intercultural communication be different today if it had been established by, say, Japanese scholars (with a collectivistic, high-context culture, and an emphasis on harmony—*wa*), instead of by Edward Hall working in the U.S. Department of State? What if Georg Simmel had been a Buddhist in Thailand instead of a German Jew?

The culture of the individual scholars who lead an academic field like intercultural communication (where culture is such a pervasive concept) exerts a strong influence on the intellectual perspectives taken. The study of intercultural communication is now spreading to non-European U.S. scholars and students. This expansion of the field may help recognize and correct the inherent biases of intercultural communication.

A more international and intercultural orientation of the entire discipline would be beneficial for communication study. Too much of what is taught in university courses is culture-bound to the United States and, in particular, to white European American people and their communication behavior. As the director of the School of Interpersonal Communication at Ohio University, Sue DeWine (1995), stated: "In interpersonal communication classes we focus on developing skills for American-based interpersonal relationships. Persuasion classes provide theoretical underpinnings for compliance techniques that succeed within an American culture but that would prove disruptive in an Asian culture, for example. Our research in interpersonal communication is based almost exclusively on American college sophomores. Studies in organizational communication are usually based on perceptions of American workers."

How did the field of communication acquire this made-in-the-United States bias? Many of the key founders of the field were North Americans (several were Europeans who immigrated to the United States). Of the sixty-six individuals credited with establishing the field of communication study before 1965, all were European Americans or Europeans, and sixty-five were men (Rogers, 1994). It would be difficult to imagine a field that began in a more restricted, monocultural way. Gradually, over the decades since its founding, communication study has attracted outstanding women scholars, individuals from every nation and culture, and it has spread to universities around the world. However, much of the theory and many of the research methods used in communication study still reflect the narrow perspectives of its beginnings. Intercultural communication should be taking the lead in the internationalization and multiculturalization of the broader field of communication study.

Summary

The roots of intercultural communication go back ninety years to the influential writings of the German sociologist Georg Simmel about the stranger. Simmel defined the stranger as an individual who is a member of a system but not strongly attached to that system. Here, we define the *stranger* more broadly as anyone who is different from oneself (Sorrells, 1997). Robert E. Park and his students at the University of Chicago eighty years ago translated Simmel's concept into empirical research. Four concepts emerged: (1) *social distance*, the degree to which an individual perceives a lack of intimacy with individuals different in ethnicity, race, religion, occupation, and other variables, (2) *marginal man*, an individual who lives in two different worlds, in both of which the individual is a stranger, (3) *heterophily*, the degree to which individuals who interact are unalike, and (4) *cosmopoliteness*, the degree to which an individual has a relatively high degree of communication outside of the system. This family of concepts, all dealing with the close/distant relationships of the individual with others, has proven to be a collection of useful analytical tools for intercultural communication scholars.

Ethnocentrism is the degree to which other cultures are judged as inferior to one's own culture. William Graham Sumner, a founder of sociology in the United States, explicated the concept of ethnocentrism as the result of people perceiving that they belonged to an *ingroup*, defined as a collectivity with which an individual identifies. An *outgroup* is a collectivity with which an individual does not identify. Ethnocentrism is learned and can be unlearned. The opposite of ethnocentrism is *cultural relativism*, the degree to which an individual judges another culture by its context. One objective of intercultural communication training and study is to decrease ethnocentrism.

Prejudice is an unfounded attitude toward an outgroup based on a comparison with one's ingroup. To be prejudiced is to pre-judge an individual or a group. While prejudice is an attitude (usually negative), *discrimination*, defined as the process of treating individuals unequally on the basis of their race, gender, or other characteristic, consists of overt behavior.

Racism categorizes individuals on the basis of their external physical traits, such as skin color, hair, facial structure, and eye shape, leading to prejudice and discrimination. *Stereotypes* are generalizations about some group of people that oversimplify reality. Such generalizations prevent accurate perception of the qualities of unalike others.

The field of intercultural communication was given its name by Edward T. Hall, an anthropologist teaching at the Foreign Service Institute from 1951 to 1955. U.S. diplomats and technical assistance workers were poorly prepared for communicating with culturally unalike others. The Foreign Service Institute sought to improve their skills. Here the *scientific paradigm* (defined as a scientific conceptualization that provides exemplary problems and methods of research to a community of scholars) for intercultural communication was formed. Starting in the mid-1960s, the new field became well established in university departments of communication, and has proven to be particularly useful to individuals living in today's culturally diverse world.

As a result of its origins in the Foreign Service Institute, the field of intercultural communication has several important characteristics today: (1) it is applied, (2) it has an international flavor, (3) it grew from its beginnings in anthropology and linguistics to become a specialty field of communication, (4) it recognizes nonverbal communication as a component, and (6) its teaching emphasizes experiential and participatory learning.

Because the field of intercultural communication developed mainly in the United States and primarily through the work of U.S. scholars, it is possible that this field has a European American perspective. As the study of intercultural communication attracts a more diverse set of scholars, this bias may be overcome.

Notes

[1] Simmel's original writing about the concept of the stranger first appeared in German in 1908 on pages 685–91 of his *Soziologie: Untersuchungen über die Formen der Vergesellschaftung*, Leipzig, Duncker und Humblot. This work was translated to English by Park and Burgess (Simmel, 1921, pp. 322–27) and by Wolff (1950, pp. 402–8).

[2] Simmel saw social distance as fundamental to his conception of human communication and to his concept of the stranger.

[3] While Lazarsfeld and Merton (1964) were the first scholars to use the concepts of homophily and heterophily, the existence of these notions was recognized by the French sociologist Gabriel Tarde (1903) over a half century earlier.

[4] Merton (1949) used the term "cosmopolitan," rather than cosmopolite, which was preferred by later scholars. Merton traced his delineation of local and cosmopolitan to Ferdinand Tönnies' (1940) concepts of *Gemeinschaft* (community) and *Gesellschaft* (society) and to Simmel. Merton acquired a copy of Simmel's (1908) *Soziologie* (which contained Simmel's concept of the stranger) on a trip to Europe in 1937. Thereafter he included Simmel's theories in his course on the history of sociological theory at Columbia University (LeVine & others, 1976).

[5] Research on both authoritarianism and dogmatism is summarized in Steinfatt (1987).

[6] Actually, the "ugly American" of the book's title was a physically unattractive practical engineer/handyman who was a very competent development worker, fashioning a village water pump out of bicycle parts.

Culture

This chapter deals with the interface of two fundamental concepts, culture and communication. *Intercultural communication* is the exchange of information between individuals who are unalike culturally.[1] This broad definition implies that two or more individuals may be unalike in their national culture, ethnicity, age, gender, or in other ways that affect their interaction. Their dissimilarity means that effective communication between them is particularly difficult. ***The cultural unalikeness of the individuals who interact is the unique aspect of intercultural communication.***

What Is Culture?

Culture is defined as the total way of life of a people, composed of their learned and shared behavior patterns, values, norms, and material objects. Culture is a very general concept. Nevertheless, culture has very powerful effects on individual behavior, including communication behavior, as we observed in previous chapters.

Not only do nationalities and ethnic groups have cultures (for example, Japanese culture, Mexican culture, African-American culture, etc.), but so do communities, organizations, and other systems. For example, the IBM Cor-

Figure 3-1.   This safety poster was displayed in an African nation in order to prevent mining accidents caused by chunks of ore on the railroad track. What message do you get from this poster? The miners who saw this poster perceived an opposite meaning because they read from right to left (as do other languages such as Arabic, Chinese, and Hebrew). Do cultural differences influence the effectiveness of a message?

poration had a distinctive organizational culture in which male employees were expected to wear dark blue suits, white button-down shirts, and conservative neckties. The gay community in the United States has a somewhat distinct culture. So do certain professions, like journalism and college-level teaching.

A co-culture (also called a subculture, although this term implies inferiority to some) is a set of shared cultural meanings held by a system within a larger system (Orbe, 1997). Thus a co-culture is a culture within a culture. Examples of co-cultures in the United States include varsity athletes at the University of Oklahoma, employees of Walt Disney Enterprises, and U.S. Marines. For example, the OU athletes' co-culture values body size, strength, and competition; academic achievement rates relatively low in this value system. To discourage the influence of these subcultural values, the NCAA has ruled that colleges cannot house athletes in separate dormitories. Walt Disney Enterprises hires clean-cut, "all-American" young people. Disney employees are expected to treat customers in a very polite manner and to smile at them in a friendly way. These qualities of the organization's culture are taught to all new Disney workers in a preservice training course. Similarly, boot camp helps the U.S. Marine Corps instill their *Semper Fi* (always faithful) subculture of discipline, loyalty, and toughness.

   Culture is created by humans. Each different group or population creates its own way of life, with the values, norms, behaviors, and material objects that they feel best fit their situation. The material objects produced by a culture, together with its musical and artistic productions, are referred to as *cultural artifacts*. The elements of a culture, like its values, are so completely accepted by individuals sharing that culture that these elements are seldom questioned or defended. As the anthropologist Ralph Linton stated: "The last person in the world to understand water is someone living at the bottom of the sea." The following sections look at some of the components of culture.

Beliefs, Attitudes, and Values

Culture is stored in individual human beings, in the form of their beliefs, attitudes, and values. There are strong similarities in the belief systems among the members of a given culture.

   Beliefs are an individual's representations of the outside world. Some beliefs are seen as very likely to be true, such as "2 + 2 = 4." Others are seen as less probable, such as "All old people sit at home in rocking chairs." Beliefs serve as the storage system for the content of our past experiences, including thoughts, memories, and interpretations of events. Beliefs are shaped by the individual's culture.

   Attitudes, like beliefs, are internal events and not directly observable by other people. *Attitudes* are emotional responses to objects, ideas, and people. Attitudes store these emotional responses in the same way that beliefs store the content of past events. People express opinions, outwardly observable verbal behavior, and engage in other behaviors, partially on the basis of their attitudes and beliefs. Attitudes and beliefs form a storage system for culture within the individual. Attitudes and beliefs are internal and are not publicly observable. I cannot know your attitudes or your beliefs directly, but I can observe what you say (your expressed opinions) and what you do (your behavior) and infer your attitudes and beliefs from these overt expressions.

   Attitudes and beliefs indicate behavioral intentions, tendencies for a person to respond to events, ideas, and people in particular ways. If I know (belief) what Thai food is and like (attitude/emotion) Thai food, then I may intend to eat (behavioral intention) Thai food. The relationship of attitudes and beliefs to behaviors is not a one-to-one equation. Numerous attitudes and beliefs are stored in a person's belief system. Just because a person likes Thai food does not mean that the person will act on that attitude. Other likes and dislikes compete for the person's time, money, and energy. Attitudes and beliefs about losing weight, spending money, and use of time may be stronger than a desire to go to a restaurant for Thai food.

Values are what people who share a culture regard strongly as good or bad. Values have an evaluative component. They often concern desired goals, such as the Christian value of salvation, or the values of mature love, world peace, or preservation of the environment. Values also concern ways of behaving that lead to these goals, such as valuing thrift, honesty, cleanliness, or speaking and acting quietly so as not to make noise that disturbs other people.

Cultural Beliefs

When a belief is held by most members of a culture we call it a *cultural belief.* Culture influences the perceptions and behaviors of the individuals sharing the culture through beliefs, values, and norms. They are important building blocks of culture.

A cultural belief may rest on a common history that a people share. For example, the Navajo believe that U.S. government programs cannot be trusted. This belief stems, in part, from the Long Walk in which the U.S. Army forced 6,000 Navajo men, women, and children in 1868 to march 300 miles from their homes in eastern Arizona and western New Mexico to internment at Fort Sumner, New Mexico. More than 4,000 Navajos died. Later, in the 1930s, the U.S. Bureau of Indian Affairs forcibly reduced the Navajo sheep population by 20 percent in order to prevent overgrazing. This policy was bitterly opposed by the Navajo. If you were a Navajo today, would you believe that the federal government could be trusted to help you and your family?

Not everyone in a society holds exactly the same cultural beliefs. In other words, an individual's culture does not totally determine his/her beliefs. But the members of a society who share a common culture have relatively more similar beliefs than do individuals of different cultures. For instance, most Japanese believe that gift giving is much more important than do people in the United States. West African people believe in magic and in the religious sacrifice of animals and chickens more than do individuals in most other cultures.

Case Illustration:
Hmong Spirits versus Western Medicine

Prior to the Vietnamese War, the Hmong tribespeople lived in the mountainous highlands of Laos. The CIA recruited the Hmong to fight on the side of the United States against the communist Pathet Lao. The Hmong were defending their homes and fought bravely. They suffered heavy losses. When the war ended in 1975, about 150,000 Hmong fled Laos. The CIA helped some Hmong escape. Others fled to refugee camps in Thailand, until they could come to the United States. They were relocated, particularly in Chicago, Minneapolis, Milwaukee, Fresno, and Merced, California. Here the Hmong tried to practice their unique culture while living an urban life.

Both in Ban Vinai (a refugee camp in Thailand) and in the United States, the Hmong were provided with free medical care. But the doctors and nurses who practiced in the clinics were perceived as enemies by the Hmong. The clinics were underutilized and were only used as a last resort when all other means of treating illness were exhausted. Why? The Hmong attributed sickness to evil spirits (called dab in the Hmong language) and to soul loss. Hmong shamans, txiv neeb, cured illnesses by the ritual sacrifice of chickens, dogs, pigs, or cows. When the Hmong went to a Western health clinic, the spirit-strings were cut from their wrists by nurses who told them these adornments were dirty and carried germs. The neck-rings that the Hmong believed held the life-souls of their babies were removed by doctors. The bloody animal sacrifices were ridiculed and discouraged by refugee camp regulations on cleanliness. The doctors prescribed drugs for their patients, which the Hmong felt did not combat the dabs and had strong side-effects.

This antagonistic relationship between Hmong cultural values versus Western medicine was finally bridged by Dr. Dwight Conquergood, an ethnographer of Hmong culture who is a professor of communication at Northwestern University. Conquergood is fluent in the Hmong language and understood the health beliefs of the refugees. He was able to look at Western medicine through the eyes of the Hmong. When he was assigned to Ban Vinai, Conquergood insisted on living in the camp, moving into a thatched hut with seven chickens and a pig (all other camp staff commuted from a nearby city). On his first day in Ban Vinai, he noticed an elderly Hmong woman, sitting on a bench and singing folk songs. Her face was decorated with blue moons and golden suns, stickers that the health clinic staff placed on medication bottles to inform patients to take their pills in the morning or at night (Fadiman, 1997, p. 27). Conquergood thought this symbol of medical noncompliance represented a delightfully creative costume design.

His first challenge came when an outbreak of rabies among the thousands of camp dogs led to a mass dog-vaccination campaign by the clinic staff. Not a single dog was brought in for vaccination. Conquergood organized a rabies parade, led by three important characters from Hmong folktales, a tiger, a chicken, and a dab, each dressed in homemade costumes, with the chicken explaining the etiology of rabies through a bullhorn as the parade wound through the camp. The next morning, the clinic staff were amazed by the turnout of Hmong who brought their dogs for inoculation. Next, Conquergood organized a parade of Hmong children led by Mother Clean, an insanely grinning figure, and a gigantic Garbage Troll, plastered with trash, who sang songs about latrine use and refuse disposal. The Hmong refugees were elated.

During his stay in the camp, Conquergood was successfully treated by a shaman with Hmong herbs for diarrhea and a gashed toe. When he got dengue fever (for which he was also treated with Western medicine), a txiv neeb diagnosed Conquergood as having lost his homesick soul, which had wandered back to Chicago. Two chickens were sacrificed, and Conquergood recovered (Fadiman, 1997, p. 28). Through his empathy with the Hmong and his understanding of their culture, Conquergood was able to bridge the culture clash between Western medicine and Hmong beliefs about evil spirits.

Cultural Values and Cultural Attitudes

Cultural values involve judgments (that is, they specify what is good or bad) and are normative (that is, they state or imply what should be). Most people in the United States feel that bullfighting is disgusting and cruel. But to many Mexicans and Spaniards, bullfighting is an important and exciting sport. Similarly, most people in the United States place a negative value on nepotism (hiring or favoring a relative) and on bribery. In other nations, these activities are valued positively and are widely practiced. In some cultures, the chief financial officer of a company is often the brother or at least a close relative of the company president, who thinks that this relative can be trusted with the company's money.

The Navajo have a strong value regarding any aspect of death. They do not want to talk about it, think about it, or deal with it in any way. Death is simply anathema to the Navajo. In a broadcast of a Superbowl football game, an English-language sports announcer might say: "The Dallas Cowboys' drive died at the 40-yard line." Radio Station KTNN (whose call letters stand for "The Navajo Nation"), broadcasting the game in *Diné*, described the same action by saying: "The football lost its vital signs on the 40-yard line." The cultural value on avoiding any mention of death is carried over to announcing a football game.

Many attitudes are based on cultural values. In the United States, freedom is a dominant value. In others, it is just one value among others. The meaning of any value, including freedom, differs across cultures. An old woman in Saigon told one of the authors that she felt that she could not tolerate the lack of freedom in the United States. In Vietnam she was free to sell her vegetables on the sidewalk without being hassled by police or city authorities. She did not have to get a permit to fix the roof on her house. She had the freedom to vote for a communist candidate if she wanted to. She believed that in the United States, where her children lived, people were expected to tell others what they thought. In Vietnam she had the freedom to remain silent. Her perceptions determined her behavior; she refused to immigrate to the United States to join her children.

When one of the authors was teaching at Stanford University, a professor friend told him about selling his daughter's horse. She loved this horse very much, rode it often, and regarded it as her special pet. When she left for college, her father decided that the horse should be sold. He placed an ad in a local newspaper and promptly received a telephone call from an interested party. They agreed on a price, and the buyers arrived shortly in a pick-up truck. They paid the $200 and then shot the horse with a rifle at pointblank range, threw the carcass in the back of their vehicle, and drove off. The professor was horrified and worried about telling his daughter about her pet's demise. The buyers were Tongans (a community of people from Tonga living in the San Francisco Bay area), who relish barbecued horse meat. The values attached to a horse are obviously quite different if it is regarded as a pet versus food.

How does the incident about killing a horse affect your attitude toward people from Tonga? Are you judging an element of Tongan culture in light of your own culture? Perhaps a person from India would be equally horrified if he or she visited a packinghouse in the United States in which cows were being slaughtered.

Norms

Norms are the established behavior patterns for members of a social system. If a cultural norm is violated, the individual is socially punished for not fulfilling the expectations of his/her system. An example of violating a cultural norm occurred when a French woman visiting Saudi Arabia used her left hand to eat out of a communal bowl of rice and lamb. Her Saudi friends suddenly lost their appetites (Seelye & Seelye, 1996, 121–22). The left hand is considered unclean in the Middle East and Asia, and cultural norms prohibit handing an object to someone with the left hand. There is a historical reason for the left-handed taboo in these cultures, related to cleaning the body with the left hand after defecation.

Thai people revere their king, so much so that they seldom talk about him and are culturally forbidden to touch him. A U.S. professor, during the first months that he taught at Bangkok University, accidentally dropped a Thai coin on the floor. In order to keep the coin from rolling under a door, he quickly stepped on it. His Thai students were shocked. Why? The king's profile is on every coin.

Individuals are often surprised when, during a communication exchange, they realize that they had incorrectly assumed that a conversation partner shared the same cultural norm. An example of such value attribution is provided by the following exchange of messages (Storti, 1994).

Alice: I heard your son is getting married. Congratulations.

Fatima: Thank you. The wedding will be next spring.

Alice: How nice for you. How did they meet?

Fatima: Oh, they haven't actually met yet.

What was the cultural norm that Alice assumed governed how young people decide whom to marry? Figure 3-2 shows advertisements for arranged marriages in India. Figure 3-3 suggests certain parallels with the personal advertisements in U.S. newspapers.

A recent university graduate from the United States was interning in a Japanese company in Nagoya. He related his experiences in violating a Japanese cultural norm about proper office behavior: "During the first week in the company, I asked a fellow employee, a young woman, for a date. She became very embarrassed and told me that she could not go out with me because we worked in the same unit. By that evening, everyone in my office

Figure 3-2.   These matrimonial ads have been placed in a major newspaper by the parents of young men and women in India. Notice how frequently caste, formal education, and physical appearance are mentioned.

knew what had happened. Several of my colleagues made jokes of rather poor taste about my mistake. For the next several months, references were made about my asking Yuki for a date, especially after my colleagues had had too much to drink. Eventually, a year later, I learned that I was referred to, behind my back, with a nickname in Japanese that connoted something like 'skirt-chaser.'"

This example shows the various ways in which an individual violating a cultural norm was punished: through gossip, joking, and by use of a humorous nickname.

Collectivistic versus Individualistic Cultures

We define a *collectivistic culture* as one in which the collectivity's goals are valued over those of the individual. In contrast, an *individualistic culture* is one in which the individual's goals are valued over those of the collectivity. Individualism-collectivism is perhaps the most important dimension of cul-

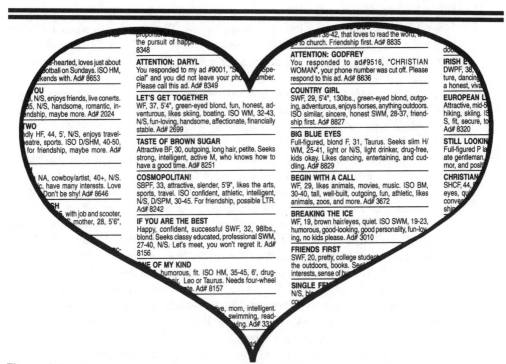

Figure 3-3. These personal ads were placed in a U.S. newspaper by individuals seeking to establish a relationship with another person. Notice the qualities described in comparison to the Indian matrimonial ads.

tural differences in behavior across the cultures of the world (Oetzel & Bolton-Oetzel, 1997). Harry Triandis, a psychologist at the University of Illinois, has written extensively about the individualistic-collectivistic classification of cultures (Hui & Triandis, 1986; Triandis, 1986, 1990, 1994, & 1995).

Japanese culture is an example of a collectivistic culture (Hofstede, 1990). Harmony (*wa*) is very important to the Japanese. The collectivistic nature of Japanese culture is evident when observing a typical business office in Tokyo. More than a dozen employees are packed into an office that in the United States might house two or three individuals. The Japanese workers sit at small desks, facing each other, clustered in the middle of the room. Their boss sits among them. Individual privacy is completely lacking; instead, much informal conversation occurs among the office workers as they help each other with various work-related tasks.

When the 5:00 P.M. bell rings, signaling the end of the workday, no one gets up to leave. Neckties are loosened and jackets are shed, and the office situation becomes more relaxed. But the employees keep right on working. Finally, hours later, at 10:30 or 11:00 P.M., the office workers go home and the office

is dark. The employees will be back at their small desks the next morning at
8:00 A.M. Perhaps one night per week, these office workers go out together
for dinner. Most individuals drink sake or beer until they are drunk. After
several drinks, the workers may play a joke on their boss or argue violently
with him/her (the following day, all that transpired will be forgotten). The
drinking session has a strong bonding effect, and the office workers regard
themselves as something like a family. All decisions are made with the group
in mind, rather than what is best for one of the workers. Thus is collectivistic
solidarity developed in Japan.

Long-term relationships based on trust are very important in a collectivistic culture. For example, many Japanese companies provide their workers
with lifetime employment. Maintaining positive long-term relationships is
stressed. An individual should not contradict another person in public, as
doing so would disrupt personal network relationships. Individuals are more
likely to say what the other person wants to hear, rather than conveying information in a more direct manner that might solve a problem. Employees are
particularly reluctant to tell their boss that the boss's pet idea is not working.

Face, a public self-image that an individual wants to present in a particular
social context, is a major consideration in dealing with others. Every effort is
made so that someone does not lose face in front of others. The Japanese pay
much attention to group memberships and to other individuals in their personal networks. Fitting in with others, creating and maintaining obligations,
conformity, and being relationship-oriented are highly prized. Individual
achievement, personal recognition, and thinking mainly for oneself are
strongly discouraged. A popular Japanese saying is: "The nail that protrudes
gets hammered down."

These collectivistic values and norms are well illustrated by the case of one
of the authors who was invited to speak at a Japanese conference. He was
asked to travel to Japan three days before the conference began so that all of
the 30 speakers (the others were Japanese) could meet in a traditional Japanese inn (*ryokan*) in order "to work out their differences" in private. Actually, there were no serious differences about the topics they were to present.
The speakers enjoyed hot baths, sumptuous meals, the traditional Japanese
tea ceremony, and took long walks through the countryside. They got well-
acquainted with each other. (This type of preconference activity fits with a
collectivistic culture.)

Finally, the speakers moved to a hotel in downtown Tokyo, where the public conference was held. The author began his speech with a profound apology,
mentioning how little he really knew about the topic that he was presenting,
how unfamiliar he was with the situation in Japan, and how sorry he was to
be wasting his audience's time (it is the custom in Japan to begin a speech
with an apology). After his talk, a number of listeners complimented him on
his apology, which they said was one of the best they had heard from a foreigner. Being apologetic is considered appropriate in a collectivistic culture,

where pride and self-centeredness might disrupt interpersonal relationships. In an individualistic culture like the United States, students enrolled in public speaking classes are told never to begin a speech with an apology.

Individualistic-collectivistic cultures strongly influence communication behavior. Reciprocally, human communication is a means through which individualism and collectivism are taught to individuals and maintained as a culture's orientation.

Nigerian students at a U.S. university have a background rich in collectivistic values versus the individualistic orientation of their classmates. Ibo villages in eastern Nigeria collect funds to send their most academically talented young people to overseas universities. When such an individual comes back to Nigeria, he/she is expected to return to his/her home village and to begin making sizeable contributions toward the university education of other talented youth. One Ibo village might boast that it has supported an MIT graduate and a Berkeley Ph.D. in astrophysics, for example. One can imagine that the Ibo students feel they are achieving their education not just for themselves, but for their people.

Another example of collectivistic culture involved a young woman from the United States, Kristen, who had been working in a Japanese company for two weeks when her boss's mother died. On the morning of the funeral, Kristen arrived in the office wearing a colorful dress, but she sensed from her coworkers that something was wrong. The others were all dressed in dark clothes. A close friend suggested that Kristen might go home for lunch, which was an unusual suggestion. Kristen took the hint, returning from lunch in a black dress. When she entered the office, all thirty colleagues gave her a standing ovation! The unpredictable stranger in their work unit had behaved in a culturally appropriate way. They felt relieved for their collectivity, which would otherwise have been embarrassed by her appearance at the funeral.

The Nature of the Self

These examples illustrate (1) the differences between communication behavior in an individualistic and a collectivistic culture and (2) the special problems of communication between individuals who do not share similar backgrounds. The nature of the self is different in an individualistic versus a collectivistic culture. Culture shapes one's self, and thus one's communication, perceptions, and other behavior. In an individualistic culture, the individual perceives himself/herself as independent. Being overly interdependent on others is considered weak or unassertive. In a collectivistic culture, the individual mainly thinks of himself/herself as connected to others. To be independent in one's thinking or actions would be considered selfish, rude, and in poor taste. An individual who is not a good team player is punished for breaking the norm on collectivism. Interaction between individuals with these different perceptions of self can easily result in misinterpreting the other's behavior.

Independence versus Interdependence at the Individual Level

Obviously, not everyone in a collectivistic culture is equally collectivistic in thinking and behavior, nor are all of the individuals in an individualistic culture equally individualistic. For example, certain Japanese are task oriented rather than relationship oriented; they are very direct in their speaking style, telling it like it is. Likewise, some European Americans in the United States are as collectivistic as any Japanese. So there is individual variation within both collectivistic and individualistic cultures, even though the average degree to which individuals are collectivistic-oriented is much greater in a collectivistic society like Japan than in an individualistic culture like the United States.

How can the degree of individualism-collectivism be measured at the individual level? A scale to measure this dimension was developed by William Gudykunst and others (1996). It has been used and modified by other intercultural communication scholars. Each scale item asks a respondent about his/her self-construal (that is, self-image) as to his/her degree of individualism (called "independence") versus collectivism (called "interdependence") (Table 3-1). Individuals with images of themselves as highly independent are more concerned with task outcomes and are more individualistic in their behavior. Individuals whose self-images are interdependent are more concerned with relational outcomes and are generally collectivistic in their behavior (Oetzel & Bolton-Oetzel, 1997). The independence-interdependence scale in Table 3-1 can help the reader understand whether he/she is more oriented to an individualistic or to a collectivistic culture.

High-Context versus Low-Context Cultures

Edward T. Hall (1976) originated the classification of high-context versus low-context cultures, based on the amount of information that is implied versus stated directly in a communication message.[2] A *high-context culture* is one in which the meanings of a communication message are found in the situation and in the relationships of the communicators or are internalized in the communicators' beliefs, values, and norms. The communication context (particularly the relationships with the other individuals in the communication situation) plays an important part in the interpretation of a communication message.

Collectivistic cultures, such as Asian and Latino, are usually high-context cultures. These cultures emphasize nonverbal communication and subtleness in communication rather than being frank. High-context cultures are extremely polite, which fits with the indirect, subtle nature of interpersonal communication. Ambiguity (the degree to which a communication message has many possible meanings to its receivers) and obscurity characterize conversations in a high-context culture. One purpose of communication is to

Table 3-1. A Scale to Measure an Individual's Degree of Independence (Individualism) versus Interdependence (Collectivism)

	Self-Image				
Scale Item	Strongly Agree	Agree	?	Disagree	Strongly Disagree
I. *Independence*					
1. Being able to take care of myself is a primary concern for me.	5	4	3	2	1
2. I prefer to be self-reliant rather than depend on others.	5	4	3	2	1
3. I try not to depend on others.	5	4	3	2	1
4. I take responsibility for my own actions.	5	4	3	2	1
5. It is important for me to be able to act as a free and independent person.	5	4	3	2	1
6. I should decide my future on my own.	5	4	3	2	1
7. What happens to me is my own doing.	5	4	3	2	1
II. *Interdependence*					
8. I consult with others before making important decisions.	1	2	3	4	5
9. I consult with co-workers on work-related matters.	1	2	3	4	5
10. I sacrifice my self-interest for the benefit of my group.	1	2	3	4	5
11. It is better to consult others and get their opinions before doing anything.	1	2	3	4	5
12. I try to meet the demands of the groups of which I am a member, even if it means controlling my own desires.	1	2	3	4	5
13. It is important to consult close friends and get their ideas before making a decision.	1	2	3	4	5

Source: These scale items are based upon Gudykunst & others (1996) and Oetzel & Bolton-Oetzel (1997).

Note: Possible scores on the total 13-item scale can range from a high of 65, indicating extreme independence (individualism), to a low of 13, indicating extreme interdependence (collectivism). A person whose self-image is equally independent and interdependent will have a score of 39.

avoid threatening the face of one's conversation partner, thus bringing shame upon oneself. What is *not* said (an unverbalized message) may be more important than what *is* said (Kim & Sharkey, 1995).

A *low-context culture* is one in which the meanings of a communication message are stated clearly and explicitly, without depending on the context of the communication situation. Examples of low-context cultures are European American, English, and other northern European countries. Reactions are expressed frankly during a conversation. Meanings are explicitly coded in a communication message. Verbal communication in a low-context culture leaves little to the imagination. A concern for clarity is highly valued, while a concern for hurting someone else's feelings or a concern for avoiding being perceived negatively by a communication co-participant is not highly valued (Kim & Sharkey, 1995). Conversations in a low-context culture are clear and to the point.

People in a high-context culture keep well informed about all aspects of the other people in their lives, such as their work associates. Thus a particular message can be brief and vague, as the recipient-individual is already well informed about the context of the message. However, in a low-context culture individuals compartmentalize their personal, work, and other relationships (Hall & Hall, 1990, p. 7). Hence a message must contain many more details than in a high-context culture. Term papers by college students in U.S. universities are often written in a high-context style which assumes that the instructor is "inside the head" of the student. Western professors constantly push their students to be exceptionally clear in their writing, attempting to move them to the dominant low-context style.

An example of how to decline a potential spouse in an arranged marriage in South India, a high-context culture, helps illustrate the coding of a high-context message. Let's say the boy's family has visited the girl's home in order to look over the potential bride. They then send an emissary who conveys this message: "We really enjoyed meeting all of your family members. Usha is a fine cook and is a very nice young woman. But we wish that tea had been served with the mangos instead of coffee." What is the real meaning of this message? "We do not want our son to marry your daughter." Subtlety characterizes communication in a high-context culture. Hurting the other party's feelings is avoided at all costs; emphasis is placed on saving face. The issue is not confronted directly; the message must be carefully interpreted.

High/Low-Context Communication Problems

In this age of globalization, interaction between high- and low-context cultures has become more frequent than ever before. International business transactions, for example, may suffer because of communication difficulties between cultures. Picture a business conversation between a U.S. executive, Smith, and her Japanese counterpart, Yamada, representing communication between a low-context culture and a high-context culture, respectively:

Smith: Yamada-san, what price per unit can you offer my company, given that we are buying in large volume?

Yamada: (smiling) We are honored to do business with such an important American company as yours, Ms. Smith.

Smith: We can pay your company $1.38 per unit, which is what we pay our present suppliers in the United States. We feel your units are of comparable quality.

Yamada: Well, our workers try very hard to produce these units so they have no defects. But of course our Japanese manufacturing equipment may not be as efficient as that of your American suppliers.

Smith: Now about the price of $1.38. . . .

Do you predict that this conversation will end with both participants feeling satisfied with the communication process? Probably not, as Ms. Smith pursues a direct, frontal approach, while Yamada is subtle and less direct.

The following conversation might occur between an Arabic and a visiting U.S. businessman (Storti, 1994, pp. 89–90). Obviously, they are operating within different cultures (high-context versus low-context).

Abu Bakr: Mr. Armstrong! How good to see you.

Armstrong: Nice to see you again, Hassan.

Abu Bakr: Tell me: How have you been?

Armstrong: Very well, thank you. And you?

Abu Bakr: Fine, fine. Allah be praised.

Armstrong: I really appreciate your agreeing to see me about these distribution arrangements. Now could we . . .

Abu Bakr: My pleasure. So tell me: How was your trip? Did you come direct or did you have a stopover?

Armstrong: No stopover this time. I'm on a tight schedule. That's why I'm so grateful you could see me on such a short notice. So about the . . .

Abu Bakr: Not at all. How is my good friend, Mr. Wilson?

Armstrong: Wilson? Oh, fine, fine. He's been very busy with this distribution problem also, which is what we need to discuss.

Abu Bakr: You know, you have come at an excellent time. Tomorrow is the Prophet's birthday—blessings and peace be upon Him—and we're having a special feast at my home. I'd like you to be our guest.

Armstrong: Thank you very much.

Here Armstrong attempts to get right down to business, while Abu Bakr thinks that there is more to business meetings than just business. He wants to get better acquainted with Armstrong. Abu Bakr is concerned with his guest's feelings. He is subtly conveying to Armstrong that he is not yet ready to talk about the business matter. Do you think Armstrong will be successful in his business negotiations with Abu Bakr?

In general, a low-context individual often becomes puzzled and frustrated when interacting with other people who have a high-context culture. Their messages seem incomplete and ambiguous. A U.S. professor of communication, teaching at a Japanese university, tells of the endless faculty meetings that he endured. Decisions were made by consensus, a process that required a great deal of discussion in a high-context and collectivistic culture like Japan. It was considered inappropriate to ask direct questions in these discussions, and often the progress of the faculty conversations drifted in what seemed to be aimless directions. Careful statements would be made by the professors, which only seemed to deal with the topic of discussion in a very oblique way. Individuals would hide their feelings to avoid hurting someone else's feelings with whom they might disagree. The U.S. professor could not even be sure as to who disagreed with whom. Faculty meetings would often continue for five or six hours, and some stretched to seven or eight hours, only ending when everyone was completely exhausted. Many faculty meetings ended without any decision being made.

Another example of a low-context individual in a high-context culture is provided by a U.S. intern working in a Japanese corporation. The intern frequently was 5 to 10 minutes late to work in the morning, but no one in his office seemed to notice or to care. Neither the boss nor coworkers suggested to the intern that he should be more prompt. In fact, he noticed that certain employees arrived an hour or two late in the morning and then worked later that evening in a kind of flex-time arrangement. The intern wondered if he could work on a flexible schedule too.

After several weeks, the intern noticed that none of the other employees at his level worked on a flexible time schedule. All arrived promptly at 8:00 A.M. Sometime later, one of his fellow employees complimented him on how well he was adjusting to Japanese culture, particularly by arriving at his desk by 8:00 each morning. The fact that the sojourner gradually learned the unwritten rule of promptness without being told and that he had observed that only senior executives could work on a flex-time schedule impressed his Japanese coworkers.

Communication problems between people of high- and low-context cultures are so common that the occupation of translator extends far beyond transcription of speeches at the United Nations. Grace Chen is a translator in a New York city hospital. She facilitates physician/patient communication for Chinese patients. The European American doctors continually demand that Grace get to the point of an exchange with a patient more quickly. Their time is valuable, and they are thinking about the other patients in their waiting room. But Grace's high-context patients insist on describing their medical problems in a spiral of widely scattered details, without actually stating what their illness is. Translating between such high-context patients and low-context doctors is very difficult. Grace is not just translating from one language to another. She is mediating between two different types of cultures. Low-context people become impatient and irritated when high-context people insist on giving them information they feel that they do not need.

Are You High-Context or Low-Context?

Perhaps by now the reader is wondering whether he/she has a high-context or a low-context culture orientation. Here are three situations, provided by Kim and Sharkey (1995), that might help you find out. What would you do if:

1. A friend of yours who worked in your department gave a very poor presentation, and then asked you, "How did I do?"
2. Another friend of yours who works in your office returns from lunch late whenever you are in charge. You have to say something to your friend about this matter. What?
3. You must write a thank-you note to a friend at work who gave you an awful gift at a department holiday party. How do you express your thanks?

In each case, do you say directly and clearly what is on your mind, without concern for the other person's feelings? Or do you try to be ambiguous and polite, so that you can maintain your friendship with the other person? Your choice is one indicator of the extent to which you are low-context or high-context.

Within versus Between Cultural Variation

Previously in this chapter, we showed that certain individuals in a collectivistic culture may be quite individualistic. Likewise, some individuals are quite collectivistic in an individualistic culture. Cultural variance may exist *within* any given group or culture as well as *between* different cultural groups. As an example, some African Americans have dark skin while others are light-skinned—a variance *within* an ethnic or cultural population, and some African Americans are lighter skinned than some European-American Whites—a variance *between* groups (Steinfatt & Christophel, 1996, p. 324). There is a great deal of cultural variance among the members of any particular ethnic population, even on variables that are the distinguishing characteristics of the ethnic group.

When people describe a culture, they describe their perceptions of its main features, its central tendencies. But these tendencies do not exist as fixed points. Rather, they vary around the central tendency, becoming greater or lesser depending on the cultural situation. In a low-context culture such as the United States, a desire for clarity and directness will occur in messages from professors to students about their term papers. But at a funeral, mourners will not be asked to express their grief clearly and directly, except by the most insensitive of their acquaintances. Cultural tendencies are neither enforced nor exhibited equally across all cultural situations.

Cultural tendencies also vary with the individual. Not all Japanese always behave in a high-context fashion, even in a situation calling for high-context behavior. Some U.S. citizens will behave in a more high-context fashion within the United States than will some Japanese in Japan. The fact that this usually does not happen allows us to make statements that Japan is a high-context culture and the U.S. a low-context culture. Our understanding of other cultures is incomplete (and faulty) if we assume that all individuals in all situations always practice the dominant features of that culture. Understanding when dominant themes are likely to be present and when they are likely to be absent is essential for effective intercultural communication.

Some behaviors and cultural styles are more related to social class and socioeconomic status than to cultural differences. The message interpretations of a Khmer in Phnom Penh can differ quite sharply from those of a foreign businessperson. But if the Khmer is poor and living on the street, while the foreigner is rich and living in a luxury hotel, the differences in interpretations between them may be more a matter of class economics than of cultural variation. In studying intercultural communication, it is important to remember that *the variation within a culture in terms of situations, individuals, and socioeconomic status may account for as much or more of the variation in intercultural interpretations of messages as does the difference between the cultures of the individuals involved.*

Cultural Clash

A *cultural clash* is defined as the conflict that occurs between two or more cultures when they disagree about a certain value. A cultural clash may involve strongly held values, such as those concerning religion. For instance, in Chapter 1 we traced the role of religious differences in past wars and other conflicts.

An example of a cultural clash is the "live animal market" in Hong Kong, Taipei, Singapore, San Francisco, and other cities with a large population of Chinese people. The live market is typically a street of small stalls where live snakes, monkeys, dogs, and other delicacies that are used as ingredients in Chinese cooking are sold. These traditional dishes have been prized for centuries by Chinese people. They believe that these dishes must be prepared with fresh ingredients. The businesspeople who manage the stalls in the live market say that their jobs depend on being allowed to sell live animals.

The Chinese perceive the public criticism of the live market as an attack on their culture. They resist the efforts of animal rights activists, such as the Humane Society, who claim that the monkeys, turtles, dogs, snakes, and other animals should not be sold for cooking purposes. Animal rights people appeal to public sympathy—imagining one's pet being sold for food. They also work to convince municipal authorities to ban the live market on the basis of its lack of cleanliness and because of cruelty to animals (such as ripping the shells off of live turtles). In certain cases, animal rights protesters have invaded a live market to smash the cages and to free the animals, birds, and snakes. In San Francisco in 1996, activists claimed that the creatures were kept in cramped, filthy quarters in Chinatown's live market. This protest led the Commission of Animal Control and Welfare in San Francisco to recommend to the city government that the live market be outlawed, but the issue remained unresolved. The underlying conflict over the live market traces to a clash of values, in this case the value of animals as creatures entitled to certain rights versus the value of animals as food.

Another example of a cultural clash is provided by Hall and Noguchi (1993). These scholars analyzed the killing of 1,000 dolphins by Japanese fisherman on the island of Iki. Their catch had declined, and the fishermen blamed it on the dolphins, called *iruka* (gangster or villain). They perceived themselves as warriors fighting off unwelcome invaders—the dolphins that they trapped in drift-nets that stretched for miles in the ocean.

Western conservationists perceived dolphins as intelligent, friendly mammals that have a special affinity for humans. They called the drift-nets a "wall of death" and protested against the actions of the Japanese fishermen. Some activists traveled to Iki Island in order to free dolphins trapped on the beaches. After lengthy negotiations, the Japanese government eventually agreed to halt the mass killing of dolphins in 1991. How do Hall and Noguchi explain this cultural clash? "'Dolphin' and '*iruka*' have a common referent; however, the meanings involved were so different that each community's common sense demanded divergent and seemingly incompatible actions."

Cultural clashes occur frequently in cities, such as Miami, that are composed of a large number of ethnic groups. For example, Suni Muslims immigrated from the Middle East and Pakistan in the 1950s. These people have maintained their culture over the several decades of living in North Miami, resisting assimilation into the dominant general culture. This cultural maintenance of the Suni Muslims, however, frequently leads to intergenerational cultural clash between youth and their parents. This conflict may center on the degree of individual freedom allowed young women. For example, a fourteen-year-old asked her parents for permission to go to a shopping mall with her friends. They refused because of the Suni Muslim value that unmarried women should not be seen in public unless chaperoned by parents or older brothers. The adolescent daughter insisted on going to the mall, so her parents chained her to her bed (Steinfatt & Christophel, 1996).

Cultural Identification

One of the important ways in which culture affects communication is through *cultural identification*, the degree to which individuals consider themselves to be representatives of a particular culture. Such cultural identification determines which ethnic groups an individual considers as ingroups and which as outgroups. How people behave depends, in part, on

Case Illustration:
Female Genital Mutilation in the United States

Female genital mutilation is the act of surgically altering a female's sexual organs. One type of genital mutilation is clitorectomy, the act of cutting off a female's clitoris. This practice is widespread among hundreds of tribes in the 28 nations across the middle of Africa. The operation is usually performed when a cohort of young women in a community reaches puberty, as part of their coming-of-age rites. The ceremony is deeply cultural and signifies a change in the status of an individual from girl to woman. The operation is often performed with a knife or razor blade that is not sterile, and infection may result. One of the main purposes in cutting off the clitoris is to inhibit a woman's sexual enjoyment, thereby making it unlikely that she can reach orgasm. Many African men refuse to marry a woman who has not undergone the operation because they fear she will not be faithful to them. Public health officials seek to prevent the operation on health grounds. Nevertheless, genital mutilation remains a strongly held norm in many African cultures. Today, a cultural clash exists in several African nations concerning this practice.

But the cultural clash regarding clitorectomy is not limited to Africa. The Centers for Disease Control and Prevention (CDC) estimated that 150,000 women of African origin or ancestry in the United States have had the operation or are at risk (Dugger, 1996). These women are scattered throughout the United States but are concentrated in Los Angeles, New York, Chicago, Philadelphia, Washington, Houston, and Atlanta.

In 1997, clitorectomy became a federal crime in the United States, punishable by up to five years in prison. African women in the United States have the operation in a secret ceremony, and the federal government's opposition to this cultural practice is deeply resented as an invasion of privacy. Medical doctors and hospitals refuse to perform the operation, and parents feel they have little choice but to ask traditional midwives to perform the ceremony. Some U.S. doctors have proposed that they cut a ritual nick in the prepuce, the fold of skin that is analogous to the foreskin of the penis. However, African parents in the United States say that this ritual act is unacceptable as a replacement for the operation. Instead, some parents fly their daughters back to their home country in Africa, where the operation can be performed legally.

Here is an extreme example of a cultural clash, a situation in which two cultures differ completely regarding a certain value. On one side of the dispute are strongly held African cultural norms requiring clitorectomy of all young girls before they are considered women and in order for them to be eligible for marriage. Opposed to this belief in the United States is the powerful force of the U.S. government, which declares that the operation is illegal. Who will prevail? How might this cultural clash be resolved?

whether they consider themselves Latinos, African Americans, or European Americans, for instance. Perceptions count in explaining how people behave, and such self-perceptions as an individual's cultural identification are particularly important in defining the individual's self and thus in determining the individual's communication behavior with others.

Case Illustration:
AIDS Prevention in San Francisco

When the AIDS epidemic was discovered in 1981, some of the first cases were identified in San Francisco. No other city in the world has been as hard hit by the AIDS epidemic, and no other urban center was as successful, eventually, in slowing the further spread of the virus. San Francisco had the highest number of HIV-infected persons per capita of any major city in the United States (including 48 percent of the city's gay and bisexual male population), as well as the highest rate of AIDS-related deaths per population. By 1997, 20,273 deaths due to AIDS had occurred among San Francisco's total population of 775,000. An Associated Press photograph in 1994 showed the 122 members of the San Francisco Gay Men's Chorus. Some 115 are dressed in black and face away from the camera. They represent the members of the chorus who had died from AIDS since 1981. Only 7 men are dressed in white and face the camera. They represent the members of the 1981 Gay Men's Chorus who were still alive 13 years later.

One of the authors investigated the relative effectiveness of HIV/AIDS prevention programs in San Francisco.[3] To his surprise, there were 212 HIV/AIDS prevention programs in this relatively small city. Why so many? One reason was the extreme cultural diversity of San Francisco. Some 25 percent of the city's residents are foreign-born (compared to 8.7 percent for the United States): Chinese, Japanese, Filipinos, and Thais. This city also has many African Americans and Latinos. Many of the HIV/AIDS prevention programs serve a particular ethnic group. For example, a Filipino organization provided a prevention program targeted to young gay Filipino males. The HIV/AIDS prevention programs in San Francisco were targeted to specialized audiences on the basis of four or five factors, such as age, ethnicity, sexual preference, gender, drug use, language, socioeconomic status, and being a sex worker. Often the audience for a prevention program was very small in number. An extreme case was one program targeted at an intended audience of 150 "Deadheads" (followers of the Grateful Dead musical group) who lived in San Francisco.

Outreach workers employed by the prevention programs sought to deliver a safe sex message including free condoms to the intended audience. Many outreach activities took place on the streets in San Francisco's low-income and redlight districts. The staff members usually shared the unique characteristics of their audience. For instance, a program aimed at Thai massage girls employed outreach workers who were former Thai massage girls who had been trained in HIV/AIDS prevention and in *outreach strategies. The cultural and linguistic homophily (similarity) of the program staff with the audience individuals meant that the messages were culturally sensitive, an important quality when communicating a topic like AIDS. Outreach workers learned not to imply in street conversations that sex work, promiscuity, or injection drug use were undesirable. They learned to be nonjudgmental.*

An especially important quality of effective outreach workers in San Francisco is that many were HIV positive or had been diagnosed with AIDS. Outreach staff frequently disclosed their status as part of their personal introduction: "Hi, my name is Sam and I am seropositive." Being identified with the epidemic conveyed credibility, the degree to which a communication source is perceived as expert and trustworthy. Audience individuals thought that outreach staff who were infected knew what they were talking about. Combining cultural and linguistic homophily with the intended audience and with high credibility resulted in successful communication—and effective HIV prevention programs.

Cultural Markers

Many people have a culturally identifiable name and, perhaps, a physical appearance that conveys, or at least suggests, their cultural identity. For example, imagine a brown-skinned, dark-haired person named Augusto Torres. He identifies himself as Latino. But many individuals are not so easily identified culturally. Two million people in the United States are culturally mixed and may identify with one or two or with multiple cultures. A person named Susan Lopez might be expected to be Latina, judging only from her last name. "Lopez" actually comes from her adoptive parents, who raised her in the Latino tradition in the Southwest. But Susan's biological father was a European American, and her mother is a Native American (Susan is a registered member of her mother's tribe). So if Susan were classified on the basis of her blood ancestry, she is Native American/European American. Her physical appearance reflects her biological parentage. However, Susan is culturally Latina, preferring to speak Spanish, enjoying traditional foods and music, and displaying other aspects of Latino culture. Yet she returns to her mother's tribe to participate in dances and other ceremonies. Here we see that blood ancestry does not necessarily dictate an individual's cultural identification. With what culture do you think Susan identifies? This question is not just a hypothetical issue, as it is asked of everyone by the U.S. Census Bureau at ten-year intervals.

Many individuals have names that do not fit exactly with their self-perceived cultural identity. For example, consider three communication scholars named Fernando Moret, Miguel Gandert, and Jorge Reina Schement. Can you guess the culture with which each individual identifies? Do you think that their first name or their surname best predicts their cultural identification? In intercultural marriages, if the wife takes her husband's surname, her cultural identity may no longer be conveyed by her married name.

When individuals change their religious and/or ethnic identity, they often change their name to reflect their new identification. For instance, when the world heavyweight boxer Cassius Clay became a Black Muslim, he changed his name to Mohammed Ali. Likewise, basketball player Kareem Abul-Jabbar was Lew Alcindor before he joined the Muslim faith. Some European immigrants had their names changed by U.S. immigration officials when they were processed through Ellis Island in New York. For example, "Kiskowski" sometimes became "Kiska," "Stein" became "Stone," and "Schwartz" was often changed to "Black." In many cases, the name change was to an Anglo-Saxon name that was easier to understand in the United States. But in some cases, the name change also altered the religious/ethnic identity of the family. Stein and Schwartz are often Jewish-German names. Some families changed their surname in order to avoid anti-Semitism; for instance, a family named "Cohen" changed their surname to "Quinn."

Sometimes an individual's self-identification may not matter as much as *others'* definition of the individual's cultural identity. An example is provided by Gregory Howard Williams (1995) in his book *Life on the Color Line: The True Story of a White Boy Who Discovered He Was Black*. Williams grew up in Virginia, thinking that he was a White European American. When he was ten, his parents separated and he moved with his father to segregated Muncie, Indiana, to live with his grandmother. To his surprise, she was an African American. Even though he was white-skinned in appearance, Williams was now categorized by society as black and treated accordingly.[4] Consider also the many thousands of Europeans in the 1930s and 1940s who were persecuted by Hitler's fascism. If they had any Jewish ancestors, whether they knew it or not, they were categorized by the Nazis as Jewish and sent to a concentration camp. Some six million people were killed in the Holocaust.

The complex interrelationships between self-identity versus other-determined cultural identity of an individual are illustrated by the "coming out" of gays and lesbians in the United States. For many individuals, the decision to come out of the closet, and thus to bring other-perceived identity in line with self-identity, is a very major event. During the 1970s and 1980s when homophobia was very strong, many thousands of gay men and women moved to San Francisco and came out. Such a public change of identity would have been much more difficult in hometowns, often characterized by prejudice and discrimination, than in a liberal setting like San Francisco. The conservative nature of small towns in the United States often necessitates that gay and lesbian people move to urban areas.

In some circumstances, an individual may be criticized for having a cultural self-identity that others perceive as inauthentic. For example, a Spanish-surnamed student at a university was criticized by Latino students for her self-identification. They claimed that she was not *really* Latino, but only claimed to be in order to become eligible for a fellowship.

Special items of clothing, haircuts, tattoos, or other aspects of appearance (like wearing a cross or a star of David) may represent cultural identification. The prisoner shown in Figure 3-4 conveys his religion and his ethnic identification with the tattoo of the Virgin of Guadalupe.

Language and Cultural Identification

The language (or languages) that an individual speaks is a very important part of cultural identification. A Spanish-surnamed person who is fluent in Spanish is more likely to self-identify as a Latino than a similarly Spanish-surnamed individual who only speaks English. We previously explained that

Figure 3-4.   This prisoner has had a figure of the Virgin of Guadalupe tattooed on his back to discourage being stabbed there. The tattoo conveys the religious and ethnic identification of this prisoner.

Source: Photograph by Miguel Gandert. Used by permission.

in the past many immigrants to the United States, once they or their children learned English, began to identify with the new culture. This melting pot process assimilated the immigrant cultures and languages into the general culture. Today, immigrants to the United States continue speaking their native tongue for a longer period of time, rejecting English, and thus are more likely to identify with their immigrant culture.

When two individuals suddenly discover that they share a common culture and/or language, a strong bond is often formed between them. A masters student at the University of Southern California's Annenberg School for Communication was being interviewed for a job at a Hollywood film company. Her interview with a top executive did not begin well. In a cynical tone of voice, he asked, "Okay, so what makes you think that your MA degree in communication has prepared *you* to work in our company? We have young women with MA degrees serving coffee to our top officials here." After several minutes of such discouraging talk, the executive asked the job applicant a question in Yiddish. Fortunately for her, her grandmother had taught her to speak Yiddish, and she was able to respond. Immediately, the relationship between the applicant and the executive warmed considerably. He offered her a job and also made several telephone calls to other film studios on her behalf.

Cultural Differences

We defined intercultural communication as the exchange of information between individuals who are unalike culturally. This is a very broad definition involving any type of cultural difference between participants who are strangers to each other. One type of difference occurs when the two or more participants in a communication situation each have a different national culture. What if the participants are of different genders and the topic of discussion is one on which men and women differ? This information exchange is also considered intercultural communication.

Perhaps the two communication participants differ in age. One individual is a teenager and the other is a parent. The younger person has been socialized into a somewhat different culture than the adult. For example, perhaps they are discussing rap music, which the parent regards as just loud noise and inferior to classical music. The teenager feels that rap is a meaningful expression of contemporary U.S. culture. This information exchange among individuals who differ in age also is intercultural communication because the teenager and the parent have somewhat different cultures.

Similarly, information exchange between individuals who differ in religion, ethnicity, sexual preference, disability status, occupational acceptability, health (such as HIV+), or in other characteristics can be affected by their cultural or subcultural differences. Now consider two individuals who differ in their socioeconomic status. Perhaps one is a homeless person and the other is the president of a corporation. This communication is also intercultural. As all these examples show, many human communication interactions can be conceptualized as intercultural communication, at least to a certain degree.

Case Illustration:
The Homeless and PEN in Santa Monica[5]

During the 1990s the use of the Internet and other electronic-mail systems spread very rapidly, rising to over 50 million Internet users in North America in 1997. These new communication technologies can link individuals who are (1) physically distant (they may live on opposite sides of the world) and (2) socially distant (they may be highly unalike). Perhaps they would never otherwise communicate on a face-to-face basis.

One illustration of the ability of electronic communication to overcome social distance is provided by PEN (Public Electronic Network), an e-mail system that is free to all residents of Santa Monica, California. When it became available in 1989, PEN was the first such system of its kind to be provided by a city government. Individuals could access PEN from their home or office computer via modem or from one of the 20 public terminals located in the public libraries, city hall, and recreation centers.

Santa Monica has a "homed" population of about 90,000 people, plus a homeless population estimated at from 2,000 to 10,000. The pleasant climate of Santa Monica and its ample public beaches, combined with city government policies that prohibit the police from hassling the homeless, make the city a center for street people. While the homeless and the homed walked past each other in the city every day, they seldom talked in any meaningful way. Certainly they did not discuss the topic of homelessness, although this issue was the main social problem facing the city.

When PEN began, homed individuals entered many e-mail messages about the homeless, stating that they were too lazy to work and that they were dirty and smelled bad. The director of a child care center in Santa Monica complained that a homeless man had defecated on the front step of her building. Within a few weeks, homeless people began to enter their messages on PEN, expressing their viewpoints. They insisted that they were not lazy, but that when they applied for a job, they seldom got past the receptionist. Both the homed and the homeless gained new understandings from this electronic exchange. The two parties talked with each other on PEN, but not in person. Why? It was impossible to know whether or not someone was homeless or homed on the basis of their messages on PEN. The lack of nonverbal cues (such as smell or appearance) in electronic communication provided anonymity. As one homeless man remarked: "No one on PEN knew that I was homeless until I told them. PEN is also special because after I told them, I was still treated like a human being" (Schmitz & others, 1995). During the first four years of the PEN system, 12,000 messages about homelessness were entered by people in Santa Monica, far more than on any other topic.

Six months after PEN began, an individual asked, "What if these people had a place to shower, a place to store their things, and a place to wash their clothes?" The idea transformed PEN into a catalyst for community action. Soon, a dozen interested people began to meet as the PEN Action Group.[6] They implemented SHWASHLOCK, a shower facility, laundry room, and storage lockers for the homeless. Then a homeless man suggested a job bank on the PEN system, which listed positions for which the homeless could apply. Soon thereafter, a computer training room was added to the SHWASHLOCK facility, so that homeless people could gain word-processing and other computer skills. Eventually, hundreds of homeless people were able to secure jobs.

How did the PEN system facilitate intercultural communication between the homed and the homeless in Santa Monica? It provided a new communication channel, one that could overcome the social distance between strangers (Rogers & Allbritton, 1997). Many homed people in Santa Monica were surprised to learn that some home-less people in their community had masters degrees and that others had been computer programmers or aerospace engineers. Once a dialogue began, stereotypes were overcome on both sides, and prejudices began to disappear. The PEN system helped both the homed and the homeless overcome their initial uncertainty as strangers. Both cultures communicated with one another and eventually worked together to solve a social problem.

The Continuum of Intercultural Differences

Think of a continuum of all possible combinations of human communication ranging from a minimum degree of cultural difference at one end to a maximum degree of cultural difference on the other. Communication between two individuals who are identical twins could represent the minimum difference end of the continuum; no intercultural communication would be involved. Near the maximum difference end of the continuum might be communication between two people from very unalike cultures, say someone from the United States and someone from Senegal. These citizens do not share a common language (Figure 3-5), and there are numerous other differences. In contrast, United States/British interaction is quite homophilous, although there are some verbal expressions that can lead to misunderstanding. For example, when a young British woman invites you to "Knock me up at my flat," she is inviting you to telephone her at her apartment. Obviously, even United States/British interaction in English is not completely homophilous. In comparison, communication between a homed and a homeless individual is relatively more heterophilous because of the socioeconomic difference between the two individuals.

As the degree of intercultural difference between any two or more people becomes wider, communication is less likely to occur. We talk most often with others who are similar to us and who think as we do. We tend to avoid contact with people who are extremely different from us. Such inter-

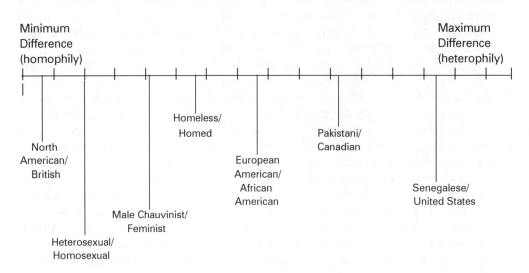

Figure 3-5.   This continuum of intercultural communication differences displays representative types of human communication that differ in the degree to which the participants are homophilous or heterophilous. For example, the individuals in the United States/British dyad are closely similar but not identical in language and culture (they are relatively homophilous). The Senegal/United States pair of individuals are extremely different (heterophilous) culturally.

cultural communication takes more effort on our part and is less rewarding than is homophilous communication. We are constantly discouraged from talking with others who are culturally very unlike us, even though there may be much interesting and useful information that we could learn from such intercultural communication.

   As the degree of intercultural difference becomes wider in human communication situations, information exchange is likely to be less effective. Meanings are less likely to be shared as the result of communication exchange. The message intended by the source participant has less probability of being interpreted predictably by the receiver if the two are culturally unalike. The basis for understanding one another narrows as cultural differences increase. As the pool of shared meanings shrinks, communication is less likely to be effective. For example, marriage advertisements in India might describe a prospective bride as "homely," meaning she is expert in domestic matters, a good cook, and a charming hostess. To someone from the United States, the word "homely" describes an unattractive person (we call homely a *false cognate*, a word that is the same in two cultures but means something quite different).

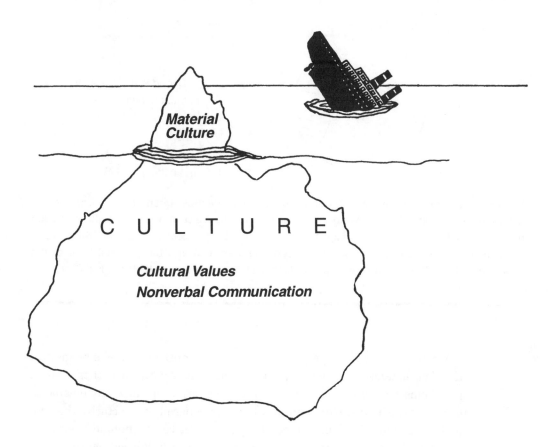

Figure 3-6. Certain aspects of a culture, like its material artifacts and verbal communication, are more obvious than others. Nonverbal communication and values, for example, often lie beneath the surface and present hidden barriers to intercultural understandings.

Overcoming Cultural Differences

When each participant in a communication exchange represents a different culture, the likelihood of effective communication is lessened. The fundamental obstacle facing intercultural communication is the cultural heterophily of the individuals involved. Figure 3-7 shows that when the message content does not intersect in the space where the two individuals' cones of meaning overlap, the attempt at communication will be ineffective.

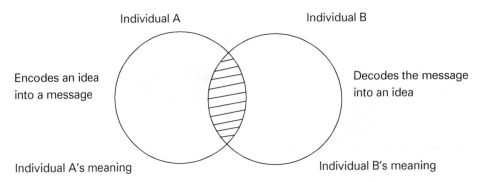

Figure 3-7. Communication is more likely to be ineffective when the participants are heterophilous. When Individual A and Individual B do not share a common culture, the perceived meanings that they attach to a message are likely to differ. So the meaning intended by Individual A when he/she encoded the message (by converting an idea into the physical form of the message) will be different than the meaning decoded from the message by Individual B.

Communication between unalike individuals does not have to be ineffective. For instance, if the participants can empathize with each other (that is, put themselves in the shoes of the other person), then they may be able to overcome the ineffective communication that generally characterizes heterophilous communication. Further, the individuals can be nonjudgmental of unalike others and can try to learn about people with different cultures.

There are a number of values shared by all cultures. Occasionally, a media person or character from one culture becomes popular in other cultures. An example of cultural shareability is a Japanese television soap opera, *Oshin*, the life story of a young girl. Her parents sell her at age seven for a bag of rice. Later she becomes rich and famous, but only after a life of sacrifice. *Oshin* has been broadcast in 47 countries, ranging from Burma to Iran to Ghana to Australia (Singhal & Udornpim, 1997). Wherever it is broadcast, *Oshin* attracts high audience ratings: 89 percent in China, 70 percent in Poland, and 81 percent in Thailand. Why is Oshin so attractive to culturally varied audiences? The character of Oshin is greatly admired for her generosity, altruism, and self-sacrifice. Older people say that Oshin represents the old-fashioned values of hard work and perseverance in the face of adversity.

Case Illustration:
The Cultural Shareability of Elvis Presley

Most communication messages, as explained previously, have different effects in different cultures (remember the miners and the safety poster in Figure 3-1)? However, certain communication messages have a similar meaning across a wide variety of cultures. These culturally shareable messages have a fundamental appeal that is able to bridge the specific values of different cultures.

One example is Elvis Presley, the rock and roll singer who died in 1977 and has since been the object of an unprecedented wave of affection and impersonation. His mansion, Graceland, is the second most-visited site in the United States (the White House is first), with over half a million tourists per year. Elvis mixed Black and White music, creating a new genre, and became tremendously popular while he lived. Since his drug-related death at an early age, he has attracted the largest outpouring of devotion that any entertainer has ever inspired. There are 500 fan clubs worldwide. Adoration for Elvis seems to cut across national boundaries as well as different ethnic groups.

Some 50,000 Elvis impersonators around the world include a Black Elvis, a Japanese Elvis, and a lesbian Elvis who calls herself "Elvis Herselvis" (Bragg, 1997). One Elvis impersonator is El Vez (whose real name is Robert Lopez); he sings variations of Elvis Presley's music. "In the Ghetto" becomes "In the Barrio." El Vez has an album entitled "Graciasland." Elvis sang, "It's now or never/come hold me tight/kiss me my darling/be mine tonight/Tomorrow will be too late/it's now or never/my love won't wait." El Vez sings: "It's now or never/please no more gangs/people are dying/don't you understand/Mañana will be too late/it's now or never/let's stop the hate."

What motivates an Elvis impersonator? Some impersonators wear chrome-rimmed dark glasses and jeweled jumpsuits and earn a living by performing at nightclubs, parties, and other events (Figure 3-8). Dennis Wise, a 41-year-old man from Joplin, Missouri, listened to Elvis Presley music daily from the age of five. When he started impersonating Elvis professionally, a promoter suggested that he have plastic surgery so that he would look more like Elvis, and Wise has since had several operations. He states, "When those people are butting, screaming and hollering, that's probably the best reward that money can buy" (Fraser & Brown, 1997). "You can portray the greatest entertainer in the world and, uh, get a little feeling of what it's like to be that man on a very small scale." To a certain extent, Wise has become Elvis.

The Elvis phenomenon provides a common experience that binds unalike people together. Elvis grew up poor, was somewhat of a rebel, and became extremely rich through his musical career. Perhaps part of his wide appeal is his Cinderella story. Perhaps one means to overcome ethnocentrism and prejudice is via the almost universal appeal of something (or someone) culturally shareable, like the late Elvis Presley.

Figure 3-8.   These people are among 50,000 Elvis impersonators worldwide; they are part of a culturally shareable phenomenon that cuts across cultural and ethnic boundaries.

Source: Photograph by Mitzi L. Gates. Used by permission.

Summary

Culture is the total way of life of a people, composed of their learned and shared behavior patterns, values, norms, and material objects. Culture is created by humans. *Beliefs* are an individual's representations of the outside world. *Values* are what the people who share a culture regard strongly as good or bad. *Norms* are the established behavior patterns for members of a social system.

A *collectivistic culture* is one in which the collectivity's goals are valued over those of the individual. An *individualistic culture* is one in which the individual's goals are valued over those of the collectivity. There is considerable variation among individuals within a collectivistic culture (with some individuals very independent) and within an individualistic culture (where some individuals are very interdependent).

Another classification of cultures is on the basis of whether they are high-context or low-context. A *high-context culture* is one in which the meanings of a communication message are found in the situation and in the relationships of the communicators, where meanings are internalized in the beliefs, values, and norms of the culture. A *low-context culture* is one in which the meanings of a communication message are stated clearly and explicitly. The United States is a low-context and individualistic culture, while Japanese culture is high-context and collectivistic.

Cultural clash is the conflict that occurs between two or more cultures when they disagree about a certain value. *Cultural identification* is the degree to which individuals consider themselves to be representatives of a particular culture. Such identification is a mix of self-perception and perception by others. Cultural markers such as names and language reinforce an individual's cultural identity.

Intercultural communication is the exchange of information between individuals who are unalike culturally. Such dissimilarity may be on the basis of national culture, gender, ethnicity, religion, age, or other factors. The difference in cultures of the individuals who interact is the unique aspect of intercultural communication. One can imagine a continuum of intercultural differences, with some pairs of communication participants very different and others quite similar. When intercultural differences are wider, communication (1) is less likely to occur and (2) is less effective.

Notes

[1] We use the concept of intercultural communication as essentially similar to cross-cultural communication, a term preferred by some scholars, especially psychologists.

[2] Edward Hall has also suggested another typology of cultures on the basis of whether they are "monochronic" versus "polychronic," that is, whether individuals carry out only one activity versus several activities at the same time.

[3] This study is reported in Dearing & others (1995) and by Rogers & others (1995).

4 Eventually, Williams became a law professor. He wrote his memoirs in 1995 when he was dean of The Ohio State University Law School.

5 This case illustration is based on Schmitz & others (1995).

6 Note that at a certain point in their dialogue the homed and homeless found it necessary to meet on a face-to-face basis. A similar process occurred for PENFEMME, a feminist group that began on the PEN system but then met on a face-to-face basis to remedy male sexual aggression against women on the PEN system (Collins-Jarvis, 1993; Rogers & others, 1994).

Chapter 4

Communication

> **"** Meanings are in people.
>
> David K. Berlo (1960) **"**

Intercultural communication is a particular kind of human communication. In previous chapters we traced the evolution of attention to particular aspects of interaction between unalike individuals. As seen in Chapter 1, cultural contact with no attempt to communicate with mutual respect brought disastrous results. Because intercultural communication is often marked with highly noticeable variance from the cultural norms to which each participant is accustomed, there is often a tendency to lose sight of the fact that the models and concepts of communication are the same for intercultural communication as they are for other types of communication exchange.

What Is Communication?

Communication is the process through which participants create and share information with one another as they move toward reaching mutual understanding. Communication is involved in every aspect of daily life, from birth to death. It is universal. Because communication is so pervasive, it is easy to take it for granted and even not to notice it.

One way to understand the crucial role of communication in all human activities is to consider individuals who have had little or no human communication. *Isolates* are children who for some reason have grown up without talking to anyone. While physically human, such isolates cannot talk or read and are completely lacking in social relationship skills. Some isolates were kept in an attic or a basement and fed regularly but not allowed contact with humans. When such isolates have been freed from their isolation, often when they are adolescents, they are socially much like infants. One example of a semi-isolate is the character "Nell" (played by Jodi Foster in the movie by the same name), who grew up in a remote cabin in the woods. Communication with others is essential to the process of personality development and socialization.

Feral children are humans who have been raised by animals. A number of accounts of feral children are available. While some may be of doubtful authenticity, several cases provide fascinating insights into what it is like to grow up without human interaction. Victor, the wild boy of Aveyron in France, is a documented case of a feral child (Rosenberg, 1979; Langer, 1957, p. 157). Feral children illustrate the essentially social nature of being human. While Helen Keller was neither an isolate nor a feral child, she was unable to participate in the process of creating and sharing information until the breakthrough moment when she associated the symbol "water" with the experience of water gushing over her hand. If one cannot communicate, one will not assimilate the qualities associated with being human.

A Model of Communication

What are the main elements in the communication process through which participants create and share information with one another in order to reach a mutual understanding (Figure 4-1)? Human communication is never perfectly effective. The receiver usually does not decode a message into exactly the same meaning that the source had in mind when encoding the message. A *code* is a classification such as a language used by individuals to categorize their experience and to communicate it to others. *Decoding* is the process by which the physical message is converted into an idea by the receiver. *Encoding* is the process by which an idea is converted into a message by a source.

Noise can interfere with the transmission of a message. *Noise* is anything that hinders the communication process among participants. Perhaps the symbol that was communicated was interpreted differently by the receiver than by the source. For instance, while the swastika has a positive meaning in India and among many Native American tribes, the swastika is abhorrent to someone whose ancestors were killed in the Holocaust. The arms of the Nazi swastika, however, point in the opposite direction (clockwise) than do the arms on the Buddhist swastika in India. When the source and the receiver do not share a common value regarding the message content (as in the case illustrations in Chapter 3 of the live animal market and clitorectomy), effective communication is unlikely to occur, leading to conflict. The more dissim-

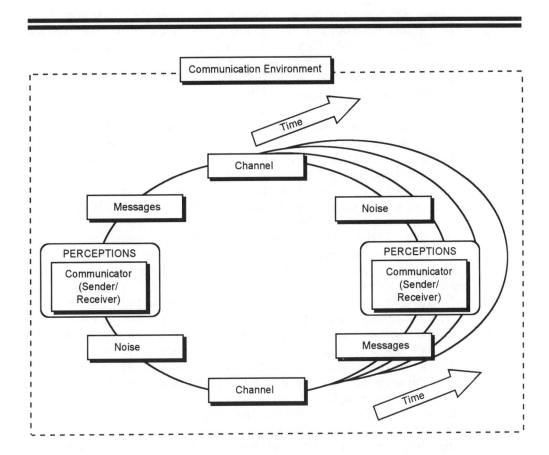

Figure 4-1.   This model illustrates the communication process between two participants who create and share information with one another in order to reach a mutual understanding. Each exchange between the participants is a communication act that may occur at a certain point in time. This act often builds upon previous communication exchanges and is followed by others in the future, thus creating a communication process over time.

Source: Based on Rogers & others (1998, p. 15).

ilar (heterophilous) the source and receiver, the more likely that their communication will be ineffective.

A *source* is the individual who originates a message by encoding an idea into a message. A *receiver* is the individual who decodes a communication message by converting it into an idea. A *channel* is the means by which a message is transmitted from its origin to its destination. *Feedback* is a message about the effects of a previous message that is sent back to the source.

Most communication research seeks to understand the effects of communication on individuals who are exposed to certain messages. *Effects* are the changes in an individual's knowledge, attitudes, and overt behavior due to exposure to a communication message. Communication scholars look at source variables, message variables, channel variables, and receiver variables in order to explain communication effects. Most of us, when we communicate, try to bring about effects in other people.

Many concepts in communication study today reflect the origins of the field in electrical engineering (receiver, noise, and feedback) and in cryptography (for example, code). A key figure in formulating the communication model was Claude E. Shannon, who earned his doctorate in electrical engineering and mathematics at MIT. Shannon worked out the basic model for communication while conducting cryptographic research at Bell Labs during World War II (Rogers, 1994). When the field of human communication study began in U.S. universities in the 1950s and 1960s, this communication model was adapted from its engineering/cryptography origins (where the interest was in understanding telephone and radio communication and the coding of secret messages) to the process of human-to-human communication. One of the major changes that human communication scholars made in the Shannon model was to emphasize the subjectivity of communication. When the source and receiver are individuals instead of machines, their perceptions, paradigms, and past experiences flavor the encoding and decoding process. This subjectivity is one reason why the receiver seldom decodes a message into exactly the same meaning that the source had in mind when encoding the message.

Further, instead of differentiating between a "source" and a "receiver" (as in the case of radio communication), the participants in most human communication exchange roles as message originators and message receivers on a second-by-second basis. Communication is an over-time, mutual process, rather than a one-way message flow. The individuals who are communicating exert mutual control over the interaction, rather than serving as an active source and a passive receiver. Most communication scholars today speak of "participants" in the communication process, rather than "sources" and "receivers."

The World War II origins of communication study (including its beginnings in cryptography) live on today in many of the concepts and perspectives that have become part of the language of communication. The larger context of communication study, of course, flavors the concepts, theories, and perspectives utilized in the field of intercultural communication.

Case Illustration:
Navajo Code-Talkers

The basic strategy used to create a secret code is to add a large amount of noise to a message when it is encoded. The intended receiver knows to discard the noise so the message can be decoded correctly. Enemies, who do not understand how to separate the noise from the rest of the message (the code) are left in the dark. Most secret codes can be cracked by cryptographers using computers to try millions of possible combinations until they find how to decode the secret message. For example, early in World War II the Allies broke the German military code that was created by the Enigma coding machine. Thereafter, the Allies had advance knowledge of every move that would be made by German planes, panzers, and submarines. The broken German code gave the Allies a decisive advantage in the Battle of Britain, the Battle of El Alemain, and other key engagements.

In the Pacific theater during World War II, the United States had broken the Japanese code well before the start of hostilities, but the Japanese were unable to break the U.S. code despite massive efforts to do so. The code used by the United States Marines during World War II represents one of the few unbreakable codes in human history. Why? Because the U.S. military transmitted their commands in Diné, the language of the Navajo. The Navajo code-talkers during World War II represent a spectacular example of how cultural factors contributed to the Allies' military victory. The story of the Navajo code-talkers has seldom been told, and in fact it was an official secret of the U.S. government for several decades after World War II.

Philip Johnston, the son of missionaries, had grown up on the Navajo Reservation. Johnston was one of only 30 non-Navajos who was fluent in Diné at the time of World War II (Aaseng, 1992). The language was unwritten at that time, and the Navajo discouraged belagaana *(non-Navajo) from learning their tongue. When World War II began, Johnston championed the idea of Navajo code-talkers to the U.S. Marine Corps at Camp Pendleton, near San Diego. Although the military brass were initially very dubious, Johnston arranged a demonstration for high-ranking officers. A Navajo Marine was asked to transmit a military command by field telephone to another Navajo about a mile away. The command that emerged at the end of this English/Diné/English process was identical with the original message. The Marine officers were convinced, and hundreds of young Navajos were recruited off the Reservation by the Marine Corps. Many joined the Marines directly out of boarding schools, where they had been forbidden to speak Diné by the Bureau of Indian Affairs, the U.S. government agency operating the schools. There were no birth records on the reservation, so many of the patriotic volunteers were underage (only 15 or 16 years old) when they joined the Marine Corps.*

The Navajo code-talkers, after completing basic military training at Camp Pendleton, were enrolled in a code-talkers' school for an additional month (Sergeant Philip Johnston was placed in charge of this code-talkers' school). The code-talkers learned how to encode military words in Diné. For example, "bomb" became the Diné word for "egg" (ayeshi), as there was no Diné word for bomb. "Submarine" became besh-lo (iron fish), and "dive bomber" was coded as gini (chicken hawk). Some 500 code-words had to be memorized. The Navajo trainees were not allowed to take notes. Fortunately, the Navajo Marines found it easy to remember the code, as the memorization of elaborate songs, prayers, and religious ceremonies is part of Navajo culture.

The Navajo code-talkers were certain that the Japanese could not decode their military transmissions. Navajo sounds are very difficult for belagaana to understand. Vowels rise and fall, changing meaning with pitch. But in order to ensure the security of their code, the Navajo code-talkers spelled out non-Navajo place names in Diné. For example, the Marines' phonetic alphabet (Able-Baker-Charlie) became Wollachee-Shush-Moasi (Ant-Bear-Cat). Then, to further complicate the task of Japanese code-breakers, the Navajo played humorous word games. "District" became "deer-ice-strict," and "belong" became "long-bee." "Bull dozer" became "bull sleep" in Diné and "dispatch" was translated as "dog is patch" (Bixler, 1992, p. 53). Finally, in order to prevent the Japanese from breaking their code through letter frequency or word frequency, a usual technique in code-breaking ("e" is the most frequently used letter in English, occurring in 60 percent of all words, while "z" occurs in only 0.3 percent of all words), the code-talkers used several Diné words for each English vowel (Paul, 1973). For example, the English letter "a" could be translated as the Diné word for "ant" (wollachee) or "apple" (belasana) or "axe" (tsenill). The letter "e" could be translated as "ear" (ahjah), as "elk" (dzeh), or "eye" (ahnah). Of the 3,600 Navajos who served in World War II, 420 became code-talkers (Kawano, 1990). The code was so complex that even a Navajo who knew Diné but who had not been instructed in the code could not break it. Essentially, the Navajo code-talkers utilized a double-code (1) by transmitting in Diné and (2) by the 500 code-words.

In 1942 with their training completed, the Navajo code-talkers were ready for action. The first Navajo code-talkers shipped out to South Pacific battlefields. Initially, U.S. military officers were skeptical, but they became convinced during the battle for Saipan, where U.S. troops on the beach were being shelled by friendly fire from their own artillery. Radio messages to "hold your fire" were disregarded by the U.S. artillery officers because the Japanese had been imitating Marine messages transmitted in English. The shelling continued. Headquarters then asked Navajo code-talkers to transmit the order to cease fire. The friendly fire stopped immediately (Watson, 1993).

A Navajo transmitted the following order to all Marine units who had just landed on the beaches of Saipan: "Tses-nah tlo-chin tsah ha-ih-des-ee ma-e ne-ahs-jah gah ne-tah al-tah-je-jay. Le-eh-gade do who-neh bihl-has-ahn" (Be on the alert for banzai attacks. Dig in and report positions). That night, when the Japanese banzais came, the Marines were ready and threw them back (McClain, 1994, p. 132). Through such effective and secure communication transmission, the Navajo code-talkers proved their worth in the battle of Saipan. Thereafter, each code-talker was assigned an armed Marine as a personal bodyguard.

Figure 4-2.   The president of the Navajo Code-Talkers' Association, Sam Billison, presents a book about the code-talkers to U.S. Senator McCain in 1997. This ceremony took place at the Navajo Nation Veterans Memorial Park in Window Rock, where the headquarters of the Navajo Nation is located.

Source: This photograph was taken by Paul Natonabah of the *Navajo Times* in which it appeared on August 28, 1997. Used by permission.

Navajo code-talkers stormed ashore in every Marine assault in the Pacific War from 1942 to 1945: Tarawa, Guadacanal, Iwo Jima, Guam, Bouganville, Peliu, Rabaul, Okinawa. Typically, the code-talkers worked in pairs, with one Navajo on board a Navy ship and his partner going ashore with an advance landing party. Eleven code-talkers were killed in action. A special hazard facing the code-talkers was that they could be mistaken for Japanese by some U.S. military personnel, and indeed a number were "captured" by U.S. soldiers.

Despite transmitting thousands of commands during the Pacific War, the Navajo code-talkers never made an important error. They were fast, consistently able to beat the U.S. Navy's mechanical coding machines. The Navajo code-talkers were an important secret weapon for the United States, contributing directly to the eventual victory. After 1945, when the Navajo code-talkers were discharged to return to their reservation, they were required to take an oath of secrecy about their role in the Pacific. The role played by the Navajo code-talkers was classified top-secret. Only after 1968 did the Pentagon acknowledge the existence of the code-talkers.

The Navajo have a well-developed sense of humor, and the code-talkers today enjoy telling their war stories. One of the authors invited a World War II code-talker, Bill Toledo, to describe his experiences to a doctoral seminar at the University of New Mexico. Toledo told of a B-29 bomber flying over Iwo Jima that picked up Navajo code-talk on the military radio band. The pilot inquired on the plane's intercom, "What is that language?" A Navajo crew member on the bomber (not trained as a code-talker), hearing the code for "bomb" ("egg" in Diné) and for "pig" (bisodih for the letter "p," used in spelling out a word with a p in it), said, "Captain, those are my people down there! I think they are preparing ham and eggs."

Initial Contact and Uncertainty among Strangers

Think back to the last time that you encountered a complete stranger whom you perceived as quite unlike yourself. Beginning a conversation with an unknown person is like navigating uncharted territory. One must have at least a certain degree of information about another person in order to know what question would be appropriate to ask initially. For example, imagine that a complete stranger sits down beside you. The individual is a well-dressed young man but has very long hair and wears a goatee. He stows an athletic bag under his seat and then begins reading a book on Confucian philosophy. He is dark-skinned, with Asian facial features. You are somewhat intrigued and would like to start a conversation, but you do not know where to begin.

Uncertainty and Information

An interpersonal communication process must have a starting place, and getting a conversation underway with a complete stranger is particularly difficult. Charles Berger and Richard Calabrese (1975) set forth a theory of uncertainty reduction that takes place in initial communication between strangers. When two individuals encounter one another for the first time, they face a high degree of uncertainty due to their lack of information about each other. This uncertainty is especially high when the two individuals do not share a common culture. If they at least share a common language and have certain common interests, they can begin talking. Their discourse then allows them to share meanings and to decrease their uncertainty gradually as they get better acquainted. We do not build an intimate interrelationship suddenly. The process typically proceeds through a series of stages over time.

Uncertainty is an individual's inability to predict or to understand some situation due to a lack of information about alternatives. The antidote for uncertainty is *information*, defined as a difference in matter-energy that affects uncertainty in a situation where a choice exists among a set of alternatives. Perhaps information is expressed as ink on paper or as a sound wave or as an electrical current passing through a copper wire. In each case, a difference in matter-energy is involved. This difference might be variations in sound or variations in ink marks on paper.

As an individual gains information about another person, uncertainty is reduced, and the situation becomes more predictable. Uncertainty is unpleasant, and individuals generally seek to reduce it (of course the complete lack of any uncertainty in a relationship can be boring). In order to communicate with another person in a smooth and understandable process, one must be able to predict how the other person will behave, what the individual will say next, and how the person will react to one's remarks.

Different cultures have developed various ways to reduce uncertainty. For example, when two Japanese meet each other for the first time, they bow and exchange *meishi* (name cards). There is a strict protocol for this exchange: The meishi should be presented with both hands, right side up, and with the type facing the other person (Figure 4-3). The name card should not be soiled or wrinkled. Initially contacting a stranger is a stressful time for a Japanese person, as he/she must decide whether the other person outranks him/her. This rapid mental calculation considers the individual's age, education, job title, and other factors (some of which are described on the *meishi*). Once their status is decided, the two people understand how to treat each other, who should defer to whom, and so forth. But what if one of the individuals makes a mistake in this ranking calculation and treats the other like a superior when he/she really is not? This error would be very embarrassing and would result in a loss of face.

To illustrate how this individual ranking system works in North Asian cultures, one of the authors was invited to visit a health research institute in Seoul. The director and the author-guest sat at the end of a long table. One by one, various researchers joined the meeting. As people entered the room, an appropriate spot was made for them to sit at the table, with the highest-

ranked individual sitting closest to the director. Employees obviously knew exactly where they stood relative to all other employees. Because of the conventions of their cultures, an initial meeting between strangers in Korea and Japan may entail even more uncertainty than does a similar situation in the United States.

Initiating Conversation with a Stranger

How does one obtain information in order to start a conversation with a complete stranger? In some cases, a mutual acquaintance may provide certain information about the stranger. An example is an introduction to a stranger at a party; the host says, "I want you to meet Holly Smith, who is studying

Figure 4-3.   In these photographs the exchange of business cards (*meishi*) between a U.S. professor and a Japanese scholar takes place. The correct etiquette for exchanging business cards calls for extending the *meishi* in both hands, while bowing. Then the *meishi* should be studied carefully in order to decide the correct level of formality for conversing with the other person.

Source: Photograph by Kathyrn Sorrells. Used by permission.

communication" (the host knows that you are also studying communication). This strategy of obtaining information via personal networks is not feasible, of course, in a chance encounter with a stranger, such as on an airplane. In that situation, one often looks for nonverbal clues to start a conversation. For instance, in the case of the stranger described earlier, you might inquire, "Are you involved in sports?" or "Pardon me, but I notice the book you are reading. Are you interested in Eastern philosophies?"

Once a conversation gets underway between strangers, the degree of uncertainty is reduced, so that further communication is facilitated. Notice that a conversation between strangers in the United States usually begins with many questions being asked, questions that typically demand relatively short answers (such as questions dealing with one's occupation, hometown, etc.). As two people gradually get acquainted, the number of questions decreases, the number of statements increases, and they become longer. Uncertainty is being reduced.

The communication situation also affects the degree of uncertainty between two strangers. Consider the example of two strangers sitting next to each other at a rally for a political candidate. Here it would be natural to begin talking about the candidate. Suppose that you learn that your conversation partner has a strong dislike for the candidate, while you are a fan. In order to maintain a smooth conversation, you might switch to another topic to avoid a likely conflict (Berger & Calabrese, 1975).

The degree of uncertainty between two strangers is greatest, of course, when they come from different cultural backgrounds. You do not even know if you share a common language with the other person. What if the other person does not speak English? In what language should you begin the conversation? When meeting a business counterpart from another culture, should you kiss, bow, or shake hands? Do you offer your business card in both hands, as is customary in Japan? Do you say, "Hello, my name is Everett Rogers?" or "Hi, my name is Ev?" These uncertainties are all inhibitors to beginning a conversation with a cultural stranger.

Case Illustration:
Don't You Want to Go to the Rat?

Rika Kumata, a Japanese student, walked into the office of one of the authors at the University of Miami. She sat down on the sofa. The professor said:

"Hi Rika. Do you have your advising folder?"

"Oh, Dr. Steinfatt, this is not about advising. Should I come back another time?"

"No, this is fine Rika. How can I help you?"

"Dr. Steinfatt, I don't know how to explain what happened last night, and I thought you might be able to help me. Drew, an American boy, lives down the hall from me in the dorm. He and a friend knocked on my door and said 'Hi Rika, we're going over to the Rat. Don't you want to go with us?'"

She paused. "Well, I did not want to go with them because I was studying, but I did not want to be impolite. So I smiled, nodded, and said 'No' and went into the other room to get my keys. But then I heard Drew say 'Oh, okay, maybe some other time,' and when I came back, the door was closed and he had gone! I don't understand, Dr. Steinfatt. I agreed to go with them, but they left without me."

"Rika, here's what I think happened. It sounds to me as though you were being polite by agreeing to go even though you didn't want to. Drew did not understand that he should talk with you for a while to determine from your feelings what you really wanted to do, before asking you the question directly. And he phrased the question negatively. Had he said 'Do you want to go?' you would have said 'Yes' out of politeness.

He would have waited for you and you would have gone to the Rat. But he phrased his question negatively. He said 'Don't you want to go?' not 'Do you want to go?'"

"In English, both of those questions mean the same thing. He just wanted to know if you wanted to go to the Rat. When you listened to his question, you were thinking about the logic of the sentence itself, because that is what you do in Japanese and in most Asian languages. You were thinking that your 'No' would make his negative question of 'Don't you want to go?' into an affirmative by canceling his negative, thereby saying that you did want to go. But he took your 'No' socially rather than logically, because in this culture people do not pay attention to the logic of negative sentences, only to their social meaning."

Rika still looked confused. All of the problems that occur in communication between persons of the same culture are even more difficult when cultural, attitudinal, and language differences are involved. The professor urged Rika to talk with Drew about what had happened. She was surprised when it was suggested that she might have unintentionally hurt his feelings by answering "No" and leaving the room.

Intrapersonal and Interpersonal Communication

"Language is primarily a vocal actualization of the tendency to see reality symbolically" (Edward Sapir, 1921). ***Communication is fundamentally intrapersonal.*** *Intrapersonal communication* is information exchange that occurs inside of one person. It is the process of selecting and interpreting symbols to represent thoughts, perceptions, or physical reality. In contrast, *interpersonal communication* involves the face-to-face exchange of information between two or more people. Interpersonal communication is the process of exchanging mutually understood symbols. You communicate with yourself (intrapersonal) as well as with others (interpersonal). Both were involved in Rika and Drew's misunderstanding.

The place to begin understanding communication is in the way that people process messages internally. Language allows humans to perceive reality symbolically. Words and their meanings allow people to be human beings. Humans use symbols as mental events to represent physical reality, as well as their hopes and dreams. If a person did not engage in thinking processes, that person could not learn to communicate using symbols.

Intercultural communication also begins with intrapersonal communication and ways of thinking. Levels of meaning (discussed below) suggests that meaning *is assigned to* messages during the decoding process, rather than *residing in* messages to be discovered. Based on our experiences, we develop attitudes, beliefs, and values that then influence the meanings we assign. Our culture accounts for a very large portion of what we experience and how we interpret the experience. Culture is critical in the meaning assignment process, which is fundamental to human communication.

Intercultural communication depends on an understanding of the belief system of the other person. Cultural belief systems serve as message filters that determine, to a certain degree, the meaning each person assigns to messages and how events are perceived. The notion of cultural-ways-of-thinking is used here in a broad sense to include religions, countries, cultures, belief systems, and behaviorally and demographically defined groups (e.g. Asian, New York, European, rural, homosexual, Buddhist, elderly, poor, etc.). This is not to imply that there is, for example, an "elderly way of thinking." Rather, it is to suggest that the concerns and concepts of specific groups and cultures act as important filters when members of cultural groups receive messages and observe behaviors. Understanding different cultural ways of thinking allows us to understand and predict, to an extent, the ways in which individuals from a given culture will respond to specific intercultural interactions.

To understand communication and how it works, we need to understand what happens within people's internal thinking processes. Rika and Drew exchanged messages and each cognitively processed them. How Drew and Rika interpreted each other's messages explains their misunderstanding.

Signs and Symbols

Communication involves signs and symbols. Rika and Drew were using both signs and symbols to communicate. Rika turned and went into another room. This action was a nonverbal sign of increasing physical distance from Drew. A sign is a physical event or action that directly represents something else. The words that Rika and Drew exchanged are symbols, something that represents something else through prior agreement. For example, Rika and Drew used the word "Rat" to refer to a student drinking place, the Rathskeller.

Prior agreement about the meaning of symbols is necessary for a language code to function. The sounds and words of a language are arbitrary and have no permanent, fixed meaning. Through prior agreement we connect the sounds to specific meanings. Agreements evolve; we sometimes change meanings. In the 1920s, for example, "dish" meant an attractive female, as well as a container for food. A few decades later the gender connotation disappeared from North American English. In the 1970s, "dish" came to mean a satellite receiver.

Language

Language is a key influence in intercultural communication. *Language* is the use of vocalized sounds, or written symbols representing these sounds or ideas, in patterns organized by grammatical rules in order to express thoughts and feelings. The people of a particular nation or ethnic group who share a language usually share a common history and a set of traditions. Speaking a particular language gives an individual a cultural identification. If the language of a cultural group disappears, the members of the cultural group find it difficult or impossible to maintain their culture, and they will be assimilated into another language/culture. An example is the Irish people, who lost their language (Celtic), and have become assimilated, at least in part, into English culture. As we have discussed, many immigrants to the United States in past decades have been assimilated into the melting pot of U.S. society.

People tend to assume that another language follows the same grammatical rules as their native language. Most Asian languages do not use articles such as "the," "a," and "an" or sounds like "r," so Rika tends to ignore their existence in English. She also must concentrate to pronounce words like "Rat," which comes out sounding like "Lat." People learning a new language tend to concentrate on what words mean and pay less attention to grammar and the meaning of sentences. Many individuals feel that they have approached fluency in a language when they begin to dream in the new language.

There is a close relationship between a language and the culture of the people who speak that language. The Whorf-Sapir notion of linguistic relativity suggests that our thinking is influenced both by language and by the culture that language carries. Can we think about something for which we do not have a word in our language? Does language influence thought? We discuss linguistic relativity more fully in the next chapter.

Case Illustration:
The Rosetta Stone

The important role of language in shaping history is illustrated by the Rosetta Stone, which unlocked the secrets of Egyptian civilization. As a result, much detail is known about the ancient Egyptians and their culture. Their role as the cradle of civilization is much better understood than other early civilizations such as the Indus Valley (whose writing has never been deciphered). The ancient Greeks and Romans knew that an even more ancient civilization had existed in Egypt. They imagined that a complex society must have been necessary to build the pyramids. But they could not understand Egyptian hieroglyphics, a pictorial language that adorned the stone remains of temples and other buildings that had been preserved in the arid climate.

Then, the world's historians got a very lucky break. Napoleon invaded Egypt in 1799 with an army of 38,000 soldiers. He was fascinated with Egypt and knew that Alexander the Great had believed that conquering Egypt was key to conquering the world. Napoleon brought 167 of France's leading scholars with his invading force.

In July 1799 while Napoleon's soldiers were building fortifications against a forthcoming British invasion, they uncovered a great stone tablet, 3' 9" by 2' 4", weighing 1,500 pounds. The site was on the banks of the Nile River, in a town called Rosetta. The Rosetta Stone was a piece broken off from a larger tablet. Three types of writing were on the stone: Greek, later Egyptian, and ancient hieroglyphics. The Greek text contained this incredible statement: "This decree shall be inscribed on a stele of hard stone in sacred and native and Greek characters." The Rosetta Stone was a linguistic key to unlocking the previously unknown past of Egyptian civilization (Hale & others, 1858). The French soldiers reported their find, and scholars set to work to decode the hieroglyphic system.

But scholars had little success for several decades. The Rosetta Stone was just a fragment of a larger tablet, sentences were incomplete, and none of the hieroglyphs could be decoded. Finally, in 1818 a British scholar, Thomas Young, identified 86 characters and was able to deduce that an oval around a certain hieroglyph signified the name of the Egyptian king (Ptolomy V). Young concluded that the hieroglyphs were phonetic rather than direct representations of meaning, but could get no further. Then a young French scholar, Jean-Francois Champollion, deciphered the remaining hieroglyphs, publishing his results in 1824 (Honour, 1968). Now the language of the ancient Pharaohs on other stone tablets and on buildings like the pyramids and temples could be read. Humans learned that the early Egyptians wrote letters to others demanding payment of a debt, to tax collectors about their assessments, and about the everyday life in this ancient civilization.

As a result, the world knows much more about Egypt's history. Notice in this case that the hieroglyphics were just carvings in stone until they were decoded. Language allowed us to ascribe meanings to the Egyptian writings, so that we could understand their culture. Today, when you learn a language, it is equivalent to finding a Rosetta Stone. You have the secret to unlocking the meanings of the culture in which your new language is spoken.

Creating Meanings

Meanings are in people. The meanings of a message are interpreted through a process in which the message content is interfaced with an individual's feelings, prior experiences, and cultural values. The late David Berlo, a communication scholar at Michigan State University, stated: "Words don't mean, meanings are in people." He meant that the meaning of a word exists only within the people who use the word, not in some other location such as in the word itself. The written symbols for the word can be expressed with ink on paper, and definitions of words can be compiled in a dictionary, but the meaning is neither in the ink nor in the dictionary. When a human who shares the meaning of that particular written code reads the dictionary definition, that person can construct a meaning for the word in question.

Communication helps people create meaning rather than just transmit meaning. Part of the intercultural mix-up between Rika and Drew concerned the meaning of Drew's question, "Don't you want to go with us?" The negative "don't" caused confusion. Drew meant one thing by the word because his culture and language use negatives in a particular way. Rika interpreted it differently because her culture and language use negatives in a different way. Interpersonal communication is a process in which the meanings of words and messages are negotiated by the parties involved. The prior agreement provided by language is a starting place, but the meanings attributed to the words in an interpersonal conversation are created in part as they are used.

Communication is a process of creating meaning for the messages received from other people. Humans are sense-makers. They decode communication messages in ways that make sense to them, thus forming perceptions that guide their behavior. The essence of intrapersonal communication is the process through which an individual creates meaning for himself/herself out of the information in a message. Much communication is intentional; that is, the source individual is trying to convey a particular meaning to the receiver individual. In this case, clear messages are desired in order to have the intended effect on the receiver. In certain situations, however, ambiguous communication may be appropriate, such as in diplomacy, business negotiation, and on romantic occasions. Recall from Chapter 3 that *ambiguity* is the degree to which a communication message has many possible meanings for its receivers.

When the two or more participants in a communication process come from different cultures, it is less likely that the attempt to convey a meaning will be effective. The importance of "meanings are in people" for intercultural communication is that people construct meanings from their language, attitudes, and their interpersonal and cultural knowledge and experience. An individual's culture shapes the meaning given to a word or other symbol. False cognates again provide an example of this point. In North American English, to be "embarrassed" is to feel mildly uncomfortable, but to Spanish-speakers, to be *embarasado* is to be "pregnant."

Levels of Meaning

The assignment of meaning in a communication process can be analyzed at six levels (Steinfatt, 1988b). Suppose that Sarah is sitting in a lecture hall next to Kyle. She leans over and whispers, "Would you like to get a cup of coffee after class?" What does Sarah mean?

#0. Signal Level of Meaning: Physical Signals

The zero level of meaning is the level of physical signals. We call it the zero level because it is not strictly a level of *meaning* but is a prior condition to meaning. The sounds that Sarah makes when she asks her question are physical signals. They do not tell us much about what Sarah means by her question.

#1. Word Level Meaning: Semantic Meaning

The first level of meaning involves the sounds or written characters which the other person uses to encode a meaning and to sort them into recognizable pieces. Human speech is an almost unbroken string of sound. The human receiver must determine the breaks between meaningful units of sounds such as words in order for a message to be interpreted.

#2. Sentence Level: Syntactic Meaning

The sentence "John hit Mary" contains the same words as the sentence "Mary hit John," but the two sentences do not have the same meaning. Obviously, the order of words influences the meaning of a sentence. This syntactic meaning rests on the grammatical structure of a language. What is the sentence-level meaning of "Do you want to get a cup of coffee after class?" It surely has to do with one person going with another person in order to drink coffee. But is that all that it means? Clearly not. A deeper meaning rests on the interpersonal, social, and cultural meanings of the question.

#3. First Scenario Level: Intent

When someone asks someone else to have coffee with them, it can mean a social get-together to talk. It might mean that one person has a potential romantic interest in the other. It might be repayment of a social debt. It could be for the purpose of obtaining a favor. When Kyle tries to interpret Sarah's question, he seeks to determine her intent in asking the question. He needs information about what is going on inside Sarah's head. He will have to guess on the basis of his past experiences with the world, with other people in general, and with Sarah in particular; based on his perceptions of himself; and based on his cultural expectations and values. He will bring these mental resources to bear on the question of attribution of intent.

#4. Second Scenario Level: Alternative Pictures

Kyle creates alternative scenarios related to Sarah's question. Suppose Kyle decides that Sarah likes him, that this meeting for coffee might be the equivalent of a first date, and that Sarah also may want to borrow his notes because she missed a previous class. When he evaluates Sarah as a date, he happens to have already noticed that she is attractive. But wasn't Sarah dating Sam? Did that mean that Sarah was just asking him to have coffee in order to get his class notes? Kyle's decisions about Sarah's intent allow him to create these alternative scenarios which serve as meanings for Sarah's question.

#5. General Theories Level: Self, Others, and the World

A final level of meaning in a communication message deals with the self, others, and the world. Sarah's message will influence Kyle's self-concept, the way that he sees himself. He may now add a new element, "I am the kind of man who gets asked for a date," and "Sarah has asked me out." Her invitation should give him an ego boost, although perhaps a temporary one. Sarah's invitation may also influence Kyle's perception of the generalized other, his beliefs and attitudes about what other people in general are like.

Kyle's processing of Sarah's invitation also leads him to change his belief system slightly regarding the world. If Kyle did not know it before, he now knows that the world is the kind of place in which women sometimes ask men to go for coffee.

Attribution

Attribution is the process in which an individual explains the meaning of others' behavior based on the individual's own experiences, values, and beliefs. In our discussion about levels of meaning in the communication process, the first scenario level (#3) looked at intent in assigning meaning to messages from other people. Attribution tells us how some of that intent assignment works. As with levels of meaning, attribution theory[1] is not concerned with the *actual* intent of the source but rather the intent *assumed* to be true by the receiver. Attribution suggests that the most important part of the meaning assignment process in human communication occurs when we attribute motives to the messages and behaviors of other people.

Attribution suggests that we usually do not attribute cause to another person if we feel the behavior or message in question was not their fault or was not under their control. Levels #3 (intent) and #4 (alternative pictures) require a judgment of whether the cause of the message or behavior itself is *internal* (lies inside the person) or *external* (lies outside the person). Among the students in a class, the teacher may observe that one of them frequently asks questions, offers comments, and makes requests of the teacher, while the others seldom or never do. The teacher might decide that the student asking the questions is more curious, more talkative, or perhaps less polite than the other students. These are each internal attributions which assume that the cause of the student's communication behavior is within that student. If this situation occurred in an Asian classroom, or with Asian students studying in the United States, the teacher might be aware that students in Asian classrooms normally select a leader to speak for them to the teacher. This knowledge might produce an external attribution—that the other students were the main cause of the questions.

Research on attribution has shown that when people attribute cause to their own actions, they tend to use external factors as explanations. When they observe the behavior of others in the same situation, people tend to attribute those actions to internal causes. I believe *I* was late because of the traffic, but I believe *you* are late because you did not plan ahead or are a "late" person. This is the fundamental attribution error: "My" actions are in response to what happens to me in the environment; "your" actions are due to the kind of person you are.

Abeyta and Steinfatt (1989) extended this interpersonal analysis to intercultural situations. They suggested that causal attributions about people from other cultures may work in the same way as the causal attributions described above. *If you are from my culture, I am more likely to attribute external causes to your actions. If you are from a different culture, then I am more likely to attribute internal causes to your actions.* The following case illustration about Pakistani engineers in Thailand illustrates these differences in the attribution of cause. People from one's own culture are given the benefit of the doubt. When they present the external reasons for their actions, we are more willing to accept those reasons as the cause. People from another culture who offer the same reasons are more likely to be seen as acting from hidden interior motives related to their culture.

Case Illustration:
From Intercultural Interaction to International Incident

International incidents frequently arise from problems in intercultural communication. In June of 1994, two Pakistani engineers working in Bangkok wanted to call their families in Pakistan. They decided to use the phone at the Asian Institute to make the overseas call. This was their usual practice, since it was much cheaper than calling from their hotel.

The Nepalese Crown Prince happened to be visiting the Asian Institute that day, and the two engineers had to pass through security to get to the telephones. They said they were engineers for a Thai company. The police were unable to confirm their employment by phone because the line was busy. The security people then requested to see the engineers' passports. The engineers did not have their passports with them (a standard precaution to safeguard their identification papers). The engineers told the police that the passports were in the safe at their hotel. They were asked to produce the passports to prove their identity.

Instead of returning with the passports, the engineers went elsewhere to make their calls in order to avoid the hassle of further questioning. This sequence of events led to an international incident. One engineer was arrested and charged with plotting to harm the Crown Prince. The other was listed as a fugitive, and the Bangkok papers reported him as having eluded the police, although he had simply gone out on a field assignment and was away from his hotel.

Rather than attributing the incident to mistaken impressions, intentional malice was assigned to the actions of the engineers. One good way to escalate the emotions in any human interaction, from interpersonal to intercultural to international, is to introduce the attribution that the other person acted "out of malice." Pakistan immediately branded the allegations of intended harm to the Crown Prince as a smear campaign by Thailand, specifically intended to sabotage Nepalese-Pakistani relations.

"This has become a very serious smear campaign," said Riaz Mahmud, Pakistani Ambassador to Thailand. "Definitely there was a motive of some kind involved." It was as unlikely that a "motive" was behind the attributions of the Thai police as it was that the Pakistanis intended to harm international relations. Attributing evil motives and intentions to the behavior of others raises the level of a conflict. The Ambassador went on to say that the Thai police had been "used by an outside agency" and suggested that "some people" were jealous of the closeness of Nepalese-Pakistani relations.

Kathmandu also called the Thai allegations "totally baseless and false." (Bangkok Post, 1994, June 24, p. 3). We tend to see the actions of those from other cultures as based in hidden motives within the foreign culture.

Power

Power is the degree to which one party controls resources valued by another party. People have power in relationship to others if they can change the other person's behavior. Financial ability is one measure of power. Unequal power affects human interaction, although this influence may go unnoticed by the more powerful person in a communication relationship. However, the power differential seldom goes unnoticed by the less powerful person who may adapt to conform to the expectations of the more powerful person.

Consider one situation in which a U.S. student on a study tour in Bangkok left a bottle of rice vodka in a precarious position on a shelf in his hotel room. When he returned later, the bottle was gone. When he answered a knock on the door, he found a maid on her knees, head almost touching the floor, her hands raised in a *wai* above her head, to ask forgiveness for breaking the bottle. She assured the student that the hotel manager would repay the cost (about one dollar U.S.) out of her salary. The student told the maid not to worry about it, but the maid was petrified. The student asked the manager not to deduct the money from the maid's salary and insisted that the maid continue to clean his room. Had he not done so, the maid might have been fired. The student had greater power due to his financial status.

In this case, the student's greater power allowed him to control the communication situation in a manner that the student thought was fair. In other situations, power differences may perpetuate racism and/or sexism.

Summary

Communication is the process through which participants create and share information with one another as they move toward a mutual understanding. A *code* is a classification used by individuals to categorize their experience and to communicate it to others. *Encoding* is the process by which an idea is converted into a message by a source. *Decoding* is the process by which a message is converted into an idea by the receiver.

A *source* is the individual who originates a message by encoding an idea into a message. A *receiver* is the individual who decodes a communication message by converting it into an idea. A *channel* is the means by which a message is transmitted from its origin to its destination. *Noise* is anything that interferes with the communication process among participants. *Effects* are the changes in an individual's knowledge, attitudes, and overt behavior due to exposure to a communication message. *Feedback* is a message about the effects of a previous message that is sent back to the source.

A sign is a physical event or action that directly represents something else. A symbol is something that represents something else through prior agreement. *Language* is the use of vocalized sounds, or written symbols representing these sounds, in patterns organized by grammatical rules to express thoughts and feelings. Language is a key influence in intercultural communication, although nonverbal communication is also very important.

Intrapersonal communication is information exchange that occurs inside of one person, while *interpersonal communication* involves the face-to-face exchange of information between two or more people. Communication helps create meaning, rather than to transmit meaning. Communication is a process of creating meaning for the messages that we receive from other people. *Ambiguity* is the degree to which a communication message has many possible meanings to its receivers. When two or more participants in a communication process come from different cultures, it is less likely that the attempt to convey a meaning will be effective.

Uncertainty is an individual's inability to predict or to understand some situation due to a lack of information about alternatives. *Information* is a difference in matter-energy that affects uncertainty in a situation where a choice exists among a set of alternatives.

Attribution is the process in which an individual explains the meaning of others' behavior based on the individual's own experiences, values, and beliefs. When we seek to attribute the behavior of a culturally unalike person to some cause, we are more likely to see the action of persons from other cultures as based on hidden motives within the other culture. *Power* is the degree to which one party controls resources valued by another party, and thus controls parts of the communication interaction.

Note

[1] Attribution theory was initially developed by E. E. Jones and Kenneth Davis (1965) and was then expanded and clarified by Harold H. Kelly (1967, 1973; Kelly & Michela, 1980).

Verbal Communication

This chapter summarizes the most important lessons learned about verbal messages in intercultural communication. Language is the fundamental tool of human communication. We begin with one of the most important ideas in intercultural communication, the Whorf-Sapir hypothesis.

Linguistic Relativity

The assignment of meaning to a message concerns human perceptions about the relationship between symbols and their referents. Language is used to think as well as to speak. *Linguistic relativity* is the degree to which language influences human thought and meanings. It proposes that in human thought language intervenes between the symbols and the ideas to which the symbols refer. Does the language in which we speak and think influence the very nature of our thoughts and the way in which we think?

Linguistic relativity proposes that language and thought are so tied together that a person's language determines the categories of thought open to the person. "We cut up and organize the spread and flow of events as we do largely because, through our mother tongue, we are parties to an agreement to do so, not because nature itself is segmented in exactly that way for all to see" (Whorf, 1940/1956, p. 239). Linguistic relativity is also called the

Whorfian hypothesis, after its main creator, Benjamin Lee Whorf.[1] Since linguistic relativity proposes that a language creates a worldview held in common by its speakers, linguistic relativity is also sometimes called the linguistic *Weltanschauung* (worldview) hypothesis.

The Whorfian hypothesis is a reaction against the *nominalist* view of language presented by Plato and Aristotle. Aristotle taught his students that knowledge of reality is not affected by language. He regarded language as an arbitrary outer form of thought. In Aristotle's view, the thought was the same regardless of the language. Aristotle's position was that any thought can be expressed in any language, and translatability between languages does not present a problem. This view went largely unchallenged until late in the nineteenth century (Steinfatt, 1988a, 1989). The primary challenge to Aristotle's view of language came from Whorf (1940/1956).[2]

Linguistic relativity proposes that language influences three different areas of human thought and cognition: (1) the *perceptions and cognitions* held by an individual such as perceptions of color, of lateness, or of size; (2) the *cognitive structure* of the individual and the *worldview* the individual holds; (3) the structure of logic itself and of what is perceived as logical (Steinfatt, 1988). For linguists, anthropologists, and scholars of intercultural communication, the Whorfian hypothesis proposed a new paradigm, a new way of thinking about language and culture. The ideas of both Whorf and Edward Sapir, Whorf's professor at Yale University, went against the conventional wisdom of their day, which denigrated unwritten and non-European languages (Kay & Kempton, 1984). The languages of native peoples in Latin America, Africa, Asia, and North America were thought by many anthropologists to be relatively simple. Following the lead of Franz Boas, Whorf and Sapir showed that unwritten languages were as systematic and logically rich as any European tongue. They just had a different logic.

Who were Benjamin Lee Whorf and Edward Sapir? How did their unusual collaboration take place? Edward Sapir (1884–1939) was born in Germany and immigrated with his family to New York as a young boy. He earned his doctorate in anthropology at Columbia University. His advisor was Franz Boas, who argued (1) that languages classify experience, (2) that different languages classify experience differently, and (3) that linguistic behavior is unconscious because talking is more or less automatic (Lucy, 1992, pp. 11–12). Boas thus laid the groundwork for the Whorf-Sapir hypothesis. However, Boas believed that language *reflects* thought; Sapir and Whorf reversed the direction, claiming that language *influences* thought. Sapir became a famous linguist and anthropologist; he taught at the University of Chicago and then at Yale University.

Benjamin Lee Whorf (1897–1941) earned a BS degree in chemical engineering from MIT. As a fire prevention engineer for the Hartford Fire Insurance Company, he travelled frequently. Evenings were often spent reading in

Figure 5-1. Benjamin Lee Whorf (1897–1941).

Source: Yale University Library. Used by permission.

a local library, pursuing questions that fired his imagination (Agar, 1994, p. 62). Whorf originally became interested in languages because of the conflict between Darwin's evolutionary theory and Biblical explanations of the origins of life on earth. Whorf thought that this conflict might stem from inaccurate translations of Biblical writings from the original Hebrew and Greek. This interest broadened into Whorf's self-taught study of linguistics and the structure of language.

An important event occurred early in Whorf's career as a fire inspector, one that was to shape his interests in linguistic relativity.[3] He investigated an accidental fire in a factory, which had started when someone threw a match into some barrels filled with gas fumes. Over the drums was a sign, EMPTY GAS DRUMS. "Yet the 'empty' drums are perhaps the more dangerous [compared to full drums], since they contain explosive vapor" (Whorf, 1940/1956, p. 135). The word "empty" had caused people to think that the drums were safe because one meaning of empty is negative, void, inert. The other meaning of the word empty is that the drums no longer contained their intended contents. The individual who wrote the EMPTY GAS DRUMS sign was thinking of the second meaning. The person who threw the match was thinking of the first meaning of "empty." Thus the hazard was created by a linguistic problem in which one word had two meanings. This defining event started Whorf thinking about the influence of language on perceptions.

When Edward Sapir joined the Yale University faculty in 1931, Whorf enrolled in his course on Native American linguistics. Sapir persuaded Whorf to begin studying the Hopi language. Later Whorf traveled to Arizona for field research in the Hopi's cliff-dwelling villages. Hopi is an almost impossible tongue for the non-Hopi to learn because it has such a different language structure than Indo-European languages. There is no verb tense in Hopi, so past, present, and future must be expressed in different ways than in English. The Hopi have two broad categories of thought and language; Whorf called them the manifest and the manifesting. The manifest includes the physical present and everything that has occurred in the physical present up to the moment. The manifesting includes everything that might be, including the wished for, and everything that is in process. Thus, for example, the dead are distinguished from the living by the Hopi but remain manifest. Unborn and unconceived children exist in the manifesting, a state which evolves over time into the manifest. Thus talking and thinking in Hopi is quite different than in English, which distinguishes between past, present, and future by using verb tenses.

Benjamin Lee Whorf became a famous scholar and was offered professorships at prestigious universities. Instead, he continued his work as a fire prevention inspector for the rest of his career. The insurance company granted him leaves to live on the Hopi Reservation from time to time. This eccentric engineer/fire inspector/linguist died young, from cancer, at age 44, in 1941 (Agar, 1994, p. 63). The title of his well-known book *Language, Thought and Reality* (Whorf, 1940/1956) summarized the essence of his main contributions to understanding human behavior.

Examples of the Whorfian Hypothesis

Language influences our thinking in an unconscious manner, which is one reason why the notion of linguistic relativity is so fascinating to most of us. "Perhaps it is the suggestion that all one's life one has been tricked, all unaware, by the structure of language into a certain way of perceiving reality, with the implication that awareness of this trickery will enable one to see the world with fresh insight" (Carroll, 1940/1956, p. 27). Whorf and Sapir claimed that a cultural system is embodied in the language of the people who speak the language. This cultural framework shapes the thoughts of the language's speakers. An individual is typically not aware of this indirect but pervasive influence. We think in the words and the meanings of our language, which in turn is an expression of our culture. Only when an individual learns a second language and tries to move back and forth to his/her mother tongue does the individual become aware of the influence that language has on perception.

Consider some examples of linguistic relativity. In India, the Hindi language has no single words that are equivalent to the English words "uncle" and "aunt." Instead, Hindi has different words for your father's older brother, father's younger brother, mother's older brother, mother's older brother-in-law, and so forth. This diversity of terms suggests that the interpersonal relationships involved between an individual and his/her uncles and aunts are much more important in India than in nations where English is spoken. Many languages in addition to Hindi are richer than English in the number of words for different family and kinship relationships.

In general, when a language has a large number of words for the same object or class of objects, that object is relatively important. Thus *Diné* (the language spoken by the Navajo) has thousands of words for the English expression "to go," the infinitive showing action. Arabic has many words for "camel," but English only has one. What if a language has *no* word for something? Could speakers of that language think of the object?

To what extent does language structure thought? Some languages have no verb tense, so the speakers do not differentiate between the past, present, and the future. To the Hopi, time is considered part of the flow of events. The Hopi expression for "he runs," *wari*, could mean he runs, he ran, he used to run, or he will run. In contrast, an English speaker *has* to put a tense marker on every verb. Further, in the Hopi language, verbs only refer to something of short duration, like a lightening flash or a puff of smoke. Anything of long duration, such as "working in the fields all summer," is a noun (Stevenson, 1994, p. 57). Such qualities of a language shape the way in which the Hopi people perceive the world. Note that it is not just the words alone in the Hopi language that shape perceptions, but also the grammar of the language, which is very different from European languages. The uniqueness of Hopi in comparison to Indo-European languages played a key role in helping Benjamin Lee Whorf create the idea of linguistic relativity.

Even among the European family of languages, however, there are important differences. Imagine the Germans looking at a masculine moon (*der Mond*). The French on the other side of the Rhine look at the same moon, but it is feminine (*la lune*). The sun is feminine in German (*die Sonne*) and masculine in French (*le soleil*). To the English across the English Channel, the moon and the sun are neither masculine nor feminine (Stevenson, 1994, p. 57). Such gender differences in languages influence how the Germans, French, and English perceive the same objects.

The most famous example used to illustrate the concept of linguistic relativity is the Inuit language. The example claims the Inuit (a tribe of Native Americans in northwestern Canada) have twelve words for "snow." To describe different types of snow—wet snow, packed snow, or powder snow—in English, speakers must use an adjective plus the noun. Because they have more options of words to convey shades of meaning about snow, one could reasonably infer that snow is more important to the Inuit.[4]

The Bororo, a tribe living in the rain forest of Brazil, call themselves "red parrots." They do not distinguish between themselves as a people and the red parrots that frequent their environment. If this identification with a bird seems strange, think of university students who call themselves "Owls," "Spartans," "Wolverines," "Hurricanes," and "Lobos." Similarly, the Bororo know that they are not birds, but the same word identifies both their tribe and the red parrots, suggesting that they think of the two together (Vygotsky, 1962).

We have been discussing languages that have many words for something but for which there is only one word in another language. Now consider the other type of evidence for the theory of linguistic relativity: a language that has a word for something for which another language does not have *any* word. An example is the Spanish word *cuates*, which means individuals with the same first name (such as two or more people named María or Juan). The names that are shared are called *homonimos*. In English, there is no word that is equivalent in meaning to *cuates*. Can an English speaker (who does not also know Spanish) think about *cuates*? Here we see another type of evidence for the Whorf-Sapir hypothesis of linguistic relativity. Can you think of other examples of a word in one language that does not have an equivalent in another language?

Linguistic relativity implies that individuals who speak different languages will think of the same world in different ways. Thus, translation from one language to another would be difficult. If there is not a word-for-word correspondence in meanings between two languages, is it futile to try to make an exact translation? In this sense the Whorfian hypothesis poses discouraging problems for effective intercultural communication across languages.

Linguistic relativity has "hard" and "soft" forms. The "hard" form is *linguistic determinism*—thinking is completely *determined* by language. This extreme perspective implies that "Language is a prison with no hope of parole. Translation and bilingualism are impossible" (Agar, 1994, p. 67). For instance, how could Whorf write journal articles in English about the Hopi language? Further, if linguistic determinism were true, how could an investigator test it? If one is trapped by one's language, any experiment that one could design would be trapped by it as well (Agar, 1994, p. 67). "Researchers themselves are not exempt from these linguistic influences. . . . A linguistic relativity, if there is such, will not only lie *out there* in the object of investigation but will also penetrate right *into* the research process itself" (Lucy, 1992, p. 2).

A great deal of research has been conducted on the Whorfian hypothesis, mainly by linguists, anthropologists, and psychologists. The findings show more support for the "soft" version of the hypothesis of linguistic relativity (language *influences* human thought and meanings) than for linguistic determinism. An individual's first language does not completely trap that person into a particular pattern of thinking. For instance, a Hopi who acquired English fluency could learn to think in past, present, and future tense. The lack of perfection in the translation process does not mean that making equivalences from one language to another is impossible (although it *is* difficult). Consider the translation of a sentence from Spanish into English. The Spanish sentence contains the personal pronoun "*tu*" (the familiar "you," conveying an intimate relationship between two individuals), which is translated simply as "you" in English (as is "*usted*," the Spanish pronoun for the formal "you," used with one's boss). How can the English "you" convey the same meaning as the Spanish "*tu*"? Or "*usted*"? It cannot. There is not a true equivalence between the English and the Spanish words.

Some of the research on the Whorfian hypothesis has been conducted on color.[5] Typically, a color spectrum (showing the various colors of the rainbow) is divided into a large number of color chips, each with a particular shade of color (for example, perhaps twenty-five color chips represent the various shades of blue-green, another twenty-five chips represent shades of red-yellow, etc.). Monolingual respondents are asked to select the color chips that they can easily identify with a single word (such as "green," "blue," "yellow," "red," "orange," etc. in English). While most Asian and Western languages break the color spectrum into the same color categories, the speakers of another language have different colors that they recognize. For instance, the Zuni Indians of the southwestern United States have a single color term for the entire yellow and orange part of the color spectrum, while English speakers distinguish between orange and yellow as two different colors. A particular color chip is called "yellow" by a native speaker of English, while the same chip is called "yellow-orange" by a Zuni. The categories formed by words influence thinking and perception.

The degree to which individuals can remember a color depends on the availability of a name for a particular color. Say that you went to a paint store and tried to purchase the correct shade of paint to match the color of your living room walls. You look at paint chips for twenty shades of white, but cannot remember the exact color of white on your walls. But if you know that the shade of your walls is called "Swiss mocha," you can bring home the correct shade.

The body of color research in the linguistic relativity tradition shows that all languages contain terms for white and black. If a language contains three color terms, one is for red. The least common colors in various languages are orange, gray, pink, and purple.

The Whorfian hypothesis of linguistic relativity has provided a major contribution to intercultural communication. The hypothesis demonstrates the importance of language in communication. More generally, Whorf and Sapir showed that language, thought, and culture are closely connected. *Language, which is a part of culture, affects human behavior through thought and perception, thus linking culture to human behavior*.

Importance of Language

Can someone understand Indian society without knowing Hindi? It would be extremely difficult, as the Whorf-Sapir hypothesis implies. *Language influences thought, and thus influences the meanings that are conveyed by words*. Becoming fluent in a foreign language is a difficult and time-consuming task, but it is essential to gaining intercultural understanding of the society in which that language is spoken. One of the authors of this book is fluent in Spanish but not in German. He realizes that he can understand Spanish-speaking cultures much more effectively than the cultures whose language he does not speak.

A few people have written about a culture without learning the language. In 1946 Ruth Benedict wrote *The Chrysanthemum and the Sword*. Benedict did not know Japanese, nor had she ever visited Japan. Instead, she based her book on various publications, mainly ethnologies written by anthropologists, about Japan. While Benedict's book is widely admired, most of us are not Ruth Benedicts. In order to understand a culture, we need first to master its language and then to experience it in a communication sense. One must live in the society on a daily basis and talk with individuals who share that culture. Once you can speak their language, you can begin to put yourself inside their skin (this ability is called empathy) and to really understand their culture more fully. Communication with members of a culture is essential to gain cultural insight, and language fluency is a necessary prerequisite for effective communication. When you can tell jokes in another language or argue on the telephone, then you have indeed reached a high level of fluency in a second language.

Case Illustration:
The Language Police in Québec[7]

The importance of language as a cultural boundary between peoples is illustrated by the French/English conflict in Canada's largest province, Québec. Language is used as the basis for the Québécois to separate themselves from the rest of Canada.

How did this zealous language policy in Québec begin? It traces to the history of Québec as a French-speaking province in the midst of an English-speaking nation. Québec was originally settled by the French. It was later added to British Canada and became a British colony. In 1812, the British forcibly removed French-speaking residents of Acadia, a Canadian island on the Atlantic Coast, to Louisiana, then a French colony (these people are called Cajuns, a corruption of the word "Acadians"). Since that time, French-speaking people in Quebec have occupied an inferior economic and political status in Canadian society. In 1967, French President Charles de Gaulle, while on a visit to Montreal—to the surprise of his Canadian hosts—declared: "Vive le Québec! Vive le Québec libre!" (Long live Québec! Long live free Québec!). De Gaulle's visit was unceremoniously ended by the Canadian government, but his speech energized and legitimized the Québécois separatist movement, which won control of the provincial government in 1976 and held power until 1985.

In order to protect their position as a French island in a sea of 300 million North American Anglophones, the Province of Québec has legislated a series of draconian laws to promote the use of French. At one time (in the late 1970s), the use of English was prohibited on all public signage. For instance, the name of a main street in

Figure 5-2.   This Québec traffic sign was bilingual, but the English word "STOP" has been defaced to "101," the law that required exclusive use of French. Law 101, enforced in the late 1970s, was later declared unconstitutional, so that today in the Province of Québec, English-language signs can again be used. Nevertheless, the language dispute in Québec is a contentious issue, with the province threatening to withdraw from Canada.

Source: Photograph by James Seeley. Used by permission.

Montreal had to be changed from St. Laurent Boulevard to Boulevard St. Laurent. All stop signs had to say Arrêt instead of "Stop."

French separatists defaced commercial signs in English. Provincial "language police" (also called "tongue troopers") issued citations to the owners of stores with English signs. The provincial government insisted that all signs had to be in large French words, but with smaller English printing allowed underneath. Student vigilantes turned in offenders. All new immigrants and their children in Québec were required to learn French. Thus, the province forced everyone in Québec toward using only French.

The national government of Canada has devoted extensive efforts to offer special protection to the French language in North America. Canada has two official languages, English and French. While French is only actively spoken in Québec, the national government, as well as the provinces and territories, all make their services available in both languages. All provinces must provide French instruction from grade school through high school. Nevertheless, there has been a growing movement for an independent Québec. A series of referenda in recent decades showed growing public support in Québec for the withdrawal of the province from Canada. The vote in a 1995 referendum was 51–49 against withdrawal from Canada. Separation would essentially cut the nation in two at the midsection, raising questions about the viability of the Canadian Federation. This development would, in turn, have dire consequences for Canada's NAFTA partners, the United States and Mexico.

The costs of the separatist movement in Québec include the loss of businesses and jobs, a decrease in tourism, and a lack of investor confidence in the Québec economy. Montreal today is a city of "à louer" (signs indicating "for rent"), and there is a 20 percent office vacancy rate. Many young people cannot find jobs in Québec and must migrate to other Canadian provinces or to the United States to seek employment in the face of double-digit unemployment. A dark economic cloud hangs over the beautiful city of Montreal. A popular joke is to ask the last person to leave Montreal to please remember to turn off the lights.

Obviously, language is a very important political issue in Canada. The French language policy issue in Québec shows that language is much more than just a means to communicate with others. Language is also a means of drawing boundaries, a symbol of political identification, and may become a basis for national dissolution. Language differences do not have to split a nation, as the case of Switzerland (where there are four national languages) shows. What will happen to Québec?

Perceptions Count

William I. Thomas, in collaboration with Florian Znaniecki, a Polish sociologist, investigated the process through which Polish people immigrated to

Chicago and other U.S. cities. Two million Poles moved to the United States from 1880 to 1910; they came mainly from villages in Europe and worked in unskilled jobs in meat packing houses, steel mills, and textile factories. Although Thomas and Znianecki did not use the term "intercultural communication," their Polish peasant investigation was one of the first empirical studies of this type of communication. Their book, *The Polish Peasant in Europe and America* (1927/1984), documented how the immigration to the slums of U.S. cities broke down the sense of solidarity among Poles, leading to a variety of social problems like crime, prostitution, and poverty. It was a social science classic and one of the first studies on assimilation (a topic discussed in Chapter 7). It was published in five volumes totaling 2,250 pages. One short sentence became a defining synopsis of perception: "If men define situations as real, they are real in all of their consequences." That is, perceptions count in determining an individual's behavior. *Perception* is the way in which an individual gives meaning to an object. Perceptions count because they form what Thomas called the individual's "definition of the situation"—how a person subjectively interprets communication messages into meaning. Communication influences perceptions; they, in turn, influence an individual's behavior.

Perceptions versus Objective Reality

Numerous scholarly investigations have established that *an individual's perceptions are more important than objective reality in determining the individual's behavior*. These perceptions, as illustrated in the following case illustration on body weight, differ from one culture to another. One of the main propositions of intercultural communication is that *culture shapes an individual's perceptions, and thus behavior*.

Case Illustration:
Perceptions of Body Weight by African-American and White Adolescent Girls

---

Intercultural differences are important not just between national cultures but also between the domestic cultures of ethnic groups within a nation, especially one that is culturally diverse like the United States. A study of body image and dieting of African-American and White adolescent girls in the United States (Parker & others, 1995) provides an example.

Body weight is a very important matter to White adolescent girls. At any given time, about three-fourths of the White teenagers in the United States are dieting. Many perceive that they are overweight, even when measurements show that they are not. Culturally defined perceptions result in constant dieting. Further, dieting and other means of having a more perfect body are main topics of conversation. These girls talk a great deal about feeling fat. Some 90 percent of the respondents in the study expressed some degree of concern about their body shape. About 2 or 3 percent of all White girls in the United States have anorexia (not eating) and bulimia (binge eating followed by vomiting).

African-American adolescent girls have strikingly different perceptions about body weight. Some 70 percent of the African-American respondents in the study were satisfied with their body weight, although measurements showed that 18 percent of those who were satisfied were significantly overweight (that is, above the 85th percentile of weight for a given height).

Why are there major differences in the perceptions and the reality of body weight between African-American and White girls? The White girls in the study strove for the bodily perfection depicted in the mass media, exemplified by model Cindy Crawford. The White respondents described the perfect girl as 5 feet 7 inches tall and weighing between 100 and 110 pounds. She should have long legs, long flowing hair, and a model's face with high cheekbones. In other words, the ideal girl was a Barbie doll. Ideal weight was perceived as a ticket to the perfect life, including popularity with attractive men.

African-American respondents in the study perceived female beauty in a very different way. Their perceptions of the ideal body centered on "making use of what you've got," and "making what you've got work for you." They expressed greater acceptance of their physical bodies than did White girls. Their self-images concerning weight were confident instead of insecure. The African-American girls stated their approval of someone "who's got it going on." By that, they meant a girl who used beauty products, had an attractive personality, and who was happy. She should be smart, easy to talk to, and have a good sense of humor. Having an attractive personal style was more important than being thin. Beauty was a personality matter, not just an aspect of bodily appearance.

Where did the African-American adolescent girls get their perceptions of body weight? Mainly from other African-American women, especially their mothers and peers, who were likely to compliment them on their appearance. They received positive feedback rather than negative comments about how they looked from family and friends. Dieting was relatively unimportant for the African-American girls. Most did not have a certain number of pounds that they considered ideal body weight.

Further, the European American and African-American girls both knew that they differed in their perceptions of female beauty. African-American girls said that White adolescents "want to be tall, thin, and have long hair." In contrast, African-American boys were thought to like girls who were "thick," who had "nice thighs," and who were "full-figured."

This research shows that perceptions count. It is her perception of body weight that determines whether an adolescent girl diets or not, rather than her actual weight. Perceptions are formed through interpersonal communication with other people like oneself. The marked differences in perceptions of body weight between the African-

American and White adolescent girls stemmed from their communication with others of their ingroup.

What if a company were marketing a dieting product and wanted to identify audience individuals most likely to buy the product? One might naturally think of identifying adolescent girls who are overweight according to objective measures, such as standardized height/weight ratios. Not so. This study illustrates that objective measures do not match perceptions. In fact, many objectively overweight individuals are not interested in dieting while many objectively average weight individuals are. It is culturally determined perceptions that count.

A classic experiment in social psychology showed the importance of perceptions and how an individual's background affects perceptions. Poor and rich children were shown a 25-cent piece. After about an hour, each child was asked to draw a picture of a quarter. The poor children perceived the quarters as huge, about the size of a coffee cup. In contrast, the rich children remembered the quarters as quite small.

A similar point about perceptions was made by Vidmar and Rokeach (1974), who studied the effects of the prime-time television show *All in the Family.* Hollywood producer Norman Lear created this program in 1971 to attack racism and sexism in the United States. The show (as mentioned in Chapter 2) featured an extremely prejudiced character, Archie Bunker, whose bigotry was ridiculed, making him a laughingstock for most viewers. Archie also was very sexist in the way he treated his wife Edith ("Dingbat"). The main foils for Archie's working-class prejudice were his daughter Gloria and her husband Mike, who represented positive role models for liberal tolerance of ethnic differences. Because of Archie's extreme behavior as a negative role model for prejudice, many viewers became less ethnocentric and prejudiced. However, Vidmar and Rokeach found that viewers who were already very prejudiced admired Archie as a hero and perceived him as a *positive* role model. These prejudiced viewers also thought that Archie won in his conflicts with Mike and Gloria about ethnic groups, which he referred to by derogatory expressions like "Wops," "Chinks," and "Coons." This tendency for some individuals to be reinforced in their existing negative behavior by a negative role model has since been called the "Archie Bunker effect" by communication scholars (Singhal & Rogers, in press).

An example of the Archie Bunker effect occurred in Jamaica among listeners to a radio soap opera called *Naiseberry Street.* This entertainment-education program (which used an entertaining radio format to promote sexual responsibility and family planning) featured a negative character named Scattershot. This dirty old man seduced young girls in his neighborhood, seeking to impregnate them as soon as they reached puberty. Although Scattershot was intended to be a negative role model for sexual responsibility and was punished for his bad behavior in the storyline, some male listeners admired him. For example, they named their pet dogs and race horses Scattershot (Singhal & Rogers, in press). Again, we see that perceptions count.

Symbolic Interaction

One of the important intellectual contributions of the Chicago School is a theoretical perspective called *symbolic interaction*, defined as the theory that individuals act toward objects on the basis of meanings and perceptions that are formed through communication with others. The founder of symbolic interactionism was George Herbert Mead (1863–1931). Mead was trained in philosophy and studied in Germany, perhaps with Georg Simmel (Rogers, 1994). He taught his theoretical perspective at the University of Chicago during the golden age of social science, in the early decades of the 1900s. *Mind, Self, and Society* was compiled from his students' notes after his death.

Mead argued that no one is born with a self (a personality), nor does it develop instinctively. Instead, an individual's self-conception evolves through talking with others (parents, teachers, and peers) during childhood. From this interpersonal communication the individual internalizes the meanings of others to form a "generalized other" based on the expectations of others. This generalized other serves as a guide to one's behavior. In the previous case illustration, adolescents in both ethnic groups formed their self-expectations for body weight on the basis of interpersonal communication with others in their ingroup, thus gradually creating their generalized other regarding ideal body weight.

Mead suggested that human behavior could be understood by learning how individuals give meaning to the symbolic information that they exchange with others (thus the phrase symbolic interactionism). Through such conversations, an individual forms perceptions which then determine actions. The symbolic interaction viewpoint has become widely accepted as an explanation of human behavior and is reflected throughout this book.

In the next section, we will look at specific communication behaviors and how they affect intercultural interactions. Before doing so, there is a particular behavior that occurs only in certain instances that illustrates intercultural communication between two skilled participants.

Code-Switching

Code-switching is the process by which individuals change from speaking one language to another during a conversation. Participants must be equally fluent in at least two languages. Intercultural communication scholars have investigated under what conditions code-switching takes place and its consequences. They have learned that code-switching has complex rules, although it usually happens naturally without the code-switchers being fully aware of why they switch when they do. The language spoken may affect the meanings derived by the conversation partners. For example, when one of this book's authors switches into speaking Spanish in a conversation, he feels closer socially to his communication co-participants. In this instance, code-switching (and therefore language) is used as a means of showing warmth and reinforcing social relationships. The choice of language may indicate formality or informality. Depending on the participants involved in a conversation, English might be the code chosen for formal discussions or in formal settings while the native language of one or both participants would be preferred for informal situations. Similarly, the topic could affect the language code chosen. If discussing the color of sunsets, for example, the two participants might automatically switch to a code that allows more differentiation and that has more words for shades of color.

Consider another case. Two people fluent in both English and Spanish are having a conversation in Spanish. A third person joins them who can only speak (or who prefers to speak) in English. The conversation rather naturally switches to English. No one states, "Okay, now let's talk in English." The change happens naturally. Now let's assume the speakers do not know the third person who joins them, but they know his name is Jesus Martinez. They could continue speaking in Spanish, assuming that Jesus knows the language, until they perceive that he does not comprehend what they are saying. Both of these examples illustrate code-switching as a desire to accommodate another participant (see Chapter 6 for a discussion of nonverbal accommodation). Code-switching occurs more frequently in cities where many people are bilingual, as in Miami, Los Angeles, or San Antonio.

Code-switching can be used in the opposite direction of the examples above. All of those situations could be viewed as a way to process symbolic information to enhance the relationships among participants. If the goal were to send a very different message, code-switching could be used to distance oneself from others. Refusing to communicate in a shared code sends a clear message that the conversation is closed to "strangers." Surveys of non-Spanish-speaking Miami residents indicate that their greatest complaints occur when co-workers and store employees speak Spanish in their presence (Steinfatt, 1994). This effect was especially strong among Black residents.

Cultural Factors in Interpersonal Communication

Some intercultural communication scholars today argue that the essence of the field is the actual dialogue between culturally unalike individuals. "The study of intercultural dialogue should be at the center of intercultural communication research and theory" (Hart, 1997). Scholars should record and analyze these conversations as the basic data of intercultural communication, so as to identify where and why miscommunication occurs. This section looks at some of the elements used to analyze intercultural dialogue.

Talk and Silence

The value of talk versus silence in a conversation varies greatly depending on the culture. For example, in comparison to European Americans, Asians are much more taciturn, or reluctant to talk. An Asian is more likely to use indirect expression to convey an intended meaning (remember our discussions about high-context cultures?). Silence itself may be a very important message.

Native Americans in the United States have a different cultural value regarding silence than do European Americans. In the early 1990s, one of the authors was involved in a government-funded communication project aimed at Native Americans with physical disabilities. A campaign consisting of radio spots and other messages urged individuals to telephone an 800-number in order to request information and technical advice about assistive technologies (such as battery-operated wheelchairs and various electronic devices) which were available at no cost to eligible individuals. The radio spots featured Native Americans with disabilities who had benefited from using assistive technologies. These messages were broadcast via radio stations that reached Native American audiences. It was expected that thousands of requests about assistive technologies would be received.

To the shocked surprise of the project staff, only a few hundred telephone requests to the 800-number were received over a two-year period. Almost none of the requests came from Native Americans. Instead, the callers were social workers and others who telephoned on behalf of disabled Native Americans. Why? Most Native Americans hold a strong cultural value against seeking information or services from a government agency. Silence, in this case, is more appropriate behavior. This important lesson about cultural differences was expensive—several hundred thousand dollars and many years of project staff time.

Reticence is generally considered by Native Americans as an appropriate mode of communicating with other individuals, especially other Native Americans. It is polite to remain silent and not to initiate a conversation. For example, a Native American student said: "I passed this Indian girl on the way to class for two months, and we never spoke—She knew who I was, and I knew who she was" (Wieder & Pratt, 1990). Another respondent stated: "When I was at this conference, this other Indian girl and I never did talk to each other until the last night. There was one girl who was there and did come up and talk to me who said she was Indian, but I could tell she wasn't, because if she was, she probably wouldn't have come up and talked to me" (Weider & Pratt, 1990).

A few years ago, Dr. Osmo Wiio, a communication scholar from Finland, came to the United States as a visiting professor. While riding a public bus to the campus, a woman sitting next to him struck up a conversation, intending to be friendly. "I see by your clothes that you may be a European. What country are you from?" Wiio replied curtly, trying to discourage further conversation: "Finland." He held his newspaper so as to cover his face. But his fellow passenger stated, "Oh, how wonderful! Please tell me all about Finland." Professor Wiio felt very angry that a complete stranger had initiated a conversation with him. In Finland, a cultural norm discourages striking up a conversation with strangers in public places.

At the University of New Mexico, a typical class may include several Navajo or Pueblo students. They are unlikely to ask questions during class sessions or to volunteer answers to the teacher's questions. To do so would be culturally inappropriate; it would not be the Native American way. When a teacher calls on one of the Native Americans with a question, there is usually a pause of several seconds. The impatient teacher is likely to call on another student rather than wait for a response. From the Native American student's viewpoint, an important question should not be answered immediately, without carefully thinking out the answer.

For the Japanese, the silence between two utterances in a conversation belongs to the previous speaker, who indicates how long the silence should continue. The listener should show respect to the previous speaker's wish for silence, especially if the speaker is older or of higher status than the listener.

As the above examples illustrate, cultural differences in talk versus silence interfere with the effectiveness of intercultural communication. Once again, respect for and knowledge about another culture's values are the keys to avoiding miscommunication.

Speaking Style

Different cultures are characterized by unique speaking styles. For example, African-American culture has an oral, rather than a written, tradition. A leader is expected to possess exceptional skills as an orator. African-American preachers often have an interactive relationship with their audiences, demonstrated by talk-back, hand clapping, and shouts of affirmation. Members of the audience may yell "That's right!" "Yes, Lord!" "Preach the truth!" and "Lordy, Lordy, Lord!" (Asante, 1987, p. 47). These rhythmic exchanges with speakers provide immediate feedback through the call-and-response pattern. Some communication scholars, like Molefi Asante (1987), note the distinctive oratorical style of African-American speakers. Two scholars of African-American speaking style stated: "To speak of the 'traditional' Black Church is to speak of the holy-rolling, bench-walking, spirit-getting, tongue-speaking, vision-receiving, intuitive-directing, Amen-saying, sing-song preaching, holy-dancing and God-sending Church" (Daniel & Smitherman, 1990). The content of Black preaching is borrowed from the Western Judeo-Christian tradition, but the emotional communication style remains essentially African. Daniel and Smitherman (1990) illustrate this distinction with the following funeral service:

Pastor: "...Who understands the Divine Plan of Justice? On the Fourth of July, Gawd reared back and said: 'Death, come here.'"

Congregation: "Wonderful Jesus!"

Pastor: "Death, go down to that place called *America*!"

Congregation: "Lissen to the Lawd!"

Pastor: "Death, find that state they call Mississippi!"

Congregation: "Gawd's a-talking!"

Pastor: "Death, go to a town called *Clintonville*!"

Congregation: "Lawd, Lawd, Lawd!"

The speaking style of African Americans is also characterized by assertiveness, intensity, aggressiveness, and, at times, outspokenness and belligerence (Hecht & others, 1993, pp. 104–105). The assertive speaking style may be expressed by using a loud voice, threats and insults (perhaps made in jest), and slang or street talk. Many African Americans speak a Black English vernacular, Ebonics, as their mother tongue.

Turn-Taking

One important and necessary behavior in every face-to-face interpersonal exchange is *turn-taking*, defined as the process through which the participants in a conversation decide who will talk first, next, and so forth. Have you noticed how individuals in a conversation decide who will talk next? Nonverbal clues may be important, such as when an individual looks at the person who is expected to talk next in a conversation (see Chapter 6).

When two people who are talking do not share a common culture, they may misunderstand each other's subtle clues as to when each should speak. As a result, both individuals may try to talk at the same time, or their discourse may be interrupted by awkward silences. As a consequence of these difficulties with turn-taking, both conversation partners may feel uncomfortable and out of synch. Again, we see how cultural differences affect communication effectiveness. For instance, when a Japanese and a North American talk in English, a pause of a few seconds' duration may frequently occur before the Japanese speaker responds. This brief delay may be vaguely disconcerting to the North American conversation partner.

Self-Disclosure

Self-disclosure is the degree to which an individual reveals personal information to another person. An individual may not want to disclose such details as sexual orientation, feelings toward another person who is a mutual friend, or some item of taboo information. Imagine a university student disclosing to another individual that he or she was sexually abused by an adult as a child. Or consider a gay man or woman who comes out of the closet. Such topics are generally not considered acceptable in casual conversation because of social taboos and sanctions. However, individuals may consciously break their silence on these subjects as a political act in order to change these taboos.

A large body of research has been conducted on self-disclosure since the psychologist Sidney Jourard (1971) called attention to this type of communication behavior with his book, *The Transparent Self*. Scholars have investigated whether or not women are more likely to disclose personal information about themselves than are men (they aren't). Generally, personal and social characteristics are not related to the degree of an individual's disclosure. The personal relationship between two or more individuals, however, does affect self-disclosure, with same-culture strangers being more disclosing about some information than are same-culture intimates. Researchers found that both men and women were more disclosing of descriptive (that is, relatively factual) information about themselves while talking with a stranger than with their spouse. The opposite was true when disclosing intimate feelings, which were more likely to be disclosed to a spouse (Dindia & others, 1997).

When an individual discloses personal information to another, such disclosure encourages reciprocal disclosure by the other party. "Disclosure begets disclosure" (Jourard, 1971, p. 66). The feeling of intimacy created by one individual's personal remarks about himself/herself seems to encourage the other person to disclose personal information.

Cultural factors strongly determine the degree to which self-disclosure is appropriate. Collectivistic and high-context cultures are not very disclosing, while individualistic and low-context cultures are relatively more self-disclosing. European Americans disclose more personal details about their health, inner experiences, intimate thoughts, and so forth than do the Japanese or Chinese. The Japanese distinguish between *honne*, one's true inner feelings, and *tatemae*, the feelings that one expresses to others so as to be consistent with others' feelings. This distinction implies that an individual may often not disclose inner feelings to others. Asians believe that self-centered talk is boastful, pretentious, and should be avoided. So when a European American discloses some personal information to an Asian American, the latter feels uncomfortable and does not self-disclose in return. Thus, Sidney Jourard's famous statement must be modified: Self-disclosure begets self-disclosure, if self-disclosure is culturally appropriate.

Content versus Relationship

Communication scholars distinguish between two dimensions of a message: (1) the message content, or *what* is said, and (2) the relationship, or *how* it is said (Watzlawick & others, 1967). This distinction was originally formulated by Gregory Bateson while observing monkeys playing in the San Francisco zoo. He noticed that one monkey would nip another in a way that looked like real combat, but both monkeys understood that the nip was just in play.

Bateson concluded that the bite message must have been preceded by another signal that established a playful relationship between the two monkeys (Rogers, 1994, p. 96). Bateson (1972) called the relationship message *metacommunication*, that is communication about communication. Humans, as well as monkeys, frequently engage in metacommunication. For example, one person is laughing while he makes a very offensive statement to a close friend, who thus understands from the smile that the remark is in jest.

Many communication scholars have investigated the content versus relationship dimensions of communication in different cultures. Collectivistic cultures put greater emphasis upon the relationship aspect of a message (as explained in Chapter 3). You will recall that individuals in a collectivistic culture form messages in a way so as not to offend or make another person lose face. Less important is the clarity of the message content because relationships are considered more important than the task at hand. In comparison, individualistic cultures stress message content over the relationship dimension of a message. Being clear, concise, and direct are prized. If someone's feelings get hurt by a communication message, too bad. Individuals generally feel that effective communication depends on being clear and avoiding ambiguity, although in an individualistic culture there are situations when ambiguous messages are appropriate (Eisenberg, 1984). For example, a certain degree of ambiguity would be appropriate when an individual refuses an invitation for a date. Explanations such as "I am too busy" or "I have to study for an exam" are more acceptable than "No, I don't like you."

Face

One of the important functions of interpersonal communication is to form and maintain interpersonal relationships (intimate or distant, friendly versus antagonistic, etc.). Culture defines the nature of these relationships between people and their intercultural interpersonal communication.

You will recall from Chapter 3 that one important dimension of interpersonal relationships, especially in most Asian cultures, is *face*, defined as the public self-image that an individual wants to present in a particular social context. Most European Americans have at best a vague idea that face is important to Asians, although Erving Goffman (1959) claims that everyone is concerned with how they present themselves in everyday life. Human behavior is acted out on the stage of life, with the "actors" often being very conscious of the audience to whom they are "playing." For this reason, Goffman (1959) titled his well-known book *The Presentation of Self in Everyday Life*.

Goffman argued that individuals engage in *impression management*, communication and other behaviors that are intended to support another person's definition of the situation. An illustration is provided by a *maq-*

uiladora (a female Mexican worker in a U.S. owned factory on the U.S.-Mexico border) who told her manager that her machine was not working right. He told her to take a break while he fixed the machine. He reported, "I messed around with the machine, and pretended to 'fix' it. When the woman came back from her break, I told her that I had taken care of the problem. . . ." (Lindsley & Braithwaite, 1996). The boss supported the *maquiladora*'s definition of the situation, so that she would not lose face.

Face is particularly important for the Japanese, Chinese, and other Asians and Asian Americans who share a collectivistic culture. These individuals are extremely concerned with how they will appear to others around them. They wish to avoid looking foolish or inept and to avoid making a social error that could lead to guilt or shame. Much attention is given to maintaining positive interpersonal relationships with peers. In order to help another person maintain face, one should pay compliments, be deferential, and offer frequent apologies for oneself. One should not criticize Asian persons in public situations, as this act might harm the individual's face. For example, a North American teaching English as a foreign language in Japan playfully said in class to a favorite student: "You are a lazy student." This student did not talk to the teacher for the next several weeks and was very hurt by the teacher's joking comment. The student had lost face.

The importance of maintaining positive relationships with others in Japan is suggested by the fact that there is no equivalent Japanese word for the English word "communication." Instead, the Japanese word meaning human relationships is used, implying that the function of communicating, at least originally in Japanese culture, was to create and maintain interpersonal relationships.

A distinction can be made between maintaining someone else's face versus your own. In collectivistic cultures like Asia, the maintenance of other-face predominates. In individualistic cultures, attention to self-face is more important. Even then, Asians attend to self-face more than do North Americans. Yet, face is not unimportant in an individualistic culture like the United States. Bosses are advised to praise their employees publicly but to offer criticism and suggestions for improved performance in private, in a one-on-one situation.

Case Illustration:
The Guest Who Came to Dinner, in Japan[8]

The first puzzle when invited to dinner in Japan is whether or not the host really means it. The invitation may be just a polite but meaningless gesture, something similar to what North Americans mean when they say, "Hi, how are you?" and respond, "Oh, I'm just fine." Etiquette requires that any dinner invitation in Japan should be declined initially. If the hostess continues to insist on the invitation, even after it is declined several times, the guest may accept.

The hostess may then ask the guest to state a food preference. However, Japanese politeness demands that one should not make demands of others. So the hostess's question should be answered by the guest insisting on a complete lack of food preference. Finally, after more urging, it would be appropriate to mention a very simple dish like ochazuke, a bowl of rice with tea poured over it.

When the guest arrives for dinner, a sumptuous meal is served, with ochazuke as the final dish. The guest, of course, expected a large meal but nevertheless should act surprised. Both host and guest say what they do not mean and understand that their counterpart is doing the same thing. Hosts and guests are thus in collusion, acting out their parts in the everyday drama of Japanese social life.

In Japanese culture, a person's home is very private, and most invitations to dinner involve going to a restaurant. The dinner party may sit on tatami mats, probably in a private room. A female waitress serves food and drinks, and participates in a passive role in the discussion. As the dinner guests become boisterous under the influence of alcohol, her initial giggles may give way to uninhibited laughter. She may accept offers of sake (rice wine) or beer, but she drinks in moderation compared to the guests.

A strict protocol governs the drinking of sake or beer. An elementary rule is that an individual never refills his or her own cup or glass. Instead, another person will do the pouring. The individual with the empty cup or glass is expected to hold it during the pouring process rather than to leave it on the table. The pourer may not even wait for the cup or glass to be empty and instead may hold the bottle in front of the other person, tilted at a slight angle, so as to suggest that that person's cup or glass should be emptied. It is socially difficult to refuse an offer of a drink. The collectivism of Japanese culture is evidenced in drinking behavior. Everyone in the dinner party consumes drinks at about the same rate, due to the custom of filling each others' cups or glasses. Also, everyone probably drinks more than they would otherwise. "In a party, it takes very little alcohol to induce loud talking, shouting, loud laughter, singing and clapping of hands in unison. . . ." (Befu, 1974).

Thus group solidarity is developed. The host orders the same dishes for everyone, so they all eat the same meal. This fosters a commonness of experience and a sense of equality. The entire party shares in a joint conversation, instead of breaking up into twos and threes (unless the party consists of a large number of people). A successful dinner entails each participant acting out his/her role. For example, individuals of higher status should be allowed to dominate the discussion most of the time. Supporting actors may introduce a topic of conversation but should defer to the principal actors when they are interrupted. The supporting cast should express exaggerated surprise and interest in the remarks of senior individuals. The drama of the dinner party cannot be enacted successfully unless all of the supporting cast follow their script, that is, the informal rules for the dinner party.

Now imagine that a principal guest at the dinner party is a North American who does not know the informal rules for a Japanese dinner party. Such visitors will not know to fill others' sake cups or beer glasses and may not hold their own cups or glasses to be filled. Also, the foreigners may not act as influenced by the alcohol as their Japanese counterparts, thus serving as a drag on the party. The social clumsiness of the guests is overlooked by the Japanese, who extend themselves to great lengths to avoid making strangers look awkward. After entertaining North Americans, many Japanese say they are exhausted.

Listening

Communication is a two-way process; for every person speaking there is usually someone who is listening. The receiving role in the communication process is just as important as the sending role, although it has received much less attention from communication scholars (at least until recent years). The average individual spends about half of all waking hours listening, and students spend much more than that.

Most of us are not very effective listeners, because we are passive instead of active listeners. One reason for our inattentiveness while listening is because humans typically speak at about 125 to 150 words per minute, while individuals can listen at a rate of 400 words per minute. During our spare time as a listener, we often let our mind wander to other topics. Such inattentive listening often occurs during lecture classes. Twenty minutes after a lecture, listeners can remember only about half of the message content. One hour after the lecture, remembering drops to 40 percent; one day later this figure is 35 percent, and after two days it is 30 percent. One week after the lecture, listeners can remember 27 percent, and after two weeks, 25 percent (Steinfatt, 1997).

These data reflect the abilities of average individuals. Certain persons have a fantastically acute ability to remember. For example, A. R. Luria (1968), a Russian psychologist, described a man he calls "S," who worked as a reporter for a Moscow newspaper. S did not take notes each morning when the editor read out a long list of story assignments. The editor thought S was being inattentive and threatened to fire him. S then rattled off not only his own story assignments, but also those of all the other reporters. The editor promptly ordered S to go to a psychologist. Luria tested S in every way that he could devise. For example, he asked S to listen to a long list of numbers, and then repeat them, forwards, backwards, crosswise, diagonally, and from a random starting point. S had a memory that was apparently unlimited.

Undergraduate students could understandably long for S's ability as a mnemonist. Unfortunately, S lost his job at the newspaper. He could only report facts and was unable to write a news story that made sense out of the facts. He could not detect relationships among the facts that he obtained to create a news article. Was S an effective listener? One principle of listening is to listen through the words in order to detect central themes. The listener should entertain various possible meanings, without filling in the gaps in what is said. A good listener demonstrates attentiveness, does not interrupt, and is cautious in asking questions of the speaker. A listener should control his/her emotions and avoid being distracted. Listening demonstrates caring for the speaker and the topic.

Active listening consists of five steps: (1) hearing, or exposure to the message, (2) understanding, when we connect the message to what we already know, (3) remembering, so that we do not lose the message content, (4) evaluating, thinking about the message and deciding whether or not it is valid, and (5) responding, when we encode a return message based on what we have heard and what we think of it.

Cultural factors affect each of these five components of active listening. In many cultures where rote learning is required, evaluating the message that was heard may be discouraged. Responding may not be valued in cultures that consider it impolite to ask a speaker (like a teacher) a question, and to disagree would be unthinkable. "How one indicates that one is paying attention is different for each culture" (Hall, 1969). Many of the difficulties in communication between culturally unalike individuals may be due to cultural factors in listening behavior. It is often problematic as to whether one's conversation partner is tuned in or not.

Summary

Linguistic relativity is the degree to which language influences human thought and behavior. Evidence for the influence of language on how people think is provided (1) by the greater richness of one language than another in the number of words for an object (for example, the thousands of words in Diné for the English equivalent of the infinitive "to go"), and (2) by the lack of any word in a language for some object, which may restrict the ability of the speakers of that language to think about the object. It is difficult to understand a culture until one is fluent in the language of that culture.

Perception is the way in which an individual gives meaning to an object. Perceptions count, in the sense that they affect individuals' behavior. Perceptions are more important than objective reality in determining an individual's behavior; what an individual perceives is what matters. Culture shapes an individual's perceptions and thus the individual's behavior. In addition, individuals negotiate meaning through communication with one another. George Herbert Mead labelled this exchange of information *symbolic interactionism*, defined as the theory that individuals act toward objects on the basis of meanings and perceptions that are formed through communication with others.

Cultural factors are important in intercultural conversation, as evidenced by (1) *talk and silence*, (2) *speaking style*, (3) *turn-taking*, the process through which the participants in a conversation decide who will talk first, next, and so forth, and (4) *self-disclosure*, the degree to which an individual reveals personal information about himself/herself to another person. Also affected by culture is the importance of *message content* versus *relationship content*. Similarly, maintaining *face*, or the public self-image that an individual wants to present in a particular situation, is a value that varies depending on the culture. *Code-switching* is the process in which two or more individuals change from speaking one language to another language during a conversation.

Listening is an often overlooked skill which can be of primary importance in learning about another culture—as long as one is careful to remember that listening itself is conditioned by culture.

Notes

[1] Earlier writers often referred to linguistic relativity as the Sapir-Whorf hypothesis. Edward Sapir was Professor of Anthropology at Yale University and encouraged Whorf's thinking, but Whorf developed the work independently of Sapir (Whorf, 1956; Lee, 1996). Nevertheless, linguistic relativity is often referred to as the Whorf-Sapir or the Sapir-Whorf hypothesis.

[2] Lee's (1996) *The Whorf Theory Complex* provides the most thorough presentation of Whorf's ideas.

[3] Whorf was later influenced to think about relativity by Sapir, who in turn was influenced by Albert Einstein's theory of relativity (Lee, 1996). Whorf's knowledge of gestalt psychology encouraged him to think about whole configurations. Whorf first used the expression linguistic relativity only in the last year or two of his life.

[4] Actually, the Inuit language does *not* have a dozen words for snow, but if it did, it would be an excellent classroom example (Pullum, 1991).

[5] Much of this research is summarized in Steinfatt (1988, 1989).

[6] A summary of this linguistic relativity research on color is provided by Steinfatt (1988; 1989) and by Lucy (1992, pp. 127–87).

[7] This case illustration was prepared by two Québécois and is used with their permission.

[8] This case illustration is based on Befu (1974).

Chapter 6

Nonverbal Communication

66 [Nonverbal communication is] an elaborate code that is written nowhere, known by none, and understood by all. 99

Edward Sapir (1935)

Most individuals, even if they have not formally studied the field of nonverbal communication, know that it is very important in everyday conversation. Nonverbal communication is particularly important when one's language ability is limited, such as when one is sojourning in another culture. But most individuals, until they have studied the topic, think that nonverbal communication is just hand gestures (such as the thumb-and-forefinger circle signalling "okay" in the United States, but an obscenity overseas). There is much more to nonverbal communication, such as space, touching, time, odors, and even the manner in which one speaks (such as the loudness of one's voice). This chapter summarizes what has been learned about nonverbal communication, especially as it applies to intercultural communication.

Why do most people find the study of nonverbal communication so fascinating? Much nonverbal communication is unintentional and unconscious—and therefore cannot be as easily controlled as verbal communication. It is difficult to lie nonverbally. Most people are not fully aware of nonverbal communication until they study it, which is why Edward Hall referred to it as a hidden dimension or a silent language. The top scholars in nonverbal communication do not feel that they understand even a small part of the nonverbal communication behavior that occurs in everyday speech. At one time, some critics of research on nonverbal communication opposed such study out

161

of concern that once the silent language code was broken, we would all be completely transparent. That criticism demeans the significance of nonverbal communication. It implies that it is a simple code which can be broken and easily understood. In fact, it is a field of multiple nuances which we have only begun to explore.

Importance of Nonverbal Communication

Nonverbal communication is defined as all types of communication that take place without words. As is generally characteristic of anything that is defined as the absence of something else, nonverbal communication includes a very wide range of communication behaviors—everything from a nod, to the wave of a hand, to wearing a new suit, to arriving five minutes early for an appointment. All of these activities and artifacts transmit meaning, so they are considered to be communication. None involve words, so they are examples of nonverbal communication.

Mehrabian and Ferris (1967) and Mehrabian and Wiener (1967) analyzed the amount of meaning that is conveyed in everyday communication situations through facial and vocal expressions (two types of nonverbal communication) versus actual words.

1. Facial expressions. 55%
2. Paralanguage (the way in which words are said, rather than their verbal content) 38%
3. Verbal communication (the words themselves) 7%

    Total   100%

While there is other evidence for the importance of nonverbal communication, especially facial expressions (Figure 6-1), the finding of 93 percent of the meaning of communication (above) may be too high. Other research suggests that about two-thirds of the meaning in an interaction is conveyed by nonverbal communication, and about one-third by verbal communication (Birdwhistell, 1955; Burgoon, 1994). The relative importance of nonverbal communication varies greatly with the communication situation. In highly technical presentations the verbal message carries the vast majority of the information, while in an intimate relationship the verbal message may be almost irrelevant. Further, nonverbal communication may be particularly revealing in some types of communication situations, such as job interviews, first impressions, expressions of attitudes, and in therapy (Burgoon, 1994, p. 235).

When conversing by telephone, e-mail, or other telecommunication channels, the social presence of one's co-participant is missing. Sensing the presence of one's communication partner is an important nonverbal influence. For instance, stutterers seldom stutter when talking on the telephone (pre-

Figure 6-1.   Facial expressions are the most important type of nonverbal communication. The six facial emotions (anger, fear, disgust, surprise, sadness, and happiness) shown here (not necessarily in this order) have been found to be cultural universals; that is, individuals in widely different cultures recognize the emotions in these facial expressions (Ekman & others, 1987; Matsumoto & others, 1989). Can you identify each of the six universal human emotions shown here?

Source: These photographs are based on research by various nonverbal communication scholars.

sumably because they do not perceive the social presence of the other person). Most individuals do not blush at something said by another person if they are in the dark. Being within sight of one's communication partner has an important influence on interpersonal communication. Nonverbals do not always overpower verbal messages, of course. In many situations, verbal communication is far more important in conveying meanings than is nonverbal communication. For example, verbal communication is relatively more important in a low-context culture like the United States than in a high-context culture.

Why is nonverbal communication so important?

1. *Nonverbal communication is present everywhere.* There is no way to avoid communicating nonverbally. Even the decision *not* to speak is a message, such as when you do not talk with the person sitting next to you on an airplane. Watzlawick, Beavin, and Jackson (1967) suggested it is impossible to not communicate. In other words, you cannot stop someone from making inferences about your nonverbal behavior, even if you are not intentionally sending a message. This statement is certainly true of nonverbal communication. Much nonverbal communication is unconscious and unintentional. As Edward Hall (1959) warned, "We must never assume that we are fully aware of what we communicate to someone else." Often, we do not know what we are saying nonverbally.

2. *Nonverbal communication usually comes first* (Burgoon & others, 1996, p. 6). Even before individuals open their mouths, they have communicated nonverbally by their posture, their clothing, whether they remain sitting, and so forth. During the initial impressions between two or more people, when there is a high degree of uncertainty in the communication situation (see Chapter 4), nonverbal communication is particularly important. When strangers meet, nonverbal communication often determines whether or not verbal interaction will occur.

3. *Nonverbal communication is especially likely to be trusted.* When nonverbal communication contradicts verbal communication, nonverbal communication wins out. Because it is difficult for individuals to control their nonverbal messages, such messages are perceived as more valid. It is difficult to lie nonverbally (because so much of nonverbal communication is unconscious), although with practice it can sometimes be done. However, under certain circumstances, even nonverbal communication can be deceptive. Facial expressions and other nonverbal cues are carefully watched in card games, such as poker, in order to determine if a card player is bluffing. Some professionals, like psychiatrists, study a patient's nonverbal behavior (such as armpit sweating and the dilation of the pupils of the eyes) in order to understand what the patient is *really* "saying."

4. *Nonverbal communication can lead to misunderstanding, especially when verbal messages are missing or limited.* Consider the

example of a young photographer who was flown to a remote location in Alaska for the summer (Burgoon & others, 1996, p. 6). When the fall weather began turning cold, his father became alarmed and sent a plane to look for him. When the pilot flew over the photographer's camp, the photographer waved his red jacket liner (which to pilots is a signal waving someone *away*), gave a thumbs-up gesture, and walked casually to his campsite. The pilot left, concluding that the young photographer was okay.

When the photographer's frozen body was found some weeks later, his diary indicated that he had been thrilled to see the plane, waving his jacket liner in the air and signaling thumbs-up to express his elation at being found. He then moved to his campsite in expectation that the plane would land. He could not believe it when the plane banked and flew away.

If two participants in a communication situation do not share the same meaning for a nonverbal symbol, the results will be miscommunication. The "language" of nonverbal symbols differs from culture to culture, just as verbal language does.

5. ***Nonverbal communication is especially important in intercultural communication situations.*** Notice that in the Alaskan example above, words were missing entirely in the communication process. When verbal and nonverbal communication are redundant, misunderstandings are less likely to occur. Each type of communication can reinforce the other. When the verbal fluency of the communication participants is limited, nonverbal reinforcement may clarify the intended meaning.

The corollary is that it is imperative to learn the nonverbal codes of the other participants. As Edward Hall (1981, p. 76) reminds us, "We have specialized the language of the body so it is integrated and congruent with everything else we do. It is therefore culturally determined and must be read against a cultural backdrop." All communication takes place in a particular context. In the United States, it is perfectly acceptable to yell in the context of a football game; the same behavior in a classroom context is not acceptable. Culture is an important aspect of the context for communication encounters. If you do not know the rules that apply to a particular context, you can unknowingly create serious misunderstanding, as the following case illustration shows.

Case Illustration:
The Meaning of Feet in Intercultural Negotiation

Bill Richardson, a former Democratic congressman from New Mexico and a relative novice at international negotiation, suddenly became a celebrity by rescuing hostages from some particularly hostile places in the mid-1990s. It began in February, 1994, when Richardson delivered a message from President Clinton to Burmese freedom leader Aung San Suu Kyi, who had won the Nobel Peace Prize for her defiant protests against the repressive government of Burma. Suu Kyi was under house arrest in Rangoon. She had not been allowed to have a visitor for five years, but Richardson was able to talk to her.

Next, Richardson managed a delicate negotiation with North Korea to release the pilot of a U.S. helicopter that had crashed after straying off course. He then secured the release of a Texas heroin smuggler from life imprisonment in a Bangladeshi prison.

In December 1996, the congressman was successful in negotiating the release of three Red Cross workers from detention in Sudan. A rebel leader, Commander Karabino, had demanded $2.5 million in ransom. He intended to purchase arms and other military equipment. Richardson learned that the rebel leader's two-year-old daughter had died two days previously from measles, and his four-year-old son was ill. Richardson asked to see the boy.

Richardson told Karabino, "You've got children dying, your own children." The congressman suggested that instead of the $2.5 million ransom, vaccines and health care workers would be of greater value to the Sudanese rebels. Then Richardson stood up and threatened to end the negotiations. Reluctantly, Commander Karabino agreed to free the hostages in exchange for the medical assistance.

Within just a few years, Congressman Richardson compiled an enviable winning streak in freeing prisoners. In December 1996, President Clinton appointed Richardson as U.S. Ambassador to the United Nations, a position in which Richardson continued to use his considerable negotiating skills for a more peaceful world.

However, Richardson has also made some monumental errors. In 1995, Richardson went to Iraq to convince Saddam Hussein to release two U.S. citizens who had mistakenly crossed from Kuwait into Iraq. After three hours of negotiations with Hussein, Richardson unthinkingly crossed his legs, showing the bottom of one shoe to Saddam (Figure 6-2). This nonverbal act is a major insult in Arab cultures. Saddam immediately stomped out of the room. When the negotiations resumed, Richardson appealed to Hussein on a humane basis, urging him to: "Think of the prisoners' families. The men are innocent. They got lost. They shouldn't have to pay for our [U.S./Iraq] differences" (quoted in Robinson, 1995). Eventually, the Iraqi leader agreed to free the prisoners. Congressman Richardson instinctively grabbed Saddam's arm to express his gratitude. This was another faux pas. The dictator's guards immediately leveled their weapons at Richardson.

How did Richardson learn to be effective in intercultural negotiation? He absorbed Spanish from his Mexican mother and studied French at Tufts University, where he earned a degree in diplomacy. Yet, learning a language does not necessarily assure the acquisition of cultural norms. On the basis of his dealings with Saddam Hussein, it seems that Richardson still had much to learn about nonverbal communication.

Figure 6-2.   Many North Americans are unaware that showing the bottom of the shoe to an individual is an insult in Arabic (and many other) cultures. Here we see an example of how the meaning of a nonverbal act varies from one culture to another.

Source: Photograph by Kathryn Sorrells. Used by permission.

The Evolution of Nonverbal Communication

The scholarly study of nonverbal communication has a long history, tracing back 140 years to Charles Darwin. More recent scholars, including Edward Hall, George Trager, and Raymond Birdwhistell, have made important contributions to understanding the importance of nonverbal communication in intercultural communication.

Charles Darwin

Charles Darwin (1809–1882) was born into a wealthy English family. He studied at Cambridge University but was not a serious student, often skipping classes in order to go hiking, hunting, or fishing. After his graduation, Darwin was invited to travel as a naturalist on the HMS *Beagle* in its five-year trip around the world. This British Navy ship sailed across the Atlantic, down the coast of South America and back up the other side, across the Pacific to Australia, past India and under South Africa, and then back to England. Darwin frequently went ashore, often for months at a time, to collect specimens and to make observations.

His most important stop was in the Galápagos Islands, in the Pacific Ocean off the coast of Ecuador. Here Darwin observed that each of the Galápagos Islands had a different species of finch. Each species had characteristics that were particularly appropriate for the ecological conditions of its island. For instance, the finches on one island had a strong beak for crushing seeds. On another island, the finches had adapted by grasping and manipulating a cactus thorn to dig insects out of plants. The way in which the birds fit into the unique conditions of each island was all the more amazing because all of the finches had evolved originally from a common ancestor. Darwin began to wonder how such evolution had occurred. The main islands of the Galápagos were separated by a distance of thirty to fifty miles, so that the finches could not fly between them. The varying conditions on each island, and their isolation, had contributed to the evolution of different species. But how had such a process taken place?

When he returned from his journey Darwin pondered over his field notes and his specimens. He began to write up his conclusions in his famous book, *The Origin of Species* (Darwin, 1859). Its publication created a firestorm of public reaction. Darwin's evolutionary theory stated that a new species originates because, given the variation within any population, certain individuals possess characteristics that ideally fit them for survival in a particular environment (hence Darwin's famous expression, "survival of the fittest"). These individuals, such as the finches with stronger beaks on one of the Galápagos Islands, become more numerous in the gene pool over time. Nature acts as a selective force, weeding out the individuals in a population who are less appropriate for a given environment. Thus a new species evolves. Darwin called his theory evolution by natural selection. Religious leaders strongly objected to Darwin's evolutionary theory, which they claimed implied that humans had descended from apes. His theory contradicted the Biblical explanation provided by the book of Genesis.

In his book *The Expression of Emotions in Man and Animals*, published thirteen years after his *The Origin of Species*, Darwin (1872/1965, p. 364) stated: "The movements of expression give vividness and energy to our spoken words." In this book, Darwin showed the basic similarity between the emotional expressions by humans and by animals. He argued that animals expressed six universal emotions of anger, fear, disgust, surprise, sadness, and happiness in a similar way to humans. Darwin compared the facial expressions of infants, children, and adults (including the mentally ill) with animals (like apes and dogs). Facial expressions of emotions appear early in life, and learning may not be required for their appearance. So the six universal facial expressions among humans must be innate, that is, inherited. The particular patterns of facial muscle movement associated with certain emotions stem from a genetic source rather than being learned. Note that Darwin's work dealt only with facial expression, not with body movements or other types of nonverbal communication. Facial expressions of emotion are by far the most important type of nonverbal communication, so it was understandable why Darwin studied them.

The fundamental similarity between the facial expression of emotions by humans and by animals, Darwin suggested, might indicate that both species had developed from a common ancestor. Darwin (1872/1965, p. 12) wrote: "With mankind, some expressions, such as the bristling of the hair under the influence of extreme terror, or the uncovering of the teeth under that of furious rage, can hardly be understood, except on the belief that man once existed in much lower and animal-like condition." Darwin felt that human emotional expressions could not be understood without understanding the emotional expressions of animals because our human expressions are in large part determined by evolution (Ekman, 1973, p. ix).

While all individuals may smile in order to show happiness, a smile may also convey quite different emotions in some cultures. For example, a smile may mean embarrassment or pain. A communication professor from the United States who was teaching in Bangkok stated: "What does it feel like to re-learn all the codes for communicating? . . . Thailand is a country where even some of the nonverbal codes are different. . . . People smile when they are angry, laugh when physically hurt or when expressing dissatisfaction. How does a Westerner avoid being confused in such circumstances?" (Judith Lee, quoted in DeWine, 1995). The professor describes hitting a pothole in the sidewalk with her child's stroller, sending the child sprawling. She cries. Half a dozen Thais are watching. They laugh or smile, leaving the professor extremely puzzled. She wondered what they found humorous about the accident to her child. Actually, the Thais were not amused; they laughed as a way of showing their embarrassment for the child and its mother and to signify relief that the child was not seriously hurt. It is easy and natural to misunderstand the meaning of nonverbal messages interculturally.

Paul Ekman, a leading scholar of nonverbal communication, summarized the details provided by Darwin a century after publication of Darwin's book, *The Expression of Emotions*. Ekman concluded that Darwin's ideas were largely supported: "Many of Darwin's observations, and a large part of his theoretical explanations and forecasts, are substantiated by current knowledge" (Ekman, 1973, p. ix). Darwin noted that facial expressions are in part unconscious and are not completely controllable, so this type of nonverbal communication is more likely to be believed by other people than are verbal statements. Darwin (1872/1965, p. 364) noted that it is difficult to lie nonverbally: "They [nonverbal facial expressions] reveal the thoughts and intentions of others more truly than do words, which may be falsified."

This hypothesis about the greater truthfulness of nonverbal communication has been studied in numerous investigations since Charles Darwin proposed it. *Nonverbal communication, compared to verbal communication, is less effective when one is trying to deceive another person* (Ekman & Friesen, 1969).

Edward Hall at the FSI

In Chapter 2, we traced the key role of the anthropologist Edward Hall in launching the field of intercultural communication in the Foreign Service Institute after World War II. In the minds of Hall and his colleagues at the FSI in the early 1950s, nonverbal communication *was* intercultural communication. Hall pioneered research on proxemics (the use of space) and chronemics (the use of time) in communication, while his FSI coworker Raymond Birdwhistell identified kinesics (body language) as a type of nonverbal communication. George Trager did original research on paralanguage, the nonvocal aspects of voice, such as loudness.

Like Darwin,[1] Hall noted that nonverbal communication was usually out-of-consciousness and thus was more difficult to fake. Hall was very influenced by Sigmund Freud, the Viennese founder of psychoanalytic theory (Rogers & Hart, 1998). In *The Silent Language*, Hall (1959a, pp. 59–60) stated: "Freud distrusted the spoken word, and a good deal of his thinking was based on the assumption that words hid much more than they revealed." Hall's expression "out-of-consciousness" came directly from Freud. The hidden dimension of nonverbal communication is particularly intriguing to individuals when first learning about communication without words.

Chapter 2 outlined the many contributions of Hall to the study of nonverbal communication. Later researchers have followed up on leads provided by Hall and his collaborators at the Foreign Service Institute. Today, nonverbal communication is a standard offering in college curricula.

Raymond Birdwhistell

Raymond L. Birdwhistell, who spent much of his career at the University of Pennsylvania, was briefly a colleague of Edward Hall's at the Foreign Service Institute in the summer of 1952. An anthropologist and linguist by training, Birdwhistell specialized in studying body movements, including facial expressions, which he called "kinesics" (Birdwhistell, 1970). Body language is particularly important to diplomats, who often may not have perfect fluency in a language and who need to understand nonverbal cues in the frequently ambiguous communication situation of international diplomacy.

The first publication about kinesics was Birdwhistell's (1952) FSI training manual, *Introduction to Kinesics*.

Birdwhistell insisted that nonverbal communication could not be completely separated from verbal communication. Both typically take place at the same time; each supplements or contradicts the meanings conveyed by the other. To separate these two types of communication, either in scholarly research or in everyday conversation, would be ridiculous. Birdwhistell pointed out that studying only nonverbal communication would be equivalent to studying noncardiac medicine (Knapp & Hall, 1997, p. 11). Evidence of the virtual impossibility of separating nonverbal and verbal communication is suggested by American Sign Language (ASL), a language used by the one million members of the deaf community (Knapp & Hall, 1997, p. 5). ASL is nonverbal communication in that spoken words are not used, although the signs have the coded meaning of words and thus are a kind of verbal communication. Are the finger and hand movements of signing verbal or nonverbal communication? Or both?

In common communication situations, nonverbal communication messages may (1) contradict, (2) complement, (3) substitute, (4) regulate, or (5) accent or moderate verbal communication messages (Knapp & Hall, 1997, pp. 13–20). Much nonverbal communication is complementary in that it adds to, or clarifies, the verbal message. This redundancy increases message accuracy. Most people gesture with their hands while talking on the telephone, even though their conversation partner cannot detect the nonverbal messages. Why? Because we become so accustomed to the complementary nature of verbal and nonverbal communication that we perform both, even when the nonverbal hand gestures cannot be seen.

Nonverbal communication may substitute for words. Perhaps you have met a friend at the end of a day. From the person's appearance alone, you could predict whether he or she was elated or depressed, tired or energized. In this situation, you were able to save words by your observations. Hand gestures are often utilized to regulate a conversation. A glance at your conversation partner may be important in signaling turn-taking. Nonverbal communication may amplify or tone down a verbal message. For example, when scolding someone, we often frown. Or, if we want to moderate the verbal scolding, we may smile at the other person. Thus nonverbal messages allow us to tweak our verbal message to "say" exactly what we wish to convey.

Cultural Factors in Nonverbal Communication

Participants in a communication process adapt to each other's speaking style—for example, by leaning forward, matching the other's speech rate, assuming a similar posture, using similar gestures, or pronouncing words with the same accent. If a communicator rejects the style of the other as culturally inappropriate—for example, by leaning away, intentionally slowing the speech rate, or assuming an uninviting posture—the flow of communication is interrupted. Edward Hall (1981) stated "People in interactions move together in a kind of dance, but they are not aware of their synchronous movement" (p. 72). He found that each culture has its "own characteristic manner of locomotion, sitting, standing, reclining and gesturing . . . Most people are unaware when these are happening. When they become aware, they are unable to pay attention to anything else" (p. 75). When someone from a low-context culture interacts with someone from a high-context culture, the rhythms are likely to be very different and may create such discomfort that communication is jeopardized.

Culture establishes standards for nonverbal behavior. We often have an involuntary reaction to someone violating our expectations about personal space. Our culture specifies behaviors that invite or discourage interaction. We learn nonverbal signals that indicate another person is receptive to being approached—for example, smiling, an open stance, and eye contact. If we use those same cues in interaction with someone from another culture, we could be quite startled by the response. If our expectations are not met, we will probably evaluate the other person negatively based on behavior that conforms to a culture different from our own.

Types of Nonverbal Communication

Throughout the text, our examples have included various types of nonverbal communication. In this section, we will identify seven types of nonverbal communication: kinesics and other body movements, space, time, touch, voice, artifacts, and physical appearance.

Body Movements

Kinesics is a type of nonverbal communication that involves body movement and activities (also called body language). The four main types of kinesic communication are: (1) emblems, (2) illustrators, (3) regulators, and (4) affect displays.

Emblems   Emblems are body movements that can be translated into words and that are used intentionally to transmit a message. One type of emblem that is particularly important, perhaps ranking second only to facial expressions, is hand gestures. People talk with their hands. Hand gestures like the thumbs up or the thumb and forefinger circle (okay) sign, the palm outward gesture (silence, or stop), and circling a forefinger near one's head (crazy) all have a widely understood meaning in the United States. But the meanings of these emblems may be quite different in another nation. For example, the thumb and forefinger circle is a sign for the sex act in some Latin American nations (Figure 6-3). So hand gestures can be very confusing interculturally. As with verbal language, nonverbal codes are not universal.

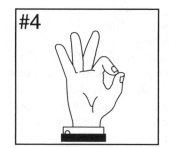

Figure 6-3. People talk with their hands, but what they say depends on their culture. Hand gestures like #1, the finger-cross; #2, the nose thumb; #3, the forearm jerk; and #4, the ring are familiar to most people in the United States. Gesture #5, the chin flick, is virtually unknown in the United States but is commonly understood in Europe. A certain hand gesture may have a different meaning, depending on where one is. For example, Gesture #6, the vertical horn-sign, has one meaning in Austin, Texas, and quite a different meaning in New York City. Gesture #7, the forefinger pointing to the nose, means "Me?" in Japan. In the United States, one would point at one's chest.

Source: These drawings are based on Morris & others (1979).

As an example, a U.S. professor teaching at Bangkok University frequently put his hands in his pockets or held them behind his back while lecturing to his class. At the end of the semester, his polite Thai students gently informed him that individuals should hold their hands in front of them. They had been embarrassed and distracted by his nonverbal cultural error during the class (a course on intercultural communication).

There are gender differences as well as cultural differences in hand gestures. An emblem unique to Japanese women is the hand held in front of the mouth when smiling or laughing. People from the United States perceive this gesture as girlish, polite, and cute. *Only* women in Japan cover their mouth when smiling. Men never do.

In addition to hand gestures, head movements can also communicate nonverbally. Like hand movements, head movements differ from one culture to another. In India the head gesture for a positive response to a question is a sideways movement which is perceived by most non-Indians as a head shake meaning no. But after visiting India for a period of time, the typical *ferengi* (foreigner) is likely to have picked up the sideways head nod. When the person returns to the home country and uses shaking the head sideways to mean yes, further confusion occurs. In Turkey, an up-and-down movement of the head conveys a negative rather than a positive expression (as in the United States).

Illustrators   Illustrators are a type of kinesic behavior that accompanies what is said verbally. As explained previously, hand and body gestures are a natural part of speaking for most individuals. Illustrators include gesturing with one's hands (such as pointing to emphasize a key point), smiling or frowning, and slouching versus standing erect. Illustrators are particularly noticeable when an individual is giving directions to a certain place. Illustrators differ from emblems in that they cannot be translated into words.

Regulators   Regulators are kinesic behaviors that control turn-taking and other procedural aspects of interpersonal communication. A practical necessity in every conversation is to determine who is going to speak first, next, and so on. This process of turn-taking is mainly an unconscious process. Sometimes problems occur, such as when two or more people talk at once and no one can be understood. Usually this behavior occurs when individuals are excited or angry (or when talking on the telephone). In most conversations, turn-taking proceeds smoothly because of regulators like the turn of a head, gaze, and other body movements.

Gaze is an important type of regulator. A speaker who maintains eye contact with members of the audience is perceived as a forceful presenter in the United States. Student teachers are taught to maintain direct eye contact with members of their class. But direct eye contact with elders is perceived as disrespectful by some Native Americans and in Asian cultures like Japan.

It is extremely impolite to gaze at one's grandparent's eyes. Japanese children are taught to gaze at their grandparent's Adam's apple instead.

Navajos avoid the direct, open-faced gaze, even when shaking hands with someone whom they are very glad to see. To maintain direct eye contact is to display anger. Hall (1969) described an adult Navajo in a pickup truck who pulled to a stop, put his head out the window, and chastised two misbehaving boys playing on the roadside. The adult Navajo did not utter a word. He just gave the boys a direct look.

Appropriate gazing behavior can have important consequences in certain communication situations. Consider the following communication exchanges between applicants for student visas to the United States and U.S. consular officers (Olaniran & Williams, 1995). The applicants are from a high-context culture in West Africa where individuals of lower status avoid direct eye contact with a superior. The officials, however, represent a low-context culture where status and power are believed to be relatively equal, and where direct eye contact is expected and is regarded as an indicator of truthfulness.

> *Official A*: You should look at me when you are speaking, and could you speak louder? I can't hear you [in a commanding voice]. How do you plan to pay for your tuition beyond the first year?
>
> *Applicant X*: My uncle is going to be responsible [looking downward].
>
> *Official A*: Which is which? Your uncle or your father [in an accusatory manner]? You indicated earlier that your father is going to pay your way.

Now consider another visa applicant interview.

> *Official B*: I'd like you to look at me when you speak.
>
> *Applicant Y*: Okay, sir, I'll try [the African visa applicant adjusts his behavior accordingly].
>
> *Official B*: Who is responsible for paying your tuition?
>
> *Applicant Y*: My uncle, Mr. Blank.
>
> *Official B*: So your uncle will be paying your tuition throughout your stay abroad.
>
> *Applicant Y*: Yes sir. There [pointing to a document in the official's hand] is the affidavit from him.
>
> *Official B*: What a nice uncle you must have. . . .

Official B believed the second applicant was truthful and awarded him a student visa to the United States. Applicant X's visa application was rejected.

Affect Displays   Affect displays are kinesic behaviors that express emotions. Facial expressions are one of the most important ways of communicating meaning to another person (see Figure 6-1). For example, surprise is conveyed by arching the eyebrows, opening the eyelids so that the white of the eye shows, and letting the jaw drop open. In contrast, the emotion of fear is shown by raising the eyebrows and drawing them together, while tensing the lips and drawing them back. Disgust is conveyed by wrinkling the nose, lowering the eyebrows, and raising the upper lip. The facial expressions for anger, happiness, and sadness are generally universal across all cultures, but other emotions are expressed differently depending on particular cultural constraints. Rules for expressing emotion vary depending on the culture. All cultures have display rules telling members when it is appropriate to show emotion and when to hide it. Affect displays can occur via crying, laughing, and even by one's posture.

Space

Proxemics is nonverbal communication that involves space. The word proxemics derives from the same Latin root as proximity, implying that one dimension of space is how close or distant two or more people are located (Figure 6-4).

One of Edward Hall's main interests in the study of nonverbal communication was space as it affected human communication. He was influenced by Heini P. Hediger's (1955) analysis of how certain animals spaced themselves. For example, Hediger, the director of the Zoological Garden in Zurich, took a remarkable photograph of a dozen blackheaded gulls spaced evenly along a rail that was suspended over the water. While living in Chicago, Hall (1966, p. 84) took photographs of people who spaced themselves equally along a streetcar waiting platform (Figure 6-5). One of Hall's research techniques in studying proxemics was to show a respondent a photograph that had been cut in half vertically; each half showed a person. The respondent was asked to move the two pieces of the photograph closer and closer until the people seemed to be spaced "about right." Then Hall analyzed why some respondents moved the two figures closer while other respondents placed them farther apart.

How physically close or distant two people stand when they talk tells a great deal about their relationship. Hall (1955) stated: "A U.S. male . . . stands eighteen to twenty inches away when talking face to face with a man he does not know very well; talking to a women under similar circumstances, he increases the distance about four inches. A distance of only eight to thirteen inches between males is considered . . . very aggressive." Yet in Latin America and the Middle East, "distances which are almost sexual in connotation are the only ones at which people can talk comfortably. . . . If you are a Latin American, talking to a North American at the distance he insists on maintaining is like trying to talk across a room" (Hall, 1955).

When a European American talks with a Latin American, the former feels that the Latin American is uncomfortably "pushy" or trying to be intimate, while the Latin American perceives the person from the United States as cold and remote. Arabic people from the Middle East do not feel that someone is

Figure 6-4. The spatial distance between the two Latino people when they converse is closer than it would be between non-Latinos. Edward T. Hall (1955) said that conversations between same-sex European Americans take place at a distance of 18 to 20 inches, while Latino individuals stand much closer while talking, perhaps at a distance of only 8 to 13 inches.

Source: Photograph by Kathyrn Sorrells. Used by permission.

friendly unless they are standing close enough to smell the garlic on the other's breath.[2] Clearly, there are strong cultural differences in perception of the appropriate space between people involved in interpersonal communication. Often this nonverbal dimension is unconscious.

People are often unaware that their culture has assigned meaning to the distances between communicators. Instead of thinking to oneself, "The person behind me in line must be from another country because he is comfortable standing shoulder to shoulder," the more common reflex would be, "what a rude person." Even if we are aware that cultures have different definitions of appropriate spacing, our emotions often override that information—visceral reactions provide further evidence of the pervasiveness of

Figure 6-5. Edward Hall, influenced by the photographs by Hediger of the approximately equal spacing of gulls perched on a rail, took these photographs in Chicago as part of his research on proxemics.

Source: Box 32 of the E.T. Hall Papers, Special Collections, University of Arizona Library. Used with permission.

cultural teachings. Proxemics convey a very important message about interpersonal relationships, but the definitions are culture-bound. In the United States, a smaller social distance indicates intimacy and communicates a close personal relationship. In other cultures, one cannot use the same standards to interpret relationships.

When people are forced by a building, a room, or other constraints to stand at a distance closer than their culture would indicate is appropriate for conversation, they seldom talk. For example, have you observed communication among people on a crowded elevator? They generally avoid eye contact, remain silent, and tense their bodies. Touching another person, even accidentally, is embarrassing and leads to an apology. Each individual acts as though he/she were surrounded by a thin bubble of space that should not be penetrated.

Most Euro-Americans view crowding as distasteful and seek to avoid it. Japanese people, on the other hand, generally prefer crowding, at least under certain conditions. There is no Japanese word for "privacy" (Hall, 1966, p. 152). Many Asian cultures place a high value on not being alone. Indonesians feel very ill at ease if they are the only person in their home at night and usually invite a friend to sleep over.

Space affects human communication in many other ways. For instance, whether or not individuals remain behind their desks when visitors enter their offices is an unstated message about friendliness or formality. Classroom arrangements of desks and chairs can determine how much discussion takes place in a class. A circular arrangement generally encourages discussion, while sitting in rows often discourages student participation. Have you noticed that where a student sits in a classroom with several rows of chairs affects the degree of participation of that student in class discussion? Nonverbal communication scholars have observed a "zone of participation" in most classrooms, which is shaped like the letter T. The most active participants sit in the front row (and hence have closer eye contact with the teacher) or in the middle of the classroom from front to back (thus just in front of the teacher when he/she is centered in front of the class (Figure 6-6).

Do students who sit in the zone of participation do so because they want to talk in class, or does sitting in this zone lead them to participate more? Classroom seating (unless it is assigned) is not random. Certain people tend to sit in the zone of participation, enjoy a greater degree of eye contact with the teacher, and thus participate to a higher degree. In one study, students who were previously identified as low and high participators were assigned to seats in and out of the zone of participation. Location in the zone of participation encouraged talking for all but the extreme low-participators (who still did not want to talk in class).

Religious values may affect spatial arrangements. For example, the Navajo always build their hogans (six- or eight-sided one-story structures) facing

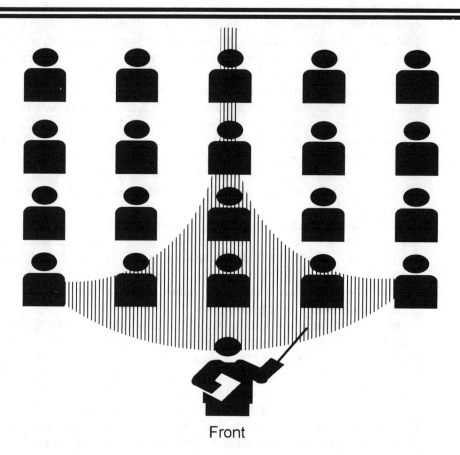

Front

Figure 6-6.   The zone of participation in the usual classroom is depicted in this diagram. The heavy participators in class discussion sit across the front and in the center of the classroom. Do you think this high degree of participation is due to these students' eye contact with the teacher or to the tendency for high participators to sit in these seats?

east, in order to face the rising sun. According to traditional beliefs, a Navajo should begin the day by running toward the sun. Islamic people believe that the main entrance of important buildings should face in the direction of Mecca.

One of the authors of this book served as a consultant in the planning of a new school of communication that was located in a Middle Eastern country. He advised mainly on the curriculum, the professors to be hired in various specialties, facilities needed for communication research, and the size of classrooms. A U.S. architectural firm then developed the actual drawings for the construction of the building that was to house the school of communication. At the last minute, just prior to showing the plans to the minister of education for approval, a very serious flaw was detected: the building did not face Mecca. The plan was shifted 90 degrees to correct for this cultural error.

Space also affects who talks to whom. For example, employees in an office whose desks are located closer are more likely to communicate. Families who live in neighboring homes are more likely to become friends than those who live farther away, even though the spatial difference may be negligible. New communication technologies like the Internet may overcome the effect of spatial distance on the frequency of communication. E-mail effectively removes spatial barriers whether two people are working in adjoining buildings or are located across the world from each other.

Space also influences human communication through territoriality—the tendency of individuals to lay claim to, and defend, a space. When one of this book's authors traveled by plane, the airline seating assignments were incorrect (due to a computer error). Many individuals found someone sitting in their seat. These individuals became extremely angry. Take-off was delayed by an hour until the airline flight personnel could straighten out the computer's seating mistakes. Of course, the most extreme examples of territoriality are the wars that have taken place when communication has failed to resolve territorial disputes. Chapter 1 briefly reviewed some of these aggressive, coercive expansions of territoriality. As Edward Hall said, "Space speaks." It does, in a variety of ways.

Time

Another important dimension of nonverbal communication is time. *Chronemics* is the way in which time affects communication. The amount of time elapsed before being considered late for an appointment varies widely from culture to culture. The Japanese are extremely prompt, often to the second, in meeting with someone at an appointed time. It is considered very rude to keep someone waiting even for several minutes. Many Japanese students have *never* been late for a class! In contrast, as we have seen, individuals in Latin America and the Middle East are extremely relaxed about punctuality. The North American guest who arrives at a party at a stated hour is likely to find the host unprepared and other guests arriving as much as several hours later. Clearly the agreed-upon time of an appointment has quite a different meaning to a Japanese, a North American, and a Latin American.

The length of time for a certain type of communication may also be culturally determined. One of the authors of this book was invited by officials in a Japanese advertising agency to a 10:00 A.M. meeting at their office in Tokyo. The topic was interesting, and the discussions were exciting. But after 11:00 A.M., the visitor noticed that he was the only one talking. The Japanese officials seemed to have suddenly lost any interest in the discussion. Later, he learned that the appointment had been pre-set for one hour. Because Japan is a high-context culture, this point was not explained to the visitor. It was assumed that he knew. The Japanese officials had other appointments at 11:00 A.M.

Another intercultural misunderstanding about time began when Edward, a U.S. businessman newly arrived in Venezuela, was having lunch with Carlos, the owner of a printing company (Tolbert & McLean, 1995). Carlos had printed the letterhead stationery for Edward's company. They developed a friendly relationship, which led to the lunch. As they were departing the restaurant, Edward thought of some layout ideas that he wanted to share with Carlos, who said he would be happy to see them. They agreed that Edward would come to Carlos's office the next day at 2:00 P.M.

When Edward arrived at Carlos's office the next day, he was not there. His secretary told Edward that Carlos had left at 1:30 and would not return for the day. Edward said there must have been some mistake because they had made the appointment the previous day. The secretary said that she did not have the appointment scheduled, and she was sorry. Edward was very angry and considered giving future printing jobs to another company. Why did Carlos break the appointment? Do you think that Carlos really was not interested in the layout drawings but did not know how to get this idea across to Edward? Perhaps Carlos forgot to tell his secretary about the appointment. Or do you think that in Venezuela secretaries handle the agenda, so if they are not told about an appointment, it does not exist?

Time can be organized into technical, formal, and informal components. Scientists developed the atomic clock to be the most accurate available; time is measured by the vibration of electrons in cesium atoms. Formal time involves the process of separating units of time into days, weeks, and months. In the United States, formal time is used for precise appointments: government hearings, court dates, job interviews. Informal time in the same culture has a more loosely defined (within limits) approximation: 8:00 can mean anywhere between 8:00 and 8:15 to 8:50. Informal time involves attitudes about punctuality within a culture.

Symbolic uses of time can be related to a person's or culture's orientation. In the West, time is viewed as a linear progression from the past, to the present, to the future. Other cultures do not segment events the same way. Some cultures have a reverence for past (to use the Western designation) experience; they value precedent and reject the present as untested. Other cultures have a future orientation—visions of how life will be. Others find both looking backward and forward irrelevant—the present is what counts.

Language can reveal a culture's attitudes toward time. In the United States we "spend" time; "time is money"; and we ask if we can "have some of your time?" As Edward Hall stated: "Time talks."

Touch

Haptics is nonverbal communication that involves touching. Individuals within a culture vary as to the degree to which they touch while speaking, and there are important differences in touching from culture to culture. Touching is usually intended to convey warmth, caring, and other positive emotions, but it may be playful (like a light slap) or show irritation (a shove). Hugging or kissing as a greeting conveys intimacy.

A set of cultural conventions guides who may touch whom, under what conditions, and where to touch. For instance, same-sex touching in the United States is more permissible than cross-sex touching. Male-to-male touching is much less frequent (except in sports) than female-to-female touching, perhaps out of fear that such touching might be perceived as indicating a sexual preference. The differences in the displays of touching are not only gender based, they are also determined by status. In business, higher-status employees generally initiate touch; lower-status employees are less likely to do so since the behavior could be interpreted as assuming a familiarity which does not exist. What does this disparity of touching behaviors communicate about the structure of workplace relationships? How do other nonverbal behaviors communicate power and/or status differences? Do you think guidelines for sexual harassment in the United States have altered any of this behavior?

Shaking hands is an example of differing cultural perceptions. In the United States, a moist handshake transmits a message that the individual is nervous or anxious. Most people in that culture feel that a firm handshake is appropriate, and that a weak handshake is wimpy. The Massai, who live in Kenya and Tanzania, barely let the palms touch during a handshake. In India, however, where handshaking is not practiced very widely as a form of greeting, a rather limp handshake is culturally appropriate. Indians generally greet each other by holding their palms together in front of their chest, while saying *Nameste* (Hello). An Indian may greet another person, such as a parent or teacher or other highly respected individual by touching his/her feet. In Korea and in Mali a person touches his/her right forearm with the left hand while shaking hands. Moroccans kiss the other person's hand while shaking. Kurdish people in Turkey bargain only while they are shaking hands, and they shake continuously until a deal is completed.

Islamic men may greet each other by embracing and kissing first on one cheek and then on the other, while saying an expression in Arabic like *Salaam aleikum* (Peace be with you). Thais greet each other with a *wai* (pronounced "wī"), which is executed by placing the hands together in a praying position in front of the chest. Greater respect for the other person is shown by doing the *wai* higher (eye level is the highest that people go). Japanese people greet each other with a bow. The depth of the bow depends on the other person's status. Bows entail bending at the waist at about 30 degrees, 45 degrees, or 90 degrees, depending on the relative status of the other person. One should not rise from the bow until the person of higher status has risen. The arms should be at the sides while bowing, and one should gaze downward. What type of greeting is appropriate between a Japanese person and a foreigner? A common greeting in this situation is for the two individuals to bow while shaking hands.

Voice

Paralanguage is vocal communication other than the verbal content. In addition to loudness, paralanguage includes the speed of speaking, accent, tone, and such non-words as grunts or "uh huhs" and other filler-words. Often, hearing a stranger's voice (in a telephone conversation, for example) is sufficient to guess the person's gender, ethnic group, age, and other characteristics. Voice is a means by which individuals can be identified nonverbally.

Loudness of voice when speaking is another type of nonverbal communication. Generally, we speak more loudly when we are more distant from the person we are addressing or when we are in a public speaking situation, such as in a classroom. Males often speak more loudly than females. Asians generally speak softly, with Asian women speaking even more softly than men. Most Thais speak very softly, and it is considered good manners to do so. Thais typically perceive that North Americans are angry, or at least rude, owing to their relatively loud manner of speaking. Emotions such as anger, excitement, or enthusiasm may be conveyed by speaking in a loud voice.

In Arabic nations, males speak loudly in order to indicate sincerity. North Americans consider this volume aggressive and obnoxious (Tubbs & Moss, 1994, p. 429). A Saudi Arabian also lowers his voice in order to show respect for a superior. This leads his North American conversation partner to raise his voice. Soon, both individuals are frustrated and confused.

Artifacts

Artifacts include an individual's clothing, lipstick, wedding ring, eyeglasses, scuffed shoes, and personal possessions like an attaché case or an expensive sports car. The clothing that one wears is an important message in a communication situation. For instance, individuals often ask, when invited to a party or some other event, whether they should dress casually or formally. In this instance, people want to know how other guests will be dressed. Have you ever forgotten to ask the question and arrived in jeans while everyone else was wearing blazers? Did you feel uncomfortable? Did people treat you differently?

Sometimes artifacts are selected for the opposite effect. Younger generations often choose clothing specifically because their parents find it inappropriate. Artifacts make statements. They can communicate belonging or independence. The most uniform dress, conforming precisely with one culture's norms, might be considered outlandish or inappropriate in another culture. Body ornamentation—including tattoos, piercing, or painting—is culturally or co-culturally based.

Physical Appearance

Physical appearance is another type of nonverbal communication. Rule-governed cultural preferences dictate the elements of appearance that are considered physically attractive. In Chapter 5, the case illustration about perceptions of body weight showed important differences between two ethnic groups in America. Physical beauty is more important to U.S. men in dating situations than is male physical attractiveness to women, who prefer intelligence, an outgoing personality, and a man who is considerate. For either gender, however, physical attractiveness is an advantage in interpersonal communication.

Physically attractive (as defined by their particular culture) individuals, particularly women, have higher self-esteem (Knapp & Hall, 1997, p. 205). In the United States, youth is valued over age. Cosmetics can mask the effects of the aging process and have a positive effect on self-image. Physical appearance is especially important during first impressions between strangers.

Figure 6-7.   Types of Nonverbal Communication

1. **BODY MOVEMENTS** (kinesics): physical behaviors such as facial movements, posture, and gestures; facial expressions are the most significant type of nonverbal communication.
   (1) **Emblems**: body movements that can be translated into words and that are used intentionally to transmit a message.
   (2) **Illustrators**: kinesic behaviors that accompany what is said verbally.
   (3) **Regulators**: kinesic behaviors that control turn-taking and other procedural aspects of interpersonal communication.
   (4) **Affect displays**: kinesic behaviors that express emotions.
2. **SPACE** (proxemics): how use of distances and space communicate.
3. **TIME** (chronemics): how orientations toward time communicate.
4. **TOUCH** (haptics): the meaning of touching behaviors and what contact is acceptable.
5. **VOICE** (paralanguage): the nonverbal aspects of voice; *how* something is said rather than what is said.
6. **ARTIFACTS**: communication through choice and arrangement of objects. Clothing, hair style, art, furniture, jewelry, and other personal possessions communicate status, social awareness, and feelings.
7. **PHYSICAL APPEARANCE**: aspects of appearance that communicate attractiveness; perceptions/expectations formulated on body type and physical characteristics.

The Truth about Lying

A great deal of research about deception has been conducted by nonverbal communication scholars in recent years. As explained previously, it is generally more difficult to lie nonverbally than verbally, presumably because nonverbal communication is often out-of-consciousness and thus more difficult for the individual to control than is verbal communication.

Lying may be a life-or-death matter, as in the O.J. Simpson trial. In some situations, such as a poker game, it may be functional to lie. Some animals, like possums, depend on lying for their survival. Individuals, usually as children, learn to lie.

Scholars have determined that the following behaviors are characteristic of individuals when they are lying:

1. More speech errors.
2. Less smiling and more fake smiling.
3. More speech hesitations.
4. Shorter answers, often yes or no.
5. Vague answers, with less specific or concrete information.
6. More slips of the tongue.
7. More allness words like "always" and "never."
8. More blinking and pupil dilation.
9. Longer pauses.

Note that many of these nine indicators of lying are paralanguage or other types of nonverbal behavior. While none of these indicators taken alone is a sure sign of lying, when several of the nine indicators occur together, the probability of lying increases. Paul Ekman found that people talk slightly more softly when they are lying, swallow more often, and drink water more often if it is available. Ekman (1985) taught these understandings to police officers and to U.S. Customs officials, who attained 80 to 90 percent accuracy using his system. The more important the lie is to the liar, the easier it is to detect, presumably because telling an important lie is more stressful.

Cultural Misunderstandings in Nonverbal Communication

How many people from the United States would make at least one of the following mistakes in dealing nonverbally with someone from Japan?

1. Should someone from the United States bow or shake hands with a person from Japan? A person who does not bow may be considered a *henna gaijin* (weird foreigner). If he/she does bow, but does so at the wrong angle or bows in some other unauthentic way, the behavior may still mark him/her as a *henna gaijin*.

2. A smile or laugh in Japan may show surprise or embarrassment and may hide anger or grief. It does not necessarily show happiness, as in the United States.

3. When Japanese want to indicate "Do you mean me?" they point to their nose, instead of to their heart, as in the United States (see Figure 6-3).

4. In the United States, people maintain eye contact when talking with another person, but a Japanese individual often focuses on the other person's Adam's apple, especially if the other is of higher status (as explained previously). This nonverbal act often conveys a sense of insincerity or shiftiness to U.S. communicators, who expect to look into the other person's eyes when talking.

5. If someone from the United States has a tattoo or walks with a slouch, their Japanese counterpart assumes that he/she is a *Yakuza* (Japanese Mafia). The *Yakuza* often have lost the final joint on their little finger, so someone with a missing digit would be very suspect. The U.S. participant is unlikely to understand why slouching, tattoos, and missing finger joints are regarded with such abhorrence by the Japanese.

These are just a few examples from one type of intercultural exchange. Many intercultural communication misunderstandings occur due to nonverbal messages. It is particularly difficult for an individual to learn the nonverbal codes of another culture. Seldom are they described in written form. They sometimes can be learned in specifically assigned training courses (many U.S. businesspeople enroll in such courses before they travel to Japan).

Even if someone knows the nonverbal code of another culture, the unintentional and unconscious nature of nonverbal communication requires that such understandings must be practiced until they become natural to the individual. For a stranger to learn to communicate effectively with the Japanese requires years of living in Japan. Is there any way to speed up this painfully slow process? Reading literature about intercultural communication and taking training courses on this topic may help, but attaining a high level of intercultural competence in nonverbal communication requires very intensive effort.

Summary

Scholarly work on nonverbal communication was begun by Charles Darwin, who studied facial expression among humans and animals. Edward Hall at the Foreign Service Institute in the early 1950s coined the term nonverbal communication. With his colleagues Raymond Birdwhistell and George Trager, Hall developed a typology of nonverbal communication.

Nonverbal communication consists of all types of communication that take place without words. The seven main types of nonverbal communication include kinesics (body movements), proxemics (which involve space), time, touch, voice, artifacts, and physical appearance (see Figure 6-7). Kinesics includes (1) *emblems*, body movements that can be translated into words and that are used intentionally to transmit a message, (2) *illustrators*, a type of emblem that accompanies speech, (3) *regulators*, kinesic behaviors that control turn-taking or other procedural aspects of interpersonal communication, and (4) *affect displays*, kinesic behaviors that express emotions.

Much of nonverbal communication is unintentional and unconscious. An interesting corollary of the unconscious nature of nonverbal behavior is that it is difficult to lie nonverbally. Although nonverbal communication is often at an unconscious level, it greatly influences the messages we send and receive. In order to overcome these hidden barriers, it is particularly important to become aware of cultural differences in nonverbal behavior.

Notes

[1] Hall did not cite Darwin's (1872/1965) *The Expression of Emotion in Man and Animals* in his *The Silent Language* (Hall, 1959a) or in any of his later publications about nonverbal communication.

[2] Olfactics is the way in which odor affects communication. Body smells, perfume/cologne, and other smells may communicate. Each individual has a unique scent, called an olfactory signature.

Chapter *7*

Assimilation, Mass Communication, and Sojourning

" *E pluribus unum* (Out of many, one).

The motto of the United States of America **"**

In 1914 a Broadway theater play, *The Melting Pot*, presented the notion that the United States was becoming a superior society because of its fusion of cultures. The metaphor became immensely popular. It was assumed that immigrants would all be assimilated rapidly—absorbed and blended with mainstream U.S. society. The belief was that "immigrants who came to the United States would, within a relatively short period of time, cast aside their European identities, cultures, and languages as they forged, or were forced to adopt, the loyalties, customs, and language of their new home" (Wilson & Gutiérrez, 1995, p. 6). Henry Ford hired thousands of new immigrants to build his Model Ts. He required all of them to participate in a ceremony on stage where they would climb a ladder into a giant pot in the costumes of their original cultures. As they emerged from the other side of the pot, they would be dressed as "Americans."

Today the United States is a nation composed of an incredibly diverse set of émigré cultures that do not seem to be "melting." As noted previously, a more accurate metaphor is a "tossed salad," as immigrants maintain their native cultures (or at least many aspects therefrom) while adapting to life in another society. The mass media play a number of roles in this process. The dominant English-language media generally encourage assimilation, while the specialized foreign-language media today often promote cultural maintenance.

Assimilation and Acculturation

Assimilation is the degree to which an individual relinquishes an original culture for another. When individuals are assimilated into a mainstream culture, they lose their previous culture. The assimilation process usually occurs as an immigrant gradually learns the language of the host culture, forms friendships with a network of host nationals rather than with fellow immigrants, becomes increasingly exposed to the mass media of the host nation, and gradually cuts ties and identification with the original homeland. This assimilation process may occur over two or more generations. Some cultures resist any acculturation into the host society even after many, many generations. Examples in the United States are Orthodox Jews and the Old Order Amish, who maintain their original culture. The Gypsies are another example (see the case illustration later in this chapter).

Native Americans have suffered greatly from attitudes toward "strangers" and from earlier concerted efforts to bring about their assimilation. We have read briefly about the forced marches to reservations where Native Americans were isolated from the society that took their lands but rejected the people. Labels such as the "Five Civilized Tribes" were applied to the Choctaw, Chickasaw, Cherokee, Creek, and Seminole because of their strong cultural heritage, Christian influences, and "cooperation" with relocation efforts (Vogt, 1998). In 1953 Congress passed House Concurrent Resolution 108 to terminate aid and protection to Native Americans. The belief was that Native Americans should leave tribal identities behind and assimilate into the general population. The only concrete results of the policy to assimilate were more lands lost by Native Americans.

Acculturation is the process through which an individual is socialized into a new culture while retaining many aspects of a previous culture. In contrast to assimilation, the acculturated individual becomes a mixture of two or more cultures. Later in this chapter we will look at sojourners who often feel like strangers caught between two worlds. The process of acculturation incorporates similar stages as the stranger modifies some aspects of the original culture, retains others, and adopts some of the norms of the new culture. Acculturation involves a less complete integration of an individual into the host culture than does assimilation.

Early Research on Mass Communication and Culture

Mass communication is the exchange of information via a mass medium (for instance radio, television, newspapers, and so forth) from one or a few individuals to an audience of many. The scholarly field of mass communication centers on understanding the effects of mass media messages on individuals who are exposed to these messages. Intercultural communication scholars are particularly interested in whether the media help (1) to maintain an individual's culture or (2) to assimilate the individual into the broader society in which the individual is living.

Although newspapers and magazines had existed for several decades previously, the first mass communication research began in the United States about the time that radio was introduced. From that point, the mass media increased exponentially. The first commercial radio station was founded in 1920 in Pittsburgh. Ten years later 46 percent of U.S. households owned radios; by 1940 this figure reached 82 percent. In the decade of the 1950s, television spread to most households in the United States. Today, the mass media of newspapers, radio, and television reach almost everyone every day, making the United States a media-saturated society.

In Chapter 2, we introduced Robert Park's concepts of social distance and marginal man which provided a foundation for future intercultural communication research. At the University of Chicago, Park taught the first course on race relations; he defined the concepts of assimilation and acculturation. Park's concept of assimilation became an important intellectual tool in understanding how, and whether, one culture dominates and absorbs another. He also contributed to one of the first research efforts on mass communication.

After the United States entered World War I in 1917, the U.S. government needed to know whether German-Americans who had recently immigrated to the United States would be loyal to President Wilson or to Kaiser Wilhelm. Would they engage in sabotage and spread German propaganda? The Carnegie Foundation funded ten studies of immigrants. Park directed the project on the foreign language press in the United States. His 1922 book, *The Immigrant Press and Its Control*, reported that newspapers in German, Yiddish, Polish, Italian, and other languages encouraged loyalty to the United States rather than to the immigrants' original homeland. By aiding the process of immigrant assimilation, the foreign-language newspapers contributed to their own eventual demise.

In the years after World War I, the number of foreign-language newspapers decreased sharply. A primary factor in the decline was that the emphasis on assimilation at that time meant that the second generation offspring of immigrant parents rarely learned their parents' language. The newspapers effectively provided a transition between the two cultures, with an emphasis on providing newcomers with the information necessary to establish themselves as members of their new culture. In order to avoid discrimination against them as strangers, immigrants learned the language and assumed the culture of the larger group.

The Continuum from Assimilation to Cultural Maintenance

Prior to the 1960s, most immigrants were assimilated but even then the melting pot metaphor was descriptive only for certain ethnicities (McAdoo,

1993, p. 11). For example, people of color such as African Americans and Asian Americans did not melt into U.S. society. They were generally excluded from the melting pot and instead maintained their cultural differences. Skin color in a biological sense is a minor genetic trait; socially it has been treated as anything but minor. "More than any other ethnic population in the United States, and perhaps in the world, African Americans have been the victims of negative beliefs and stereotypes" (Aguirre & Turner, 1995, p. 5).

Think of adaptation to a new culture as a continuum ranging from assimilation at one end, various degrees of acculturation in the middle, and *cultural maintenance* at the other end. Table 7-1 shows a measure of assimilation/acculturation/cultural maintenance for Chicanos in the United States. Individuals who tend to answer these ten questions by saying "English" (rather than Spanish) are descendants of more generations of ancestors in the United States, have more formal education, and have a higher average

Table 7-1.   A Scale to Measure the Assimilation/Cultural Maintenance of Chicanos in the United States

Scale Item

1.	What language do you speak?	Mainly Spanish/mainly English
2.	What language do you prefer?	Mainly Spanish/mainly English
3.	How do you identify yourself?	Mainly Spanish/mainly English
4.	What is your music preference?	Mainly Spanish/mainly English
5.	What is your TV viewing preference?	Mainly Spanish/mainly English
6.	Where were you raised?	Mainly Mexico/mainly U.S.
7.	What contact have you had with Mexico?	Number of years lived in Mexico Visits to Mexico
8.	In what language do you think?	Mainly Spanish/mainly English
9.	Which language do you read better?	Spanish/English
10.	Which language do you write better?	Spanish/English

Source: Dawson & others (1996). These ten scale items were selected as the best indicators of cultural assimilation of Chicanos from a much longer scale. Note that most of the items measure communication behavior.

income. As an example of differences between the two groups, individuals who are more assimilated go more immediately to a medical doctor if seriously ill. Those who maintain their native culture's norms about medicine often wait longer to seek medical care, sometimes suffering serious consequences as a result of the delay (Dawson & others, 1996).

The Latino people, who now comprise the second-largest ethnic group in the United States, offer a prime illustration of the movement away from assimilation toward cultural maintenance. The political consciousness-raising events of the 1960s led to the designation Chicano. It denotes the multiple heritages—Native American, Spanish, Mexican and Anglo—of Mexicans in the United States. Using the term Chicano is a declaration of independence. Diego Vigil (1998, p. 270) writes, "The term 'Chicano' implies pride in a background of many and mixed heritages and the versatility to widen one's sociocultural persona. This orientation of national acculturation, in which the dominant cultural mode is learned and the native style kept," provides a path away from ethnocentrism.

Case Illustration:
Maintaining a Distinctive Culture: The Gypsies

One of the most successful societies at resisting assimilation, not only in the United States but throughout the world, is the Gypsies. How do they do it? Gypsies live in almost every country of the world, but little is known about them. The history of the Gypsies is a story of cultural survival despite many concerted attempts to destroy their culture. "Gypsy" is a word used by outsiders, not by the Gypsies themselves. Their name comes from the mistaken belief that the Gypsies were Egyptians. Others erroneously think that Gypsies come from Romania, and indeed the set of moral codes that guides Gypsy behavior is called the Romania *by Gypsies. Actually, the language of the Gypsies, called Romani, is closely related to Hindi and Sanskrit. It is certain that the Gypsies originated in India.*

Presumably the Gypsies left India twelve centuries ago and have since lived a life of almost constant travel. Such traveling is a key part of Gypsy culture and is one means of avoiding assimilation in the culture in which they reside. Most Gypsies believe that they were healthy when they were travelling continuously, and those who are now settled feel their lack of travel is why they become sickly. So the Gypsy means of coping with an illness is to travel and thus to outrun the inauspiciousness of non-Gypsy diseases.

Prior to World War II, many Gypsies traveled in Europe. Hitler considered them subhuman and put half a million Gypsies to death in the Holocaust. Today eight million of the twelve million Gypsies in the world live in Europe (Fonseca, 1995). About one million Gypsies live in the United States, where they practice fortune telling, sell used cars, and engage in a variety of other occupations. Most are illiterate. Gypsies prefer not to have contact with non-Gypsies, whom they view with contempt. This strong ethnocentrism is a fundamental reason for the nonassimilation of Gypsies into U.S. culture (Banks & Banks, 1995).

Another strategy employed by Gypsies to avoid contact with the larger culture is to disguise their identity. For example, Gypsies regularly present multiple identities through using a variety of non-Gypsy names and obtaining false records of birth dates, parents, place of birth, occupation, and national origin. Gypsies sometimes deny that they are Gypsy, feign imbecility, and may even pretend to have heart attacks (Banks & Banks, 1995). Such deception is considered by Gypsies to be the equivalent of traveling. Mystification of others is one strategy for resisting assimilation. The Gypsies protect their cultural boundaries against outsiders in order to maintain their unique culture.

The Gypsies are permanent strangers in the sense described by Georg Simmel (see Chapter 2). They may reside in a system but do not consider themselves to be a part of that system. Gypsy culture contains certain elements, like the constant traveling, the high rate of illiteracy, and their separate language, that help isolate the Gypsies from the larger society in which they live. Do you think that the Gypsies will ever be assimilated into U.S. (or some other) culture?

Changing Demographics

Immigrants to the United States today often maintain their native language and cultural uniqueness. The movement on the continuum from assimilation toward cultural maintenance has been facilitated by the mass media. Demographic changes led to the reversal of the situation that had developed with the immigrant press during the 1920s and 1930s. Two scholars of the media and cultural maintenance in the United States stated: "Rapid and sweeping change in the demographic composition of the United States would force change in the way the media do business. . . . The media's approach would shift from seeking to appeal to a homogenized 'mass' audience to a strategy of targeting audience segments along racial and/or other demographic lines" (Wilson & Gutiérrez, 1995, p. xii).

One example of the ethnic segmentation of U.S. media is provided by the *Los Angeles Times*, which publishes a Spanish-language and a Korean-language supplement. In the 1970s, the *LA Times* dominated the suburban areas ringing the central city, where several million white, middle-class families lived. Meanwhile, a huge area along Vermont Avenue filled with more than a million Korean immigrants. The news information needs of residents of Koreatown were provided by the *Korean Times*, a newspaper published in English and Korean. Southeastern Los Angeles contained large numbers of Latinos and African Americans. Latinos read *La Opinión*, published in Spanish and specializing in news about Spanish-surnamed people.

The *Los Angeles Times* employed few reporters who were culturally able to cover Spanish-language news. Their news staff, like the reporters of many other big-city papers, were mainly "male and pale." In the 1980s the circulation of the *LA Times* was dropping in the central city. The newspaper's sales began to look like a doughnut, hollow in the center. Along with many other urban newspapers, the *Los Angeles Times* began a concerted effort to employ staff members who were Koreans, Latinos, and African Americans.

Case Illustration:
Ethnic Media in New York City

Just how out-of-date the melting pot model is in the United States today is exemplified by the numerous ethnic media in New York. One indication of the importance of ethnic media is that the New York City mayor's office deals with 143 newspapers and magazines, 22 television stations, and 12 radio stations. More than 30 different languages (Dugger, 1997) are represented by these media outlets.

For instance, there are 38 Russian-language newspapers, including the Novoye Russkoye Slovo *(New Russian Word) which has a daily circulation of 65,000 copies. In 1997, this newspaper gave front-page coverage to the flap concerning parking tickets issued to the Russian ambassador's limousine (a news event that did not appear in English-language newspapers in New York). Every weeknight, a half million New Yorkers watch the evening television news on one of two Spanish-language television stations. In addition, there are 56 Spanish-language publications and 5 radio stations. Many New Yorkers regularly buy a newspaper from their native country, which may be Puerto Rico, the Dominican Republic, or Argentina.*

In 1997, one of the three Chinese daily newspapers in New York reported that Taiwan's vice president, Lien Chan, would have an audience with the Pope. Another of the Chinese newspapers questioned this news, and a dispute evolved. Two days later, the first newspaper triumphantly carried a front-page photo of the Taiwanese official with the Pope. So the foreign-language press in New York carries news of special interest to its audience segments. India Abroad *and* News India-Times *gave major attention to accusations that a former Pakistani cricket star running for prime minister had had a love child (Dugger, 1997). More attention is generally given to news from the subcontinent of Asia than to news events involving Indians, Pakistanis, and Bangladeshis in the United States.*

What role do you think the foreign language media play in maintaining diverse cultures in New York City and in other cities?

Ethnic Groups in the United States

One factor in the slowing of the melting-pot process is that some "minority" populations in the United States are becoming "majority" populations. More than half of the population of Miami is Spanish speaking in origin. We feel that the term "minority" should be laid to rest. We do not use it in this book. "Minority" or "minority group" has often been utilized as a synonym for an ethnic group. The term "minority" is misleading in a number of senses. People of color constitute a majority of persons in the world (Figure 7-1), as they do in large U.S. cities and in several states. Further, "minority," as used in the United States, means those persons most affected by racism and may have a connotation of inferiority (as perceived by those of "majority" status).

An *ethnic group* is a set of people who share a common culture that is usually based on nationality or language. Self-identification with an ethnic category often determines which individuals are members of the ethnic group and which individuals are not. Also important is how others in a society perceive various individuals as members of ethnic groups. So ethnic identification is mainly self-defined but may also, in part, be other-defined. Sometimes the self and other identifications conflict. For example, many Native Americans believe that numerous individuals who are not official tribal members identify themselves as Native Americans.

In an ideal society, individuals would be accepted regardless of their cultural background, religious preference, and lifestyle. No preference would be given to any particular ethnic group. All would be treated equally. Certainly the United States is far from this ideal.

In the United States, the terminology commonly used to categorize ethnic populations is:

1. "Asian American" or "Asian"—terms used to describe the people who trace their origins to the Asian continent or to the Pacific Islands (for example, Japan, Korea, China, or Samoa).

2. "African American" or "Black"—terms used to describe the people who trace their origins to the sub-Saharan part of Africa. *African American* is often the preferred term by Black citizens of the United States, while *Black* is the preferred term by Black citizens of the Caribbean and Latin America. We generally use "African American" in this book.

3. "Latino"—a term used to describe people who trace their origins to Latin America (including the Caribbean and Brazil) or to Spain. "Chicano," as described earlier, refers to Mexican heritage. "Hispanic" is the term used by the U.S. Census Bureau for all of these individuals.[1]

The global village is composed of:

Speaking these languages:

And affiliated with these religions:

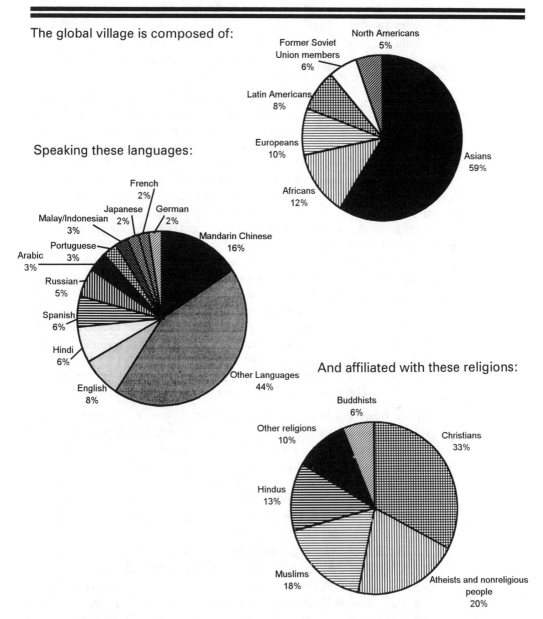

Figure 7-1.   People of color are the majority of people in the world today. Note the numerical dominance of Asians (59 percent) in the world, which is one reason why Asian Americans are an increasing portion of the U.S. population. Only 5.3 percent of the world population lives in North America.

Source: Based upon Lustig & Koester (1996, p. 7).

4. "Native American"—a term used to describe the native peoples of the American continents.
5. "White," "Anglo American," and "European American"—terms used to describe persons of European background other than Spanish. We mainly use "European American" in this book.

Like any set of categories, the above taxonomy has many problems. For example, which of these five labels best fits an individual who traces his/her origin to *both* European American and African-American ancestors? How does one classify an individual with a Native American mother and a European American father? Is an individual classified on the basis of blood lines, self-identification, physical appearance, or some other basis? Many individuals in the United States move in and out of a particular ethnic group, including those marked by racial characteristics. Recall the experience of Gregory Williams in Muncie, discussed in Chapter 3. Such are the troubling questions of determining ethnic categories.

A further complication with the above categories is how to classify Jews. They have often been considered a "race," but that is a biological term rather than a social, cultural, and religious designation. No distinguishing physical trait makes it easy to designate someone as a Jew. The main basis of Jewish self-identification is a shared history of persecution over past centuries. Some six million Jews live in the United States, about 3 percent of the total population (and about half of the world's Jewish population).

What is the makeup of each of these ethnic groups in the United States' population? The U.S. Census of 1990 provides the following answers:

1. Of the total population of about 249 million people, 200 million were White European Americans, about 80.3 percent of the total (down from 83.1 percent in 1980). By 1995, this percentage was down to 74 percent, and by 2025, the U.S. Census Bureau predicts that it will be only 62 percent. In other words, the non-White components of the U.S. population are growing much faster than are European Americans.
2. Some 29.9 million (12 percent of the U.S. population) were African Americans in 1990. By 2025, this category will increase somewhat.
3. About 22.3 million (9 percent) were Latinos, up from 6.4 percent in 1980. By 2025, Latinos will be 17.6 percent of the U.S. population.
4. Some 7.2 million (2.9 percent of the U.S. population) were Asian Americans and Pacific Islanders. This category grew from 1.5 percent of the total population in 1980 and was the most rapidly growing ethnic group on a percentage basis. By 2025, this category will be 6.2 percent.
5. About 1.9 million (0.8 percent of the U.S. population) were Native Americans. About half live on reservations.

In addition, the Census Bureau counted 9.8 million people (3.9 percent) of "other races." Many of these individuals are of mixed ancestry. In the year

2000 population census, the U.S. Census Bureau will no longer force people living in the United States to classify themselves into one of the five ethnic groups. Instead, individuals will be able to identify with more than one ethnic group.

In general, demographic trends show that the United States' population is increasingly composed of people of color, with Latinos, Asian Americans and Pacific Islanders growing most rapidly in numbers. As the melting pot boils more slowly, U.S. society is becoming more and more culturally diverse. As these population changes occur, intercultural communication becomes increasingly more important.

The dramatic demographic changes underway in the U.S. population are reflected in the gender and ethnic makeup of the organizational workforce. In the past, organizations have been male-dominated and mainly peopled by European Americans. In recent years, this domination has decreased. In the 1970s, 1980s, and 1990s, increasing numbers of women entered the workforce. While salaries for males are still much higher (by half again), greater gender equality has been achieved. Compare the gender and ethnic makeup of the workforce in 1985 and as estimated by the federal government (Lambert, 1992) for the year 2000:

	1985	*2000*
1. White European American males	47%	32%
2. White European American women	36%	35%
3. Ethnic populations (Latino, African American, Asian American, and others)	17%	33%
Totals	100%	100%

The number of ethnic group members in the U.S. workforce is estimated to double from 1985 to 2000! This change results from the swelling ethnic population in the United States and the Civil Rights legislation that mandated equal employment opportunities for all. The increasing diversity of the U.S. workforce means that intercultural communication has become more common in U.S. work organizations, creating a need for diversity training and other interventions that facilitate more effective communication.

The Role of Language in Cultural Maintenance

The most important single factor in the rate of assimilation versus cultural maintenance of an ethnic group is whether it can continue its distinctive language. Earlier, we learned that the loss of the ability to speak the parents' language often resulted in the assimilation of second-generation offspring into mainstream culture. As discussed in Chapter 5, language is one of the important bonds between people. Because it is a key component in a culture, losing the ability to communicate in the native code means losing more than just the ability to speak another language. The media can help sustain and extend opportunities for the use of native language. For example, the Navajo Nation publishes its own newspaper, *The Navajo Times*, and operates a radio station (KTNN in Window Rock, Arizona) that broadcasts in *Diné*. Navajo children are taught in *Diné* in elementary schools. Thus the Navajo hope to maintain their culture over future generations. The Navajo have carefully preserved an important part of their heritage, *Diné*.

Spanish-language media flourish in a variety of forms in the United States. Because Latinos are a fast-growing segment of the U.S. population (and will be for at least the next two decades), television, radio, and newspapers (in both Spanish and English) target the Latino audience. The message content provided by Latino media includes the usual news topics of politics, sports, and entertainment in the United States, but these media also focus on topics specifically related to Latin America: migration to the United States, the environmental problems of the U.S./Mexico border, and Latin American sports and entertainment news (Rodriguez, 1997; Soruco, 1996).

The largest Spanish-language television network in the United States, Univisión, is 25 percent owned by Televisa, the Mexican television conglomerate. Televisa produces more than half of the programs that Univisión broadcasts from its 600 stations in the United States. Univisión's nightly newscast, *Noticiero Univisión*, has a regular audience of about 1.2 million viewers. About half of each newscast is Latin American news, and a fifth is news from U.S. Latino communities. In comparison, ABC's evening newscast devotes only 1 percent of its broadcast time to news of Latin America and Latinos. Like the three largest U.S. television networks, Univisión is "an audience-maximizing, advertiser-supported enterprise" that seeks profits by providing a professionally objective account of the news that will appeal to the broadest possible number of people (Rodriguez, 1997). Univisión shuns the advocacy role sometimes played by ethnic group journalism.

What characterizes the Latino audience in the United States? Compared with others, Latinos are poorer (with a median family income of $23,900 compared to $37,000 for non-Latino families) and have less formal education (only 44 percent have completed high school, compared to 88 percent of the general population). The lower socioeconomic status of Latino people in the United States is in part due to the history of discrimination over the past one hundred years or so.

Somewhat more than half (54 percent) of U.S. Latinos speak Spanish at home. There are three distinct Latino populations in the United States: (1) Chicanos, Mexican Americans who comprise about two-thirds of all the Latino population; (2) Puerto Ricans, constituting about 10 percent, living mainly in New York City, and representing the poorest Latinos; and (3) Cuban refugees, also representing 10 percent of the Hispanic population, residing mainly in Miami and South Florida, and characterized by relative wealth and political power (Rodriguez, 1997; Soruco, 1996). When asked in a 1992 survey to self-identify, 10 percent of Latino people said "American," 20 percent said "Hispanic" or "Latino," and the remainder self-identified by saying "I'm Mexican," "I'm Cuban," and so forth (de la Garza & others, 1992). Like some other muted groups in the United States, Latinos generally wish to maintain their unique cultures and to avoid assimilation (Figure 7-2).

Networks in the Assimilation Process

Past research shows the crucial role of interpersonal networks in the assimilation process, as a new immigrant gradually shifts from having a personal network composed mainly of old-world friends to a network made up of

Figure 7-2. The cultural identification of Chicanos may be displayed by artistic expressions on vehicles or by graffiti on walls and buildings. The proud owner of this 1959 Chevrolet lives in Barrio San Jose, Albuquerque. In the background is graffiti by gang members.

Source: Photograph by Miguel Gandert. Used by permission.

individuals from the new culture. Peer networks often determine whether assimilation does or does not occur.

When a new immigrant arrives, the individual may have a relative who has lived in the United States for several years and who can provide advice on how to get a job, purchase food, and find a bank and other services. The new immigrant may learn English and gradually get to know members of the new culture, who exchange information and provide social support to the newcomer. These interpersonal exchanges are the mechanism through which the assimilation process occurs (Kim, 1987). As networks expand to include more individuals from the host culture, the immigrant is more likely to develop good communication skills and to expand ties with the host culture.

In contrast, the new immigrant may develop a personal communication network composed mainly or entirely of other unassimilated immigrants. They will continue to speak their native tongue rather than English, insulate themselves from the broader culture, and maintain their original culture. They will expose themselves mainly to mass media in the language of their country of origin. Thus their previous culture is maintained.

Contemporary Migration to America

Which decade in U.S. history is characterized by the highest rate of migration? If you had been asked this question before 1980, the correct answer would have been the decade around 1910 (Figure 7-3). After that period, immigration to the United States declined for the next 60 years or so, due to the enactment of harsh immigration laws. Today, the number of migrants to the United States is larger than it has ever been. In recent decades, as discussed earlier, the assimilation process has changed in a fundamental way. Many immigrants now maintain their imported culture. As a result, many U.S. cities are "cultural salads," a collection of different cultures that are only very slowly becoming assimilated (Figure 7-4).

One indicator of the end of the melting pot era is the changing role of the English language. In the decades following the Civil War, most immigrants learned English as soon as possible; many present-day immigrants maintain their original language. Some 32 million (about 13 percent of the U.S. population) speak a mother tongue other than English, and another 14 million are not very fluent in English (Chen & Starosta, 1998). Some 17 million people in the United States speak Spanish, and 4.5 million speak an Asian or Pacific Island language, mainly Chinese or Japanese.

Contemporary migration consists mainly of people from Latin America and Asia. As recently as 1940, 70 percent of the immigrants to the United States came from Europe. In 1990, this figure had dropped to only 15 percent, with 44 percent of immigrants from Latin America and the Caribbean and 37 percent from Asia (Chen & Starosta, 1998). Immigration to the United

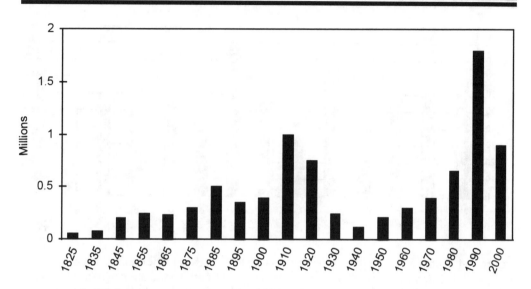

Figure 7-3. Legal Migration to the United States. An early peak in European migration to the United States occurred in the several decades following the Civil War. Most were European peasants who settled in U.S. cities, where they experienced poverty, crime, and exploitation of their labor. The largest number of legal immigrants occurred in 1991 when 1.8 million people arrived on U.S. shores. This number dropped somewhat in the late 1990s due to the effects of the 1990 Immigration Act, although this decrease was probably more than compensated for by illegal migration, which the U.S. Immigration and Naturalization Service estimates are an additional 20 percent of the total number of legal immigrants.
Source: U.S. Bureau of the Census.

States became an important policy issue. The topic is widely debated and much disputed. Should the United States welcome anyone who wishes to immigrate? Should preference continue to be given to certain individuals, such as medical doctors, engineers, and others in skilled occupations? Should people from certain countries be excluded from migration to the United States? Is the end of the melting pot a problem for U.S. society?

The U.S. government, for many years, implemented immigration policies to limit the number of newcomers based on two criteria: (1) to discourage individuals with only manual work skills (while allowing people from the professions noted above to enter), and (2) to restrict the number of people of color (for example, Asians and Latin Americans). U.S. immigration policy displayed discrimination in who was allowed to arrive in the United States, and who was kept out. These policies were far from effective; several million illegal residents are presently living in the United States, having slipped through the nation's borders (Figure 7-5).

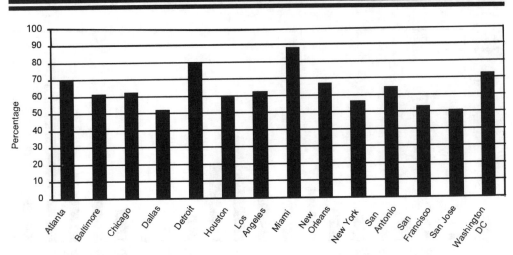

Figure 7-4. The majority of the population of large U.S. cities were non-European Americans in 1990. The 1990 U.S. Census showed that more than half of the population of large U.S. cities was composed of African Americans, Latinos, Asian Americans, and Native Americans, ranging up to 88 percent in Miami and 79 percent in Detroit.

Source: U.S. Bureau of Census.

Miami, Florida (and Miami-Dade County which surrounds it) is one of the most ethnically diverse urban areas in the United States. A wave of immiration swept over the Miami area in the past several decades, changing the ethnic composition of the city. In 1950, only 20,000 people of Spanish-speaking origin (4 percent of the population) lived in Miami-Dade County. In 1959, the Communist revolution of Fidel Castro in Cuba set off a massive migration to Miami, with the Mariel boatlift of the early 1980s creating the largest spurt in migration. Today, over half of Miami-Dade County's population is from the West Indies, Mexico, Central, and South America. Some 60 percent are Cuban refugees, with others migrating from Puerto Rico, the Dominican Republic, Mexico, Guatemala, Honduras, Nicaragua, Colombia, and Peru. Some 19 percent of Miami-Dade's population is African American, and there are sizeable numbers of Southeast Asians and other Asian Americans. Only 12 percent of Miami's population in 1990 was composed of European Americans, the lowest percentage of any large U.S. city.

The Policy Issue of Immigration

In recent years, immigration to the United States has become a very contentious policy issue. A basic problem is that the standard of living in the United States and the availability of jobs attract immigrants from Mexico, Central

Figure 7-5. A Mexican national attempts to cross the border at El Paso/Juarez while the U.S. Border Patrol watches. The only land border in the world between a developing country and an industrialized nation is the U.S./Mexico frontier. The extremes of poverty versus wealth provide a powerful attraction for Mexicans and other Latin Americans to cross into the United States. El Paso/Juarez is one of the main points at which illegal immigration occurs.

Source: Photograph by Miguel Gandert. Used by permission.

America, China, and other nations. The number of immigrants attracted to the United States is greater than the number of immigrants legally allowed into the United States.

Despite intensive efforts by the U.S. Border Patrol and the U.S. Immigration Service, millions of undocumented workers have crossed the nation's borders and now live in the United States. They are often illegally employed and do not pay income tax, nor do they receive health or retirement benefits. Some observers feel that these illegal immigrants are taking jobs away from U.S. citizens. Others argue that these jobs are work that no one else wants. Certain industries such as wine production and orange-growing in California rely on the economics of hiring workers who do not earn the minimum wage.

Not only has the number of immigrants to the United States (both legal and illegal) increased sharply in recent years, but the average age dropped from 46 in 1980 to 28 in the late 1990s (Chen & Starosta, 1998). The youthful trend means that the fertility of the immigrant population will increase.

The changes in immigration to the United States mainly reflect the changes in immigration laws in recent decades. The Immigration Act of 1965 (1) eliminated country-specific quotas (which had favored European nations), and (2) allowed the immediate family members of U.S. citizens the opportunity to immigrate without numerical restrictions. Individuals who were engineers, doctors, or in other occupations that were in short supply were still given priority, but they could constitute only 20 percent of all visas. The Refugee Act of 1980 encouraged immigration from Vietnam, Laos, and Cambodia in the aftermath of the Vietnam War. A 1986 law allowed long-term illegal residents already in the United States to gain amnesty and thus avoid deportation. Many of these individuals were agricultural workers from Mexico and other Latin American nations. Finally, the 1990 Immigration Act allowed immigration to increase substantially. As a result, the U.S. population in the future will include more Latinos and Asians (Aguirre & Turner, 1995, p. 235).

How do U.S. citizens, almost all of whom are either immigrants or the descendants of immigrants, feel about the current wave of immigration to the United States? A 1994 national survey showed that 34 percent said it is now time to halt all immigration to the United States! About 43 percent of the survey respondents said that some but not all immigrants should be welcome. They justified this belief on the basis of the economic position of the nation and claimed that immigrants take jobs away from U.S. citizens. Half of the survey respondents said that immigrants cause trouble, and 22 percent stated that immigrants of the past five years should be ordered to return to their home countries.

A common perception is that new immigrants are poorly educated and that many go on welfare. Actually, only three out of one thousand new immigrants go on welfare, and 20 percent have university degrees (about the same percentage as individuals born in the United States).[2]

These issues are often the subject of media stories. In instances of referendums such as California's recent referendum on immigration, the media reports are constant. The drama of adversarial demonstrations floods newspapers and local news coverage. Conflict is highlighted, and the opportunities for reasoned communication dwindle. The mass media can set the agenda for attitudes toward ethnic groups. The stories they choose to present influence public opinion. The fear that results from stories about street crime can lead to hostility and hardened attitudes about spending tax dollars to improve schools in neighborhoods composed primarily of one ethnic group.

The Role of the Media

As we learned in the early chapters of this book, cultures must communicate their content to future generations if they are to survive. The socialization process works through society's institutions: the family, peer groups, schools, and religious institutions. The media are major players in communicating culture. They offer steady streams of information in appealing formats, capturing the attention of children over long periods of time—more time than is often spent with parents or teachers. Entertainment, including television, comic books, music, movies, and Internet chat groups, carries potent messages about politics, economics, and social behavior.

Because culture is not stagnant, the means of communicating attitudes and values often create their own contributions to the culture. The media as an institution reinforce a culture's beliefs and values. As a powerful channel transmitting cultural norms, the media can also generate new attitudes that become part of the general culture. One small indication of the influence of television was its power to rearrange living rooms (Jeffres, 1994). When introduced in the 1950s, this artifact became a focal point and furniture was grouped accordingly. Television influenced nonverbal behavior, family interactions, and leisure patterns. In providing a range of cultural information to children, the electronic media also blurred the lines between childhood and adulthood that existed previously. Ease of use and the demands of programming to fill hours of broadcast time meant that multiple topics from which children had been shielded previously were available at the flip of a power button.

Most individuals rely on the mass media for perceptions of others with whom they do not have regular interpersonal contact. Thus the media play a major role in forming and maintaining stereotypes. If journalists do not share the cultures of the society whose news they report, then society will not see itself reflected accurately in the news. In an ideal world, the media would serve as mirrors of society, accurately conveying the reality of different cultures to their audience. This is not the current state of affairs.

Reports about certain nations like Japan, Germany, and England appear far more frequently in the U.S. media than their population or economic size would seem to justify. Other nations such as Mexico and Canada, which border the United States and are very important trading partners, appear in the news only rarely. When the developing nations of Latin America, Africa, and Asia are covered by the U.S. media, the news is usually negative and mainly concerns wars, military coups, and disasters.

Bias in the Media

There is a strong bias in the mainstream U.S. media against non-English-speaking nations. U.S. media reporters often do not know the language of a developing country, so they search for English-speaking respondents to interview about a news event. Unfortunately, such individuals are highly untypical of their compatriots.

Comparative studies of the public's knowledge of international affairs consistently show that people in the United States are much less informed than are people of Germany, England, France, or Italy. Why is this so, given that the United States has a high level of formal education and is such a media-saturated society? The main reason is that the U.S. mass media do not carry nearly as much international news as the media of other nations. The lack of knowledge about foreign affairs is especially important to the world because in a democracy like the United States, public opinion is reflected in government foreign policy. The United States is the major world power, so its international policy affects everyone.

Why don't the U.S. media provide more international news to their audience? It is not because the public is not interested. Surveys of media audiences consistently show they want more international news. Gathering international news is costly, and U.S. journalists have been poorly prepared for working overseas. They seldom have ability in a language other than English, and they know little of the history and culture of other nations.

The U.S. mass media do not do a much more effective job of accurately reflecting the culture of various ethnic groups in the United States. Media stereotypes from an earlier era, such as Charlie Chan, the Frito Bandito, and "Amos 'n Andy," were particularly insensitive. A noted case of the inauthenticity of Hollywood films in representing Native Americans is *Cheyenne Autumn*. The Native Americans in the movie were portrayed by Navajos (the film was shot on location near Gallup, New Mexico). Today, Navajos enjoy watching a videotape of this film. To counteract the stereotyped plot, the Navajo actors amused themselves by uttering ribald lines in *Diné* about John Wayne and the other actors in the film.

Latinos and Native Americans are particularly underrepresented in media newsrooms. Very few news stories appear in the U.S. media about Native American communities, and when they do, the subject is often violence, graft, casino gambling, or alcoholism. Underrepresentation results in misrepresentation as evidenced by U.S. media coverage of the Hantavirus epidemic that struck the Navajo population in the Four Corners area of the Southwest in May–June, 1993.

Navajo tribal leaders strongly objected to the epidemic being termed the "Navajo epidemic" by the *Arizona Republic* (many of the victims of the Hantavirus were Navajo). The Navajo Nation despised the culturally insensitive news-gathering procedures by the media. Reporters from *Time, Newsweek*, and *The New York Times* flew into New Mexico and sought to interview personally the next-of-kin of Navajos who had just died from the Hantavirus. Navajos believe that it is inappropriate to speak of the dead, especially in the period just after death has occurred. Media reporters did not understand Navajo culture and misrepresented it in their news stories about the Hantavirus epidemic. Much was made of the role of Navajo "medicine men." The tribe's complex theology was treated as if it were a set of primitive superstitions. Had the news media been able to assign a Native American news reporter to cover the Hantavirus epidemic, the news stories would have been more accurate and less offensive to the Navajo. The distorted news coverage of the 1993 Hantavirus epidemic had serious, negative effects for New Mexico. Millions of dollars in tourist income were lost due to individuals who cancelled their travel plans out of fear that they might contract the disease (actually, Hantavirus is transmitted by infected deer mice, not by human contact).

The mass media can maintain the notion of race, or they can question whether racial categories should exist. We know that race is a social construction, a classification that is arbitrarily based on such visible features of people as their skin color, eye shape, and so forth. Should the media describe a criminal as "African American" or "Chicano"? Should the individual be identified by his/her ethnicity at all? The media—and the audience—should weigh these issues carefully. When ethnic people appear in the news, are they depicted in stereotypic and demeaning ways?

The color of words is equally important in international news reporting (Herbst, 1997). Cultural biases are revealed in the vocabulary chosen to describe the same event. For example, the *Jerusalem Post*, reporting an armed attack on a settlement in Israel, called the participants "terrorists." *Alharam* (a leading Egyptian newspaper) reported that "freedom fighters" stormed the settlement.

Recall in Chapter 3 that gender can be considered a co-culture. Cultural bias in the media is just as pervasive when it comes to gender as it is with ethnic groups. How are men and women portrayed in the U.S. mass media? Not very equally. Women appear in the news media much less frequently than do men, although they constitute an equal portion of the population. A 1996 study of the front pages of U.S. newspapers found that women constituted only 15 percent of the individuals mentioned. "Male voices, activities, and images saturated newspaper front pages" (*Media Report to Women*, 1996, p. 9). When women do appear in the news, often they are portrayed as incompetent, frequently as individuals who are victimized, trivialized, and denigrated. "When females were covered on key pages as the main figures of a story, more than half were victims or perpetrators of crimes or alleged misconduct, rather than persons of accomplishment or achievement" (*Media Report to Women*, 1996). Gender stereotypes, as well as ethnic stereotypes, can be created and maintained—or destroyed—by the mass media.

Impacts of the Mass Media

Although the growth of cable and satellite broadcasting has curtailed the monolithic power of the major networks that existed through the 1980s, the mainstream mass media still can counteract the effects of specialized media. The expansion of media outlets has allowed Univisión, for example, to gain a strong foothold, but think of other cultures that do not have the same economic and political strength as the Latino population. Are they as well represented? Are they represented at all? The bulk of U.S. advertising dollars still goes to programs and networks dominated by mainstream U.S. culture.

In a media-saturated society, what are the effects of an endless stream of images on viewers and listeners? What are the prevalent images projected? What values are reflected? Imagine a Pakistani child watching television in Chicago, or a Navajo child in Gallup, or an Indonesian child in San Diego. Depending on the amount of time spent watching the media, the child will copy the speech mannerisms of television characters, adopt their clothing styles, and beg his/her parents for the toys, sweetened drinks, and other products advertised on television. Even if the child's family members speak their own language at home, cook native recipes, and consider themselves to be Pakistani, Navajo, or Indonesian, their child is likely to grow up with a self-image as a European American. Such is the potent process of assimilation, driven in part by the ubiquitous nature of the dominant mass media.

Who gathers and produces the news and who appears in the mass media have an important impact on society. In an ideal world, people of color would be represented in the media in the same proportions as in the populations that the media serve. In the media of the United States, this ideal is far from being reached, although progress is being made in recent decades.

The underrepresentation of ethnic groups in the media is not in the economic interest of the media. The experience of the *Los Angeles Times* maps what may happen as demographics change. ***When the media do not have a workforce that reflects the audience that they seek to serve, news coverage is unbalanced and ethnic groups in the audience tune out.*** General newspapers have been particularly hard hit. With the growth of new media forms such as the Internet, and facing competition from evening television news, many of the general-circulation newspapers have disappeared, especially big-city afternoon newspapers. Few U.S. cities have more than one newspaper today. In the late 1990s, only 62 percent of adults in the United States read a daily newspaper, down from 75 percent 20 years previously.

Some of the lost readership has been recovered by special-interest publications.

The effects of the mass media on intercultural relations are not easy to characterize. The messages they communicate often depend on the perceptions of the audience. As we have already seen in this chapter, foreign-language newspapers once served the process of assimilation; today they facilitate cultural maintenance. Communities and societies are made up of forces that pull people together and forces that push them apart. In the 1930s, Herbert Blumer viewed the broadcast media as the bulwark of social solidarity (Leach, 1986). From this view, the insistently omnipresent, standardizing influence of the media was a means to counteract disruptive forces. Today, new communication technologies support the creation of interest groups that often promote their own interests to the exclusion of all others. Both positions can harm efforts to exchange culturally different views.

The contributions of the media to the assimilation process will continue to be a focus of intercultural communication researchers. The opportunities and risks inherent in the ability of the media to reach limitless audiences supply rich veins to tap in the exploration of how culture is communicated. The remainder of this chapter looks at a unique group of people whose experiences clearly illustrate the pervasive influence of culture.

The Sojourner

A *sojourner* is an individual who visits another culture for a period of time but who retains his/her original culture. The sojourner typically is a visitor or traveler who only resides in the other culture for a relatively specific time, often a year or two, with the intention of returning home. Sojourners may be businesspeople, diplomats, students, military personnel, or guest workers.

Many U.S. citizens experience sojourning (Storti, 1997, p. 2):

1. Over two million people from the United States work overseas. The average company spends $250,000 per year for salary, benefits, and expenses to keep a U.S. employee and dependents overseas; some 25 percent of returnees leave their company within one year of coming home (many sojourning businesspeople expect that their experience in another culture will benefit their career and are disappointed when they find that it does not).

2. More than half a million U.S. military personnel and their dependents are stationed abroad.

3. Some 30,000 high school students and 75,000 university students study abroad each year.

Large numbers of sojourners come *to* the United States:

1. About 450,000 international students study in the United States. The majority come from China, Japan, Taiwan, and India.

2. Over 12 million international visitors come to the United States each year. Japan, Britain, and Germany are the leading nations from which these sojourners come.

Sojourners are a favorite topic of study by intercultural communication scholars. Sojourners represent a unique situation in which most everyday communication is intercultural. The sojourner is a particular type of stranger.[3] While immigrants decide the degree to which they will become assimilated, sojourners know that their stay in the new culture is temporary. Regardless of their intent to learn the new culture, they will eventually return to their original culture. This "escape clause" can affect adjustment to the new culture. The sojourner is a stranger caught between two worlds.

Past research shows that sojourning is a very difficult process, especially when an individual is sojourning for the first time. Sojourning threatens the self-worth of many individuals. The degree of culture shock that many individuals experience tells us that culture *is* important and that intercultural adjustment is not easy, although it can be a valuable learning experience. Some individuals perceive the sojourning experience as negative and personally painful, at least during their sojourn. However, if one has the desire to understand a different culture, sojourning can be an exciting and wonderful event once the period of adjustment passes. Some sojourners thrive on the experience (Furnham, 1987, p. 53). Sojourning can change one's life by giving a feeling of self-confidence and self-efficacy, a sense of controlling one's life and overcoming difficult situations. Many sojourners look back on their intercultural experience as something resembling a profound religious rebirth.

Culture Shock

Culture shock is the traumatic experience that an individual may encounter when entering a different culture. We often become anxious when we lose our familiar surroundings. This fish-out-of-water feeling is due to losing the familiar signs and symbols of everyday communication (Oberg, 1960). Alvin Toffler (1970) described culture shock as what happens when one finds oneself "in a place where yes may mean no, where a 'fixed price' is negotiable, where to be kept waiting in an outer office is no cause for insult, where laughter may signify anger." The shock of finding oneself in unfamiliar territory, overloaded with stimuli one cannot process, unable to ask directions or to understand the answers to carefully rehearsed questions, in weather more extreme than ever experienced at home, with food that is unrecognizable and water that cannot be used to brush one's teeth, is somewhat like experiencing a maelstrom while everyone around you calmly negotiates daily activities. After the basics are finally mastered, the sojourner will eventually confront differences in attitudes and values that may seem even more jarring.

The term culture shock was coined by an anthropologist, Cora DuBois, in 1951. Much of the early research on culture shock was conducted by social psychologists who investigated individuals' adjustment to new cultural settings. As the field of intercultural communication got underway in the 1960s, culture shock became a favorite topic of research. In these investigations, sojourners are typically personally interviewed (1) before their departure for another culture, (2) while they are suffering from culture shock, and (3) upon their return to their home culture, where they often experience reentry problems (also called reverse culture shock). For some individuals, the reentry process is more serious than the earlier shock of living in another culture. ***Both culture shock and reverse culture shock show us that culture is an important influence on human behavior.***

Culture shock can be very serious. Over recent decades, the Peace Corps has had to return about 30 percent of its volunteers to the United States before the end of their two-year overseas stay. Volunteers (as well as other sojourners) return home due to the mental problems caused by culture shock. Paul Bohannan and Dirk van der Elst (1998) describe the mental and emotional discomfort as the result of "finding yourself understanding behaviors resulting logically from premises alien to your own culture" (p. 52). As they warn, no amount of training prepares you to look into yourself and become aware that you have cultural limitations.

When your beliefs and values are knocked askew and your capacity to predict what might happen disappears, you feel as though your existence is threatened. Different people react differently. Some are devastated; some are outraged; and some learn to expand their capacities beyond the limitations of their particular culture. As Bohannan and van der Elst (1998) phrase it, "You have to be willing to admit that there are aspects of the human experience about which you know very little—that you have much to learn. You can learn a lot of it by allowing yourself to experience the weightlessness that comes when your sense of cultural gravity is knocked out" (p. 54).

Most individuals are able to cope with culture shock, but some sojourners encounter severe problems. Culture shock is a primary reason why employers generally prefer to hire individuals for overseas work who have had previous experience in living and working in a foreign culture. These individuals are less likely to have the props knocked out from under them. Individuals who are self-efficacious (that is, who feel they can control their future) suffer less culture shock. Predeparture training can help prepare individuals. Just by knowing about culture shock, a sojourner may better understand the sojourning process and thus suffer less disorientation.

What are common symptoms of culture shock? Excessive washing of hands; extreme concern over drinking the water, eating local food, and the cleanliness of bedding; an absent-minded, far-away stare; loss of appetite; an overdependence on being with long-term residents of one's own nationality; fits of sudden anger over minor delays; overwhelming fear of being cheated or robbed; great concern over minor skin irritations and slight pains; and a terrible longing to be back home (Oberg, 1960). Most individuals who travel to another country, especially for the first time, experience at least a certain degree of culture shock. Some individuals are rendered completely incapable of daily functioning. For example, the wife of a U.S. military attaché in Bogotá, Colombia, remained in bed for two years, fearful of the germs that she felt pervaded the local environment. Her husband's Colombian friends and acquaintances considered her behavior shocking.

A spectacular example of culture shock entails a highly experienced CNN newsperson who traveled to Lagos, Nigeria, in order to report an important news event. He had not worked previously in Nigeria. Other newspeople warned the CNN employee that he should arrange for a security service in advance of his arrival, but he pooh-poohed this advice. When he arrived in Lagos International Airport at 10:00 P.M., the CNN reporter encountered few difficulties, other than a demand for a bribe from customs officials for allowing him to bring his television camera into the country. He took a taxi from the airport and settled down for the 30-mile trip into the city.

A few miles from the Airport, the taxi driver turned into a side road and stopped the vehicle. The driver then put a revolver to the sojourner's temple and politely invited him to step outside of the car, to strip naked, and to toss his clothes inside the taxi. Then the driver sped off in the night, laughing. How would you cope with this reception in a strange country?

Culture shock can be a useful learning experience. An individual can gain important understandings about cultural relativism and become better prepared for a next sojourning experience. Some individuals start out by sojourning in a culture similar to their own. Most sojourners from the United States experience relatively little culture shock in England. However, there are cultural differences which must be learned; sometimes survival depends on it. If you are from a culture where people drive on the right-hand side of the road and then spend time in a country where people drive on the left-hand side, you will learn just how habitual behavior becomes. If you try to cross a street without specifically and carefully reminding yourself of the cultural difference and what it means, you could spend your sojourn in a hospital.

Learning about differences within a culture that shares some similarities with your own allows you to cope with cultural uncertainty on a gradual basis. However, in some instances the comfort level may obscure cultural differences, contribute to a false sense of awareness, and be counterproductive. International reporters are often not sufficiently skilled in the culture in which a story is breaking to report accurately. The overseas correspondents are often headquartered in major, cosmopolitan cities where cultural differences are less noticeable. They fly to crisis areas on assignment and then return to the more hospitable locale.

The U-Curve of Cultural Adjustment

How and why does culture shock occur? One useful way to understand culture shock is to dissect it as a process composed of several stages, which form a U-curve of cultural adjustment over time.[4]

1. The first step in the process leading to culture shock occurs over the weeks and months prior to departure from the individual's home culture (Figure 7-6). The excitement of living and working or studying in a new culture leads the prospective traveler to be exuberant with anticipation. Perhaps the individual reads books or other publications about the destination culture and talks to individuals who are especially knowledgeable. High expectations are created, and the traveler builds up an idealized mental picture of what his/her daily life will be like in the new culture. Unfortunately, many or most of these expectations will turn out to be unrealistic, as the traveler will soon learn.

2. Finally, the day arrives for travel to the new culture. On arrival, the sojourner begins to discover that the host culture is markedly different from the individual's home culture. The familiar markings of ordinary daily life are suddenly, dramatically, and completely changed. These differences are perceived by the sojourner as odd and as inferior (this is ethnocentrism). The sojourner initially has few friends in the host culture and seeks out other people from his/her passport culture. The expatriots get together to grouse about the odd nature of the culture in which they are living. If the sojourners are from the United States, they glorify that country irrationally. They reject the local environment, which they perceive as causing their discomfort (Oberg, 1960). They are accustomed to instant gratification; they don't like being in a culture where the pace is much slower and waits are long. The sojourner takes refuge in a cocktail circuit of compatriots, which prevents making new friends with individuals from the host country. The individual feels very lonesome for the home culture that he/she was extremely happy to leave only a few weeks previously. The sojourner becomes depressed and may experience such physical symptoms as fatigue, nausea, and headaches. A loss of control and a sense of helplessness is experienced, in the face of unfamiliar cultural cues.

3. Eventually, after several weeks or months, the visitor begins to appreciate certain elements of the new culture and to form gradually more accurate expectations. Friendships with a growing network of host-culture acquaintances serve as a social cushion, minimizing the shock when differences in customs surface. Relatively less time is spent with compatriots and more with people of the host culture. The sojourner even begins to joke about the initial difficulties in the host culture. Fluency in the local language improves. The host culture is accepted as different but as coherent within itself. The individual may even begin to feel some pride and a sense of accomplishment in adjusting to the host culture and in overcoming culture shock. A few sojourners "go native," as they enthusiastically identify with the host culture and inauthentically think of themselves as having become members of

the local society. Peace Corps volunteers who adopt the dress of the villagers or urban poor with whom they work are examples.

4. As the sojourning period nears its end and the day approaches to return home, the individual feels regret at the forthcoming departure. Yet, expectations build up about the individual's return home, and positive and nostalgic aspects of the home culture are recalled. The sojourner is excited about returning home.

5. On arrival home, the sojourner is surprised to find that the home culture is not as remembered! These unfulfilled expectations are due to faulty memory, to selective recall, and to the fact that the home culture has changed in noticeable ways while the sojourner was gone, even though it was only for several months or a couple of years. The sojourner's old friends are not interested in hearing about the sojourner's experiences in the other culture. The traveler's expectations do not fit reality, and he/she again becomes depressed. This reverse culture shock is caused by the absence of familiar cues in the environment. This reentry period may last for several months before

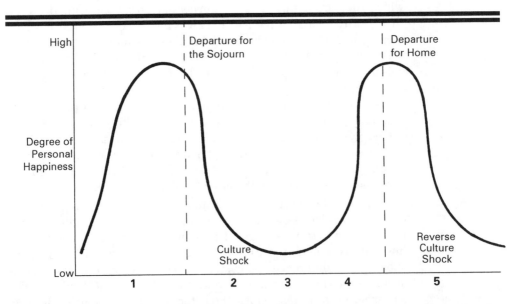

Figure 7-6.   The U-Curve of Adjustment. A sojourner typically passes through a series of stages: 1, preparing to travel to another culture; 2, arriving and experiencing culture shock; 3, gradually fitting into the host culture; 4, looking forward to return; and 5, returning home and experiencing reentry shock (or reverse culture shock).

the traveler once again feels at home. The individual's feelings of well-being during these five phases, when plotted over time, look U-shaped (or perhaps like a "W.")

Reentry

Reentry is the process that an individual goes through when returning to the home culture after a sojourn. Returning home is often more difficult than going overseas, in part because reentry shock is usually a surprise to the individual, who does not expect to have adjustment problems in going home (Martin, 1984; 1986). A returned Peace Corps volunteer commented:

> When I got back to my hometown in Ohio and went to work, I fell back into hanging out evenings in the neighborhood tavern with my old buddies. After about two weeks of that I gave up on the tavern. They didn't care about the problems of the Indians in Peru, and I didn't give a damn about what happened to the Indians in Cleveland (Calvert, 1966).

Reverse culture shock or reacculturation is experienced by about half a million people in the United States each year. Sixty-two percent of Peace Corps volunteers said they found reentry to be difficult, and half of U.S. business executives said they experienced problems upon repatriation. Despite the troubling difficulties of culture shock and reentry, Storti (1997, p. 9) concludes: "Reentry *is* an experience to be reckoned with, but when the reckoning is done and the accounts are cleared, you'll likely find that the price you paid for your overseas sojourn was the bargain of a lifetime."

Case Illustration:
You Gotta Have *Wa*[5]

Baseball is the national sport in Japan, as it is in the United States. The rules by which baseball is played, the dimensions of the playing field, and the size of the baseball are identical in the two countries. But in many other ways, besuboru *in Japan and baseball in the United States are as different as night and day.*

Each professional baseball team in Japan is allowed to hire two foreign players, usually players from the United States whose careers are fading. One exception was Bob Horner, who had hit 215 home runs in nine seasons with the Atlanta Braves before he played in Japan for the Yakult Swallows in 1987. He was 29 years old and at the top of his game. The Swallows paid him $2 million for the season, more than twice the salary paid the top Japanese stars. The Swallows's owner told Horner that he expected him to hit 50 homers and to make winners out of the Swallows, Tokyo's perennial losing team. The club's owner issued him a Swallows uniform with number 50 on the back.

Horner arrived in Tokyo Airport to great media attention. Sports writers dubbed him Akaoni, *"the Red Devil," an allusion to a fairytale figure of great strength in*

Japanese popular culture. His fellow players on the Yakult Swallows baseball team called him sensei, meaning "teacher" or "master," because he shared his considerable knowledge of baseball with them. As the season began, Horner fulfilled everyone's high expectations. He homered in the Swallows's first game, and then hit three baseballs out of the park in the second game. At the end of the first week, he had seven home runs and was hitting .533. And the Yakult Swallows were winning.

Horner became an obsession of the Japanese media. When he got his blond hair cut in Sapporo, the media discussed the possible effects on his hitting. A crowd of reporters followed him everywhere, allowing him little privacy. "The hyperactive Japanese media had locked on to him like a heat-seeking missile" (Whiting, 1989, p.14). Horner retreated to his tiny apartment in Tokyo, only occasionally going out for drinks with his one teammate from the United States on the Swallows—Leon Lee, a first baseman who had played in Japan for ten years.

Opposing pitchers soon became cautious in pitching to Horner, due to the special shame of giving up a home run to a gaijin batter. Horner was fed a steady diet of balls. He was walked frequently and began to swing at bad pitches in frustration. Horner expected the pitchers to throw their best pitches and challenge him to hit them. That's the way it was in the United States. That's big league baseball! But the Japanese game is cautious, designed to avoid embarrassing mistakes, with emphasis on walks, singles, and sacrifice bunts.

After his initial hitting streak, Horner fell into a slump, hitting only three more home runs in the next month while his average dropped to .300. Horner's batting became one of frequent walks and many strikeouts, with very few homers. He began to gripe about the umpires, who gave him an extra big strike zone because, they said, gaijin are bigger than Japanese players and have longer arms. Horner strained his back going after a bad pitch and went on the disabled list in July. The media crucified him for what they interpreted as cowardly behavior.

The media also criticized Horner for disturbing the wa (harmony) on the Swallows team. For instance, he did not participate in the exhausting two- or three-hour grind of pregame drills. Instead, Horner slept on the trainer's table in the team's clubhouse. The Japanese press was horrified and considered this flouting of pregame drills to be sacrilegious. The rigid system of Japanese baseball demanded that playing the game was a ten-hour-day grind for the players. Harmony was achieved by incessant team meetings: pregame, during the game itself, and postgame, when the team's mistakes were reviewed. Horner disdained these endless conferences, asking why baseball couldn't just be played for fun. After all, wasn't it a game? He began to think that besuboru in Japan was ridiculously rigid.

Ask any Japanese manager the most important factor in a winning team and they would reply wa. Horner's manager believed that such harmony resulted from a delicate balance among the team members, in which each player devoted himself to the pregame drills, to the team meetings, and to achieving his greatest effort. Horner seemed to disturb this delicate balance of the Yakult Swallows. He did not have wa. To Horner, Japanese baseball seemed formal and incredibly uptight (Whiting, 1989, p. 24). He began to think about going home to the United States. He complained incessantly to his teammate Leon Lee and to players from the United States on other teams. He had culture shock.

Japan is a collectivistic culture in which the collectivity's goals are valued over those of the individual. One reason for Bob Horner's cultural conflicts with his manager and the press was that he represented an individualistic culture in a collectivistic society. These incompatibilities affected not only his home run production and his batting average, but also the Swallows's wa, and consequently their won-lost record.

Horner actually finished the 1987 season with a respectable batting average of .327 with 31 home runs. The media calculated that had he played every game in the 130-game schedule, his home run production would have totaled 51. The Yakult Swallows offered him $10 million for a three-year contract. Instead, Horner accepted a one-year contract to play for the St. Louis Cardinals for $950,000, thus showing his disdain for Japanese baseball.

Had Horner more fully understood U.S./Japanese cultural differences, how might he have conducted himself during his sojourn in Japan?

Summary

Assimilation is the degree to which an individual relinquishes an original culture for another. In past decades, the United States was a "melting pot" in which immigrants from Europe were assimilated within a generation or two. Today, however, the assimilation process has slowed down, in part because of the large number of immigrants who have retained their ability to speak their native language, the most important factor in resisting assimilation. *Acculturation* is the process through which immigrants adapt to the host culture while retaining aspects of their native culture. At the other end of the continuum is *cultural maintenance* where immigrants reject assimilation and maintain a separate culture.

Mass communication plays an important role in the assimilation versus maintenance of émigré cultures in the United States. *Mass communication* is the exchange of information via a mass medium (like radio, television, newspapers, and so forth) from one or a few individuals to an audience of many. The mass media are both mirrors and makers of the ethnic composition of the population. On the one hand, the media display and reinforce the dominant values and beliefs of the U.S. public and the various ethnic groups of which it is composed. On the other hand, the mass media shape the perceptions of ethnic groups in the nation. If an ethnic group is underrepresented on the television screen and on newspaper pages, the U.S. audience is influenced to think that the group is not a very important part of the nation's population. People of color make up about 25 percent of the U.S. population, but only 11 percent of the personnel in media newsrooms.

A *sojourner* is an individual who visits another culture for a period of time but who retains his/her original culture. Many sojourners encounter at least some degree of *culture shock*, defined as the traumatic experience that an individual may encounter when entering another culture. A similar type of culture shock (reverse culture shock) may be encountered upon *reentry*, defined as the process that an individual goes through when returning to his/her passport culture after a sojourn. Sojourning and reentry show that culture is an important influence on human behavior.

Notes

[1] In the Eastern United States (particularly the Southeast) and in New Mexico, the term *Hispanic* is preferred over *Latino* (Soruco, 1996). In Miami, *Latino* is perceived as somewhat negative and possibly implying lower-class status. While Oboler (1995) uses *Latino* in the title in her book *Ethnic Labels, Latino Lives: Identity and the Politics of (Re)Presentation in the United States*, she argues that *Hispanic* is the preferred term by most Latin Americans in the United States as a group identifier, with the exception of persons of Mexican descent living in the Western states. *Latino* refers to persons of Latin American descent, while *Hispanic* includes Latin Americans but also includes persons of Spanish descent. Once again, intercultural communication can be a matter of location and perception.

[2] A study cited by President Clinton in a June 1998 Springfield, OR speech on immigration indicates that, on average, immigrants pay $1,800 more in taxes each year than they receive in government benefits.

[3] A 1989 film, *Iron and Silk*, portrays a U.S. citizen teaching English as a foreign language in China, while studying Chinese martial arts. Mark Salzman (1986), who wrote the book on which the film is based, played himself.

[4] Gullahorn and Gullahorn (1963) introduced the idea of the U-curve of cultural adjustment.

[5] This case illustration is based on Chapter 1 of Whiting (1989). The reader may note the similarity of the Bob Horner case to the role played by actor Tom Selleck in the film *Mr. Baseball*.

Chapter 8

Becoming More Intercultural

> ❝ It really does little good to talk or lecture to people about prejudice. Tolerance has to be lived. ❞
>
> Edward T. Hall (1948)

This chapter provides guidelines for the individual who wishes to become more interculturally competent in a communication sense. How does one become more capable in intercultural communication? Does intimate contact with another culture lead to better intercultural communication? How can one overcome the obstacles that prevent effective intercultural communication?

Intercultural Competence

Intercultural competence is the degree to which an individual is able to exchange information effectively and appropriately with individuals who are culturally dissimilar. Individuals vary widely in their ability to communicate with culturally unalike others. As we noted in previous chapters, there is much evidence that intercultural communication is a difficult process.

The stated or implied purpose of most research, training, and teaching in the field of intercultural communication is to improve the intercultural competence of individuals. This objective has been apparent since the beginnings of the field of intercultural communication at the Foreign Service Institute in the 1950s. One of the most important skills for cultural competence is the ability to suspend our assumptions about what is "right." The greater the range of alternatives to which we are exposed, the more choices we have for deciding what makes sense for us. "Knowing another culture gives you a place to stand while you take a good look at the one you were born into" (Bohannan & van der Elst, 1998, p. 6). Anthropologists are taught to be nonjudgmental about cultural differences. Even though they may study a culture that has sexual practices considered bizarre by European/North American standards, anthropologists seek to understand the functions fulfilled by these sexual practices from the point of view of the culture in which they occur. Hall and his anthropological colleagues who founded intercultural communication were nonjudgmental, and the new field took on this attitude.

We live in a world that is increasingly diverse in a cultural sense. Large U.S. cities, for example, have populations that are extremely diverse. Improved communication technologies and transportation make intercultural contact increasingly common (see Chapter 9). This trend will continue in the future; the "global village" becomes more real every day. If individuals could attain a higher degree of intercultural competence, they would presumably become better citizens, students, teachers, businesspeople, and so forth. Society would be more peaceful, more productive, and become a generally more attractive place in which to live. Individuals would be better able to understand others who are unlike themselves. Through such improved understanding, a great deal of conflict could be avoided; the world would be a better place.

Most North Americans *want* to become more interculturally experienced. College students, for example, want to learn about individuals unlike themselves. They often attend religious services of religions other than the one in which they were raised. They make friends with individuals from nations other than their own. They may date someone from another ethnic group, attracted to someone who does not think exactly as they do. Many students take vacations in other nations, go on student exchanges, and/or study at foreign universities. ***Heterophilous contacts with culturally different people provide an opportunity to become more interculturally competent, but they do not guarantee it.*** Our ability to learn from other individuals depends on our ability to overcome the barriers of culture.

Willingness to expand one's skills to include intercultural communication is an essential first step in overcoming barriers to intercultural communication. However, despite good intentions, we should be mindful of possible negative outcomes. ***Intercultural contact in many cases leads an individual to become more ethnocentric, prejudiced, and discriminatory***. Even when we are aware of the barriers that make intercultural communication particularly difficult, we may mistakenly attribute problems to other people rather than examining our own skills or lack of them. Misunderstandings are as likely to result from intercultural contact as are understandings. How do we develop sufficient intercultural communication competence to ensure more successes than failures? The following sections revisit major barriers to intercultural communication and suggest ways to improve one's skills.

Overcoming Ethnocentrism

One of the most important barriers to intercultural competence is ethnocentrism, the degree to which other cultures are judged as inferior to one's own culture. As explained in Chapter 2, ethnocentrism can lead to racism and sexism. As defined previously, racism categorizes individuals on the basis of their external physical traits, such as skin color, hair, facial structure, and eye shape, leading to prejudice and discrimination. Sexism is the assignment of characteristics to individuals on the basis of their sex, such that the genders are treated unequally. In many cultures, the female gender is treated as inferior and subjected to prejudice and discrimination.

How can ethnocentrism, and its attendant racism and sexism, be decreased or eliminated? Decreasing ethnocentrism is usually not just a matter of increased information but rather one of bringing about an emotional change on the part of the individuals involved. Greater contact between unalike individuals may be one means to lessen ethnocentrism, as Gordon Allport's (1954/1979) contact hypothesis suggests (see Chapter 2). Many individuals study other national cultures or travel to visit them because they think that closer contact will help them toward better understanding of an unalike culture. However, the nature of such intercultural contact is an important determinant of whether such travel decreases or increases ethnocentrism toward the culture that is visited. Many tourists who visit another culture for a brief period, often without knowing the language, become *more* ethnocentric toward that culture. Touristic sojourning often does little to decrease ethnocentrism toward a national culture. Language competence, contact over a lengthy period of time, and a more intense relationship with members of the foreign culture (such as through close personal friendships) can help decrease ethnocentrism. The key is that only positive contacts produce positive feelings about another culture.

The various elements of a culture are integrated so that each element generally makes sense in light of the other elements. When a stranger encounters only one cultural element, independently of the other elements, it may seem exotic, unusual, or weird. Only when the outside observer experiences and understands *all* of the cultural elements, does that culture make sense. This level of cultural understanding can be achieved more fully if an individual has fluency in the language that is spoken and has had extended personal contact. Only then can the stranger perceive all of the elements of an unfamiliar culture and understand that the totality is coherent.

The nature of contact also applies to the case of ethnocentrism toward another religion, race, or any outgroup *within* one's own society. Just as most individuals have only limited, and socially distant, contact with foreigners, so do most North Americans communicate mainly with others who are ethnically much like themselves. The degree of interpersonal contact with heterophilous others is infrequent, but when interpersonal relationships occur, they have a rich potential for behavior change. ***Direct, personal (one-on-one) contact with an unalike other can decrease ethnocentrism***.

More individuals today have the opportunity to meet people from another culture. Frequently the reasons for increased contact are related to studying or working abroad. Sojourning *can* be an effective type of intercultural communication in decreasing ethnocentrism, especially if the stay is long enough. The special cultural patterns created, shared, and learned by individuals who have lived in a culture other than their own have been termed "third culture" (Useem & others, 1963). Even though the sojourning individuals may have a different first culture (the culture into which they were born and reared) and a different second culture (the culture in which they sojourned), they learn to share a world-encompassing perspective (the third culture). Someone who was born in the United States and then lived in India has a third culture experience in common with another individual who was born in Japan and then sojourned in Mexico.

Most people learn the third culture as adults when they sojourn abroad. Their children may learn the third culture by accompanying their parents on the sojourning experience. Third culture young people have much in common and, in fact, often marry each other. Third culture individuals are unusually tolerant and understanding of cultural differences. They are less likely to think in terms of borders between ingroups and outgroups.

Some individuals have a third culture from birth. Biracial children, for example, can often operate effectively within each of their parents' cultures and can connect the two. Biracial people, who never leave their home nation, have a third culture. In the United States, the number of interracial marriages is increasing, as is the number of multiracial children. Today there are more than two million people of mixed racial ancestry in the United States; this number may be a substantial underestimate.

Experiential Training

Ethnocentric attitudes are firmly entrenched in cultural norms and thus are extremely difficult to change. Change is not, however, impossible. One means of decreasing ethnocentrism is intervention through training. There are courses designed to help individuals understand the nature of their ethnocentric beliefs. One example of an ethnocentrism intervention is a two-week training course in India that is designed to decrease the sexism of male government employees. This Women's Awareness Training puts the male trainees in the daily role of an Indian woman. The trainees carry water from a distant well, wash their clothes and dishes, cook, and clean their living quarters. The male trainees are not allowed to go outside of their residences without permission of a female trainer. Nor are the trainees permitted to drive a vehicle. Thus, the Indian men are taught to empathize with the subservient role of Indian women. Individuals who have completed this training say that it has a powerful effect on their sexist attitudes and, more generally, in decreasing their ethnocentrism. The training is intended to increase empathy not just with women but with all heterophilous others, including lower-caste individuals and others considered inferior.

Intercultural communication training must be highly experiential in order for it to increase intercultural competence. Thus intercultural communication courses often use simulation games, exercises, videos, and other types of learning in which another culture can be experienced by the learner. In other words, if intercultural communication training is to have an effect on individuals' behavior, the unalike culture must be experienced. One cannot just talk about intercultural communication. One has to *do* it.

Cultural Relativism

As defined in Chapter 2, *cultural relativism* is the degree to which an individual judges another culture by its context. One can then understand the behavior of another individual in the context of the other's culture. Thus cultural relativism is in a sense the opposite of ethnocentrism. Rather than picking out a specific cultural element as unusual or odd, the individual who is culturally relativistic considers that element in light of the total culture of which it is a part. When judged from the viewpoint of the entire culture, the cultural element usually can be understood for the functions that it serves.

For example, the Hindu value on sacred cows seems bizarre to many visitors to India. In a land where millions of individuals go hungry, cows roam the streets of large cities, causing traffic problems, but cannot be slaughtered for meat. To Westerners who are accustomed to an entirely different culture, one that stresses eating steak and hamburgers, the beliefs about cows seem illogical. But the sacred cows are very functional for Indian society. Their manure is gathered and used for fuel and fertilizer. Sacred cows are milked to provide an important source of protein for the human diet in a largely vegetarian society. Hindu religion, which believes in reincarnation, preaches that the cows may represent a former (or a future) form of human life. So the idea of sacred cows makes sense in light of the total culture of India, including its dominant religion, its vegetarianism, and the need for protein in the diet.

Differences surface in routine activities. For example, a European American may greet another person simply by saying, "Hi, my name is Sam Hill." In contrast, a Navajo living in Window Rock, Arizona, may respond by stating, "I am Tom Begay, by the Two-Who-Came-to-the-Water Clan [his mother's clan], for the One-Walks-Around Clan [his father's clan]." Many non-Navajos find such a lengthy introduction unnecessary and irrelevant. A culturally relativistic individual, however, would note that the identification of a Navajo's parental clans is functional in a society in which incest (marriage or intercourse with an individual perceived to be a relative) is a very strong taboo. The lengthy personal introduction establishes, from the initial contact between Navajo strangers, the ground rules for any future relationships.

The Navajo approach to housing is another example of a behavior serving a germane function within a culture. Tom Begay lives in a hogan. We learned in Chapter 6 that the door faces east because the Navajo feel a spiritual closeness with the sun. The hogan belongs to Tom's wife; the Navajo are matrilocal, which means that when they marry the husband goes to live in the wife's mother's hogan. All of these elements of Navajo culture make sense to a culturally relativistic individual who understands this culture and who appreciates its coherence.

Cultural relativism means that we understand a culture from the inside and that we look at the behavior of people from their point of view. Further, we respect the differences that contrast with our own culture.

From Ethnocentrism to Ethnorelativism

The variable of ethnocentrism versus ethnorelativism (that is, cultural relativism) is marked by a series of stages through which an individual may pass (Bennett, 1986):

1. A parochial *denial* of cultural differences, in which there is little contact with unalike others. For example, when Edward Hall (1957) was training diplomats and technicians at the Foreign Service Institute, many of the trainees initially insisted that all people are alike, once you get to know them.

2. An evaluative *defense* against understanding cultural differences, because they may be threatening to one's view of the world. An individual may say, "I don't want to understand what those people think. They are so different from us."

3. A *minimization* of cultural differences, through which cultural similarities are stressed. Edward Hall found that the mid-career agricultural technicians that he was training at the FSI frequently stated: "I have worked extensively with U.S. farmers in the past, and I expect that Latin American farmers will be about the same."

4. The *acceptance* of cultural differences, which are acknowledged and understood. Here a trainee in a cultural diversity workshop might say, "Okay, people in India do not use their left hand for eating, and I understand why."

5. The *adaptation* of one's thinking and behavior to cultural differences. A trainee might state: "Now I understand why women in the United

States feel they are underpaid for doing the same work as a man."

6. The *integration* of cultural differences into one's own worldview, so that one's identity is both a part of, but apart from, the different culture, and a new "third culture" perspective replaces the native culture perspective. A returned Peace Corps volunteer from Nigeria explained that she now felt she viewed North American culture from a different perspective than before her sojourn in Africa.

Training can move an individual through these six stages toward a greater degree of cultural relativism.

Pluralism is the degree to which an individual is open to others' points of view. Such broadmindedness is closely related to cultural relativism but may be even wider in scope. For example, one could be pluralistic regarding another individual's point of view on some issue like abortion. An ethnnorelativistic individual would accept a viewpoint if it were coherent with the rest of the culture of which it is part.

Societies, as well as individuals, can be pluralistic. Often a system that is characterized by *diversity* (defined as the degree to which a system is composed of a variety of individuals with different cultures) is also pluralistic. In Chapter 7, we reviewed how the United States is becoming increasingly diverse. Diversity can encourage tolerance for other points of view. Of course, diversity can also lead ethnocentric individuals to think in terms of ingroups and outgroups.

Overcoming Stereotypes

In order for individuals to become more interculturally conscious, they must learn to question stereotypes, the building blocks of prejudice, and to break through the arbitrary borders that have been taught to separate people from one another. The interculturally competent communicator judges each individual on a person-to-person basis, rather than categorizing people into stereotypes.

Derivation of Stereotypes

What is the origin of the word "stereotype"? In the early history of U.S. newspapers, more than 100 years ago, cartoons were extremely popular. Photography was not yet well developed, and newspapers were eager to publish illustrative material. The works of famous cartoonists were syndicated in a number of newspapers. The cartoonist's daily cartoon was distributed by sending a papier mâché mirror image of the cartoon through the postal service. A stereotype was made of the cartoon by converting the cartoon to lead type, and the cartoon was published in the local newspaper. The cartoons often featured exaggerated images of Uncle Sam, John Bull, the cunning

Asian, bloated politicians, and other social figures. Gradually, these cartoon images came to be called "stereotypes."

As explained in Chapter 2, a *stereotype* is a generalization about some group of people that oversimplifies their culture. Many stereotypes are completely incorrect and others greatly distort reality. For example, many North Americans have a stereotype of the college athlete as an individual who is not a serious student. The authors of this book have taught hundreds of athletes, many of whom were outstanding students. The stereotype was generalized from well-known examples. While there may be some truth in the stereotype (some athletes, like all other students, may not be exceptional scholars), it is greatly exaggerated. A stereotype is often self-fulfilling. If we accept a stereotype as an accurate description, we tend to see only evidence that supports it and to overlook the frequent exceptions to it.

In *Public Opinion*, Walter Lippmann (1922) spoke of "the pictures in our heads," and the role of the mass media in forming such stereotypes. One of the most shameful episodes in U.S. history resulted from the stereotypes depicting the enemy during World War II. Anti-Japanese propaganda convinced many people in the United States that the Japanese were cunning, tricky, and willing to fight to the death to win. The negative stereotype was mainly formed by news accounts carried by the media about warfare in the Pacific theater, by cartoons and posters, and by interpersonal communication influenced by the predominant beliefs of the time. Attitudes help us determine appropriate behavior. Nationalistic sentiments—protecting one's country by uniting against an enemy that threatens its national security—are essential during a war. However, those stereotypes created an atmosphere in 1942 in which U.S. citizens did nothing while the federal government put 110,000 *citizens* of Japanese ancestry in internment camps. Japanese-Americans were forced to leave their homes, their businesses, and their possessions behind because the stereotype portrayed them as threats to their own country (Figure 8-1).

Stereotypes as Codes

What is a code? A *code* is a classification used by individuals to categorize their experience and to communicate it to others. A code is a kind of shorthand that enables an individual to convey a range of phenomena in a single word. For example, ducks, geese, and swans are three variations of waterbirds. Adults are generally familiar with the general category and the three subcategories. A child may learn one of the subcategories and apply it to the other two, calling all birds paddling in a lake "ducks," for example.

A stereotype is a special kind of code. The term stereotype evolved from the printing process of repeatedly casting the same image—often exaggerated and usually negative. It is easier to communicate if we don't need to describe every nuance of difference. Rather than exerting the mental effort

Figure 8-1. Prejudice against Japanese Americans was very strong during World War II. The United States government officially apologized in 1988, 36 years after the government's relocation order, for violating the civil rights of Japanese Americans. A compensation of $20,000 was paid by the federal government to each survivor of the relocation camps.

Source: UPI/Corbis-Bettmann. Used by permission.

to evaluate all incoming information carefully and critically, we often resort to categorizing certain information into familiar patterns. Stereotypes are one of these patterns, and they can be positive or negative. For example, many people in the United States think that Asians have a gift for mathematics and science. Another stereotype is that Germans build the finest automobiles; the French have the best chefs; the Italians the finest opera singers.

We learn stereotypes as one part of our culture. Standardized mental pictures held in common by members of a group make it easier to decide what behavior is appropriate and what behavior to expect. The problem with such an oversimplified approach is that it distorts the reality of what we are perceiving. During initial contact with someone of a certain race or lifestyle, you may have reacted toward the stranger in a way determined by the stereotype that you held. The stereotype may have prevented you from ever getting to know the other individual. On the other hand, if you got to know the individual better, you might first believe that the stereotype did not apply to him or her and, eventually, that the stereotype incorrectly categorized all members of the group. We should recognize that within any stereotyped set of individuals, there is wide variation.

Forming codes and thinking in terms of these categories is a necessary aspect of human communication. Culturally sensitive individuals guard against the dangers of thinking in stereotypes; they remain flexible in changing these classifications. Culturally competent people use stereotypes as tools with limited functions. Cultural relativism is one means of questioning existing stereotypes. As we learn the codes of other cultures, we can evaluate our own more critically.

Overcoming Prejudice and Discrimination

Certain countries like the United States have a national policy objective to lessen discrimination. The Civil War of the 1860s, the Civil Rights movement of the 1950s and 1960s, and the equal opportunity legislation of recent decades are important landmarks in this historical movement toward lessened discrimination. But making discrimination illegal does not make it disappear. In order to decrease discrimination, individuals and systems must change. Such a shift in attitudes (prejudice) and in overt behavior (discrimination) ultimately can be encouraged by intercultural communication.

Prejudice

As explained in previous chapters, *prejudice* is an unfounded attitude toward an outgroup based on a comparison with one's ingroup. Prejudice is usually expressed through communication. For example, an African-American student attending a mainly White university stated: "In my freshman year, at a university student parade, there was a group of us standing there not knowing that this was an event that not a lot of Black people went to. Our dorm was going, and . . . we were students too! . . . A group of White fraternity boys—I remember the Southern flag—and one of them pointed and said, 'Look at that bunch of niggers!' I remember thinking, 'Surely he's not talking to us!' . . . I wanted to cry" (quoted in Feagin, 1992).

After several such unpleasant experiences, an individual develops an expectation of experiencing prejudice in similar situations. Another African-American student attending a predominantly White university explained: "I still find myself uncomfortable if I walk into a strange environment where there are only Whites and I'm the only Black. And unfortunately, usually someone, at least one person in that environment or in that situation, will say or do something that's negative, if it's no more than just ignore you. So, if you come in defensive . . . your fear is reinforced" (quoted in Feagin, 1992).

There are many types of prejudice in the United States, but one of the most obvious is prejudice by European Americans toward African Americans. In the 1940s Gunnar Myrdal (1944) identified racial prejudice as *An American Dilemma*. In recent decades, White North Americans' negative perceptions of African Americans have softened as part of a general liberalization of racial attitudes in the United States and as segregation has decreased (Sigelman & Tuch, 1997). However, many prejudiced Whites still cling to negative stereotypes. A national survey of ethnic images found that African Americans are more likely than European Americans, Latinos, Asian Americans, or Southern Whites to be perceived as poor, violent, unintelligent, and welfare-dependent (Smith, 1990). A 1991 national survey found that 31 percent of White European Americans perceived African Americans as lazy, and 50 percent thought they were aggressive (Peffley & Hurwitz, 1993).

This kind of prejudice leads to discrimination. Whites who perceive African Americans as lazy are less supportive of government programs to alleviate poverty. Those who perceive African Americans as unintelligent and violent are less supportive of school integration (Smith, 1990). Public opinion polls in the United States show that the nation is actually two societies: One Black and one White, separate and unequal (Kinder & Sanders, 1996). The two groups differ markedly in socioeconomic status and are divided by residential segregation. The public opinion polls show that Blacks and Whites disagree, even on topics that have no explicit racial content (Kinder & Sanders, 1996). So the "American dilemma" that Gunnar Myrdal wrote about 50 years ago still exists.

Prejudice can take as many forms as there are groups who perceive difference as a threat. Earlier we looked at the prejudice against Japanese Americans from 1942 to 1945. Despite the unimaginable discrimination against citizens in a democracy, some 33,000 Japanese Americans enlisted in the armed forces, some of them serving in the much-decorated 442nd Regiment in Europe. When U.S. President Harry Truman welcomed home this regiment in 1946, he said: "You fought not only the enemy, you fought prejudice—and you won" (quoted in Takaki, 1993, p. 384).

Prejudice is a kind of cultural blindness. It prevents us from seeing reality accurately. In order for individuals to become more interculturally competent, they must avoid the prejudiced attitudes that often lead to discrimination and the unequal treatment of others.

Discrimination

Discrimination, as defined previously in this book, is the process of treating individuals unequally on the basis of their race, gender, or other characteristics. In the United States, federal laws state that discrimination is illegal in

---

Case Illustration:
A Navajo Perspective on Prejudice[1]

When I was in junior high school in Gallup, New Mexico, White people were racially biased against Native Americans and Hispanics, but especially against we Navajos. White kids made fun of the way that Navajo kids talked and of their clothing. Their criticism was even stronger in high school, but I could take it because my grandparents raised me to be strong. I had to chop wood, bring coal in to our hogan, and take cold showers. We did not have running water. This hard life and the demanding work of herding sheep would kill a White man. Navajos live in the Third World.

But in Gallup High School, the Navajo students could not display pride in being Navajo, or they were criticized. My grandparents were a medicine man and a medicine woman, and I was raised to believe in the traditional Navajo way. I am proud that I am Navajo. Our teachers in high school did not teach us the history of Native people. They skipped an entire chapter in our history book on the Holocaust of the Native Americans [such as the massacre at Wounded Knee]. Many Navajo kids did not honor our traditional ways, looked down on our culture, and felt embarrassed by it. In high school, White people hung out with White people, Hispanic people were friends with Hispanics, and Navajo people mingled with Navajo people. Hispanics outnumbered the other two groups. This did not matter to me because I felt that no one really knows their cultural identity until they go to college.

Politics on the reservation are simply corrupt. People embezzle money, and use their power to get government housing for their family members. This is disgusting, but it happens everywhere in the United Sates and in other nations.

Interracial marriages are highly discouraged by Navajo culture, especially with a White man or a Black man. Such a marriage brings a taboo into your life, and eventually will kill you or put you in the hospital with a terminal illness. This belief has some recent exceptions [Miss Navajo of 1997 was of Navajo and Black ancestry, and she is well accepted]. I might marry a White man because Navajo men do not communicate what they feel. Also, I don't want to marry an alcoholic. But there is always that one good man in a million.

---

housing, hiring, schooling, and in other aspects of daily life. The Civil Rights Act of 1964 prohibits employment discrimination on the basis of race, color, sex, marital status, religion, or national origin. Such laws, even when vigorously enforced, however, have by no means eliminated discrimination. Such behavior change usually requires a dramatic, emotional type of communication. Information alone seldom leads to change in individuals' discriminatory behavior. ***Laws alone cannot change cultural norms on discrimination.***

The positive movement toward lessened discrimination in the United States suffered a major setback in April, 1992. Four White Los Angeles police officers were found not guilty of brutality against Rodney King, an African American who had been beaten by the policemen, an event documented on videotape. The trial results immediately set off widespread rage on the part of African Americans and Latinos in Los Angeles. Violence, burning, and looting occurred in many parts of the city over the next several days, with the Los Angeles Police Department unable to control the angry crowds. Some 58 people were killed in the rioting, 5,500 individuals were arrested, and one billion dollars worth of property was destroyed, mainly by fires. Especially hard hit were Korean-owned businesses; some 2,000 were destroyed or demolished. The 1992 Los Angeles race riots turned entire sections of the city into burned-out war zones. Rodney King pleaded for calm: "We can all get along. I mean, we're all stuck here for a while. Let's try to work it out."

Why does racial violence erupt in situations like the 1992 Los Angeles riots? Discrimination and violence often result from a sense of threat (Aguirre & Turner, 1995, p. 39). For example, the passage of Proposition 209, the California Civil Rights Initiative, in 1996 was fueled by the public belief that Latinos, African Americans, and Asian Americans in California had received more than their share of resources, at the expense of European Americans. California voters feared reverse discrimination, which occurs when programs intended to overcome past discrimination deny equal access to valued resources to members of the dominant ethnic population. This perceived threat leads to support for policies like the California Civil Rights Initiative, which, despite its name, was a setback for antidiscrimination programs.

Mahatma Gandhi championed reduced discrimination against the untouchable caste in India (Figure 8-2). He renamed them *Harijans* (children of God) and insisted that they must be treated by upper-caste Indians as equals. Gandhi also took direct action against discrimination. For example, on one occasion Gandhi was traveling by railway across southern India. The leaders of a village in West Godavri District in Andhra Pradesh state heard that his train was coming and lay down on the railroad tracks so that the train was forced to stop. The high caste leaders pleaded with Gandhi to visit their village, which he agreed to do. As he strode into the village, Gandhi offered a drink of water from the well reserved for Brahmins to a Harijan. Then he led a group of Harijans into the Hindu temple, from which they had been barred, effectively desegregating it. He then made the village leaders promise they would not discriminate against the Harijans in the future.

One of the authors visited this village several decades later. The wells and temples remained open to all. During a five-minute visit, Gandhi had ended the discrimination in this Indian village that had been maintained for many centuries.

Gandhi is credited with convincing the British to give India its independence. He involved the huge lower class of millions of Indians in his efforts

Figure 8-2.   Pictured on the left is Mahatma Gandhi, the leader of the Indian Independence Movement. He was also famous for his role in decreasing religious and caste prejudice and discrimination in the 1930s and 1940s. On the right is Martin Luther King, Jr., leader of the U.S. Civil Rights movement in the 1960s. He studied Gandhi's strategies for peaceful social change, and applied these strategies in the South. Both Gandhi and King show the tremendous influence that an individual champion can have in improving society.

Source: Drawings by Corinne L. Shefner-Rogers. Used by permission.

to end colonial status. In 1915, Gandhi stated: "India is not 200 elite lawyers arguing in New Delhi." Through organized demonstrations which received extensive news coverage from the world's media, Gandhi and his followers protested British rule. On one occasion Gandhi resisted British discrimination represented by a sign "English Only" on a footbridge in an Indian city. Gandhi walked across the bridge and was arrested by the British. Then 200,000 of his followers walked across the bridge and were also jailed. No one resisted arrest. Soon, all of the jails were filled. Yet more of Gandhi's followers walked across the bridge. The British were forced to remove the discriminatory sign.

Thus did Gandhi work out strategies of peaceful social change. Eventually, in 1947, he and his followers were able to gain independent nationhood in India. But Gandhi was unable to solve the religious hatred between Muslims and Hindus in former British India, and so the new nation was divided into Hindu India and Muslim Pakistan. Enmity between these two neighboring countries continues to this day.

Martin Luther King, Jr., the famous African-American leader of the Civil Rights movement, studied Gandhian strategies of peaceful social change. King then applied these strategies to oppose racial discrimination in the United States. For example, King and other Civil Rights leaders organized restaurant sit-ins and public marches in order to call attention to the Jim Crow discrimination in the South. These demonstrations received massive news coverage in the U.S. mass media: police dogs, water cannons, and electric cattle prods were used by White sheriffs on Black men, women, and children. The media, especially television, showed the South and the rest of the United States an image of themselves of which they could not be proud. The strategies of social change that had been formulated by Gandhi were applied by Martin Luther King, Jr. and his followers to achieve similar ends in two different cultures.

King and Gandhi show the importance of champions in combating discrimination and in changing human behavior on a massive scale, even when they lack formal power or authority. These cases of bottom-up social change in India and the United States show again that changing laws does not necessarily change the norms of a system. Many of the Civil Rights demonstrations in the South were intended to end discrimination that was illegal (under federal laws that were not enforced).

Gender discrimination is an important problem throughout the world. In the United States a survey of men and women showed that most women were quite angry about being treated as inferiors by men. Most of the female respondents in the survey could cite specific examples of discrimination. In comparison, men were not interested in talking about their discrimination against women. The men acknowledged that gender discrimination occurred, but they were not bothered by it. We noted in the previous chapter that women in the United States receive an average salary that is three-fourths that of men. In other words, if a man and a woman both perform the same job, the male is paid $1.00 while the female is paid 75 cents. Stated another way, women with a university degree are paid the equivalent of what men earn who have only a high school degree. The feminist movement in the United States, inspired by the Civil Rights movement and using some of its strategies, seeks to end gender discrimination.

A strong son-preference exists in India. Male babies are given more food than female babies, and so males are more likely to survive. As they grow up, girls are less likely to be sent to school. Females often have little or no say in whom they will marry. Child marriage (under the legal age of 18) is frequent, especially in villages. A dowry is usually paid by the bride's family to the groom's family. A serious social problem has arisen in India in recent years in the form of "dowry deaths," which occur when the bride's family agrees to pay an exorbitant dowry. If her family defaults on the payment, the groom's family mistreats the new wife. On some occasions, they burn her to death in a supposedly accidental kitchen fire (by drenching her with kerosene). Ironically in recent decades, technological development has increased sexist practices. Once the medical equipment for amniocentesis became widely available, it was used to determine the sex of unborn children in India so that female fetuses could be aborted. As a result, many more male babies are born than are female babies.

How would you go about changing sexism in India so as to eliminate the dowry deaths and the abortion of female babies? Both acts are illegal, but they are supported by the patriarchal values of Indian society. Reversing the trend toward dowry deaths and female abortion in a nation of one billion people might strike one as being impossible, but efforts are being made in India to decrease sexism.

The social problem of dowry deaths in India can be overcome. One of this book's authors helped evaluate the effects of a radio soap opera, *Tinka Tinka Sukh* (Happiness Consists of Small Pleasures) that was broadcast in 1996-1997 in North India. This entertainment-education[2] soap opera taught the value of gender equality through its storyline and its characters, who were positive and negative role models. The "dowry death" of a young bride takes place in the soap opera, in this case by suicide after the bride is abused and mistreated by her husband's family. Of 120,000 letters mailed in response to the program by Indian listeners, many dealt with the issue of dowry. One Indian village, Lutsaan, sent a huge poster-sized letter signed by 184 residents of the village stating that they would neither pay nor accept dowry from that day onward. The residents of Village Lutsaan also agreed by consensus to treat their girls equally with boys (such as by sending them to the village school) and to oppose child marriage. *Tinka Tinka Sukh* featured positive role models for gender equality, such as a daughter who refused a child marriage and who withstood family pressures for marriage so that she could pursue a career. She becomes a medical doctor (Papa & others, 1998). So the mass media can alter sexism and other types of ethnocentrism, if they communicate involving, emotional messages about these topics.

However, while the dowry concept is abhorrent to many Indians, they still feel that they must pay dowry in order to get their daughters married. Thus their individual wishes are entrapped by cultural norms, which they feel they cannot change. Even in Village Lutsaan, where many individuals rejected dowry, this illegal practice was not stopped entirely because brides must marry husbands outside of their village. Thus to halt completely the practice of dowry, all of the villages in the Lutsaan area would have to reject the norm on dowry.

Many groups experience discrimination in today's world. Homosexuals are one of the groups most discriminated against in U.S. society. Religious prejudice still exists, particularly against Jews and Muslims. People with disabilities, people with AIDS, people who are overweight, people who work in the sex industry, and people who are old all experience discrimination. As a result, they lose jobs, are refused opportunities to rent or purchase homes, and must struggle to maintain a positive self-image and worldview in the face of relentlessly unfair characterizations and behavior.

Overcoming Conflict

The world is filled with conflict, racial tension, and war. How can such conflict be dealt with, avoiding the escalation that leads to violence? How can conflict be transformed into positive and constructive directions?

Negotiation is the process of settling a conflict by facilitating understanding between the disputing parties. The negotiation process involves each disputing party listening carefully to the other party and then reaching some compromise.

A related means of overcoming conflict is *mediation*, the process of finding peaceful solutions to a conflict through a neutral, third party intervention. The mediation process is confidential and private. First, one of the disputants is asked to describe the conflict. The mediator then summarizes this side of the story. The other disputant then describes the conflict from the other point of view. Again the mediator summarizes the main points. Then the two parties identify the main issues of contention, which are listed by the mediator. The two disputants decide which issue to begin resolving, usually starting with the easiest. When all of the issues have been discussed and settled (if possible), the mediator puts an agreement in writing that the two parties each sign. The agreement specifies exactly who will do what in order to resolve the conflict.

The mediation process is nonbinding in that the participants are not forced to accept the mediated resolution of their conflict. The purpose of mediation is to provide each side of a conflict with an improved understanding of the other party's point of view and thus to resolve issues before they escalate into a legal dispute or a more serious type of conflict. Mediation is more difficult when the parties in conflict do not share a common culture. Reaching an understanding is more difficult when cultural differences divide the two parties.

The mediation process, as described above, may have limited application in cultures other than European American. For example, the success of the mediation process rests on the willingness of the two disputants to engage in direct communication about the conflict. In many cultures, however, conflicting parties prefer to deal through intermediaries, rather than to meet directly. Individuals in some cultures (such as collectivistic cultures) are more relational-oriented, rather than task-oriented, and would fear the loss of face if they participated in a mediation process. Further, certain cultures may doubt that a neutral, fair mediator could exist. Most experts on mediation believe that we have far to go toward achieving a mediation process that is not culturally limited.

Resolving conflict is the final measure of how competent we are as communicators. Some conflicts may never be resolved. One of the reasons for that negative prognosis is that the emotions attached to most conflicts often override much of the knowledge we have learned about communicating with others—alike or unalike. This text has introduced a number of seemingly routine behaviors—introductions, invitations for coffee, standing in line, crossing the street—that become barriers to communicating competently and developing relationships. If expectations are violated in those instances and we find it difficult to reduce the uncertainty experienced, what happens when life-threatening situations arise? Although simplistic, the adage of "one step at a time" applies. If we develop a habit of viewing behavior with an open, flexible approach, we have a better opportunity to apply the communication skills most likely to lead to an understanding with others.

Toward Multiculturalism

Multiculturalism is the recognition that several different cultures can exist in the same environment and benefit each other. The cultures may be national cultures or may be those of various ethnic groups within the same nation. For example, in 1960, the U.S. workforce was dominated by European American White males. One could stand in the lobby of an office building at the end of the workday and observe people exiting elevators. Well-dressed White men stepped out of the elevators that descended from the executive floors. Women, mainly European Americans, came out of the elevators from the floors of the building on which the typing pool was located. The men from the loading dock and the furnace room, dressed in work clothes, were often members of ethnic groups.

Today, the composition in the scene of people getting off the elevators is much different. The genders would no longer be segregated on the executive floors versus the typing pool, nor would members of different ethnic groups be limited to manual occupations. Today, about 80 percent of the additions to the U.S. workforce are women, members of ethnic groups, and immigrants. Male European Americans are now a minority of individuals entering the employed ranks. This dramatic change in the U.S. workforce is one evidence of multiculturalism in the United States.

Brazil is often held up as an ideal society in a multicultural sense and one that might hold useful lessons for the United States. The largest country in

Latin America in territory and population size, Brazil's history parallels that of the United States. European colonizers, the Portuguese, overwhelmed the native people, whose population dropped precipitously in the 1800s due to the spread of European diseases. The Portuguese imported slaves from Africa to work on plantations and in businesses. Brazil imported eight times as many slaves as did the slave states in North America. Then, about 100 years ago, large numbers of Italians, Germans, Spanish, and Portuguese immigrated to Brazil, as occurred in the United States at about the same time (in the late 1800s).

Unlike the United States, however, Brazil is characterized today by relatively smooth race relations. Some 40 percent of the total population are of mixed ancestry, due to widespread intermarriage between the European immigrants, African Americans, and the native people (Aguirre & Turner, 1995). Black and White are not perceived as a dichotomy. Why is Brazil so unlike the United States in its race relationships? Historically, many former slaves were freed in Brazil, and a smooth transition took place when slavery ended in 1888, unlike the U.S. Civil War of the 1860s. Blacks and Whites were economically dependent on each other in Brazil, and people of African ancestry were highly valued as employees. So the European Brazilians were much more dependent on the slave population to sustain the economy. Slaves were perceived as humans and attitudes toward them were not as harsh as in the United States.

Brazilian society has long pursued a policy of assimilation, in which all people, including those of African descent, were expected to share a common culture and to intermix physically as well as culturally. In contrast, in the United States the "melting pot" policies of assimilation applied to European Americans, and perhaps Asian Americans, but not to African Americans. Many states had laws against miscegenation until recent decades. Cultural blending was expected, but the intermarriage of Black and White Americans was not allowed. Despite more favorable attitudes resulting from the historical experiences described above, Brazil has not completely eradicated prejudice. Most of the higher socioeconomic positions are filled by lighter-skinned people. As in the United States, the government is committed to pursue policies that reduce discrimination, but these policies are not very effective.

Looking at other systems can often provide lessons about how to encourage multiculturalism at a societal and an individual level. How can an individual become more multicultural?

1. Communicate with culturally heterophilous others. Seek friends who are culturally different from yourself. Travel. Learn languages other than your native tongue as a means of better understanding cultures in which these languages are spoken.

2. Work at understanding people unlike yourself. Reading about their culture may be helpful, but you can also learn by getting to know members of another culture on a personal basis. Go out of your way

to develop close relationships with unalike others. Participate in intercultural and diversity training courses that help you become less ethnocentric and more understanding of unalike others.

3. Empathize with heterophilous others so that you can look at the world from their point of view. Be pluralistic and culturally relativistic. Do not think of ingroups and outgroups, but instead perceive of a continuum of cultural differences, such as on the basis of individualism/collectivism or other dimensions.

4. Capitalize on the natural curiosity that we all have in learning about other people who are different from us. Encourage your friends and family members to become multicultural. Set an appropriate example for them to follow.

5. Understand yourself, particularly your degree of ethnocentrism, prejudice, and stereotyping versus cultural relativism, tolerance, and understanding.

6. Recognize and appreciate the cultural differences among people in your environment.

7. Be nonjudgmental of others and their cultural values.

Summary

Intercultural competence is the degree to which an individual is able to exchange information effectively and appropriately with individuals who are culturally dissimilar. If you can be effective in intercultural communication, you will be better able to learn from others who are culturally different.

Throughout this book, we have shown that cultural differences between people pose difficulties for intercultural communication. Ethnocentrism rejects others as inferior to one's own system. Stereotypes, the building blocks of prejudice, categorize others into familiar patterns. These standardized mental pictures distort reality and can lead to discriminatory behavior. Cultural relativism counteracts the effects of ethnocentrism, prejudice, and discrimination, as does experiential training.

Multiculturalism recognizes that several different cultures can exist in the same environment and benefit each other. Cultural differences can provide a rich resource for creative learning about the world, if culturally unalike individuals communicate effectively. Communication opens the door to developing closer relationships—the most powerful means of expanding understanding and becoming multicultural. Competence in intercultural communication is an important quality for an individual living in today's world. It will be even more valuable for our children.

Notes

1   This case illustration was written as a longer paper by a Navajo student enrolled in a course in intercultural communication at the University of New Mexico.

2   *Entertainment-education* is the process of purposely creating a media message to both entertain and educate in order to change audience members' behavior (Singhal & Rogers, in press).

Chapter 9

The Global Village

> Knowledge of the cultural dimension as a vast complex of communications on many levels would be virtually unnecessary if it were not for two things: our increasing involvements with people in all parts of the world, and the mixing of subcultures within our own country as people from rural areas and foreign countries pour into our cities.
>
> Edward T. Hall (1966)

We began our investigation of intercultural communication with a look at the historical context of intercultural contact that formed the background of present-day patterns of thinking about unalike others. After reviewing the main concepts and areas of intercultural communication, we here look at the key issues that intercultural communicators will confront in the increasingly smaller world of tomorrow.

The channels for communication have proliferated at dizzying speed. Transportation links formerly remote locations. The mass media provide instant information from the opposite side of the globe. Have abilities to communicate with unalike others matched the advance of these new technologies? We begin this chapter with development communication, a specific application of intercultural communication that is important to the world. We then look at ethical issues of using intercultural communication to change someone's culture and at other aspects of the global village of today.

Development Programs in Third World Countries

In Chapter 1 we read about the imperialism of European countries during recent centuries in expanding their authority across the globe. When the former colonies of Latin America, Africa, and Asia obtained their political independence, the main problem facing the new national governments was development. These were countries characterized by poor health, low levels of formal education, inadequate housing, and the low productivity that accompanies low income. The new governments turned their efforts to mounting development programs to remedy these socioeconomic problems. They took the richer, industrialized countries of the West as their models for development and pursued national policies to become more like them. They invited the Western nations to assist them in designing and implementing development programs in the decades since the end of World War II. These development programs brought together culturally unalike people in a unique kind of intercultural contact.

What Is Development?

Development is defined as a widely participatory process of social change in a society intended to bring about both social and economic advancement for the majority of people through gaining greater control over their environment (Rogers, 1995, p. 127). In the 1950s and 1960s, development programs were mainly directed by economists and technicians skilled in agriculture, education, medicine, and health. These early development programs were generally disappointing. Many failed. They did not reach their goals of raising per capita incomes, lowering child mortality rates, and boosting literacy rates in Latin America, Africa, and Asia. Gradually in the 1960s and thereafter it was realized that more attention needed to be paid to communication processes in development, especially at the point where development workers interacted with the people who would be most affected by the social change.

What Is Development Communication?

Development communication is the exchange of information between two or more individuals in which one individual (a change agent) seeks to assist the other individual to achieve a higher socioeconomic status by changing his/her behavior. A *change agent* is an individual who influences clients' decisions to adopt innovations (Rogers, 1995, p. 27). Client populations often consist of rural villagers or the urban poor. An *innovation* is any idea perceived as new by the intended audience. For example, a change agent may introduce a higher-yielding crop variety to village farmers or an improved tool or a new piece of equipment (Figure 9-1). Perhaps the development program concerns public health, and the change agent seeks to persuade individuals to adopt family planning, to prevent HIV/AIDS, or to immunize their children.

The change agent works for a change agency, which may be a government agency, an association of professionals, or a nonprofit organization—any

Figure 9-1. An Asian woman using an improved water pump, a foot treadle, to irrigate her rice field. Development programs in Latin America, Africa, and Asia introduce technological innovations in agriculture, health, and education in order to raise incomes and levels of living of the world's poor.

Source: IDE. Used with permission.

organization attempting to disseminate technical competence in some area. The change agent is the communication link between a resource system of some kind (the change agency) and the client system. He or she is responsible both for introducing the ideas to the clients and for providing feedback to the agency so that development programs can be adjusted to meet the needs of the clients.

Change Agent/Client Heterophily

Development programs always entail the communication of information between change agents and the members of the group they seek to help. When a change agent does not share a common culture with his/her clients, communicating with them so as to bring about change in their behavior is particularly difficult. Because the two parties often have very different perceptions regarding the innovation and the problem it is designed to address, effective communication about the new idea faces a number of problems. The participants are thus involved in intercultural communication.

As we learned in previous chapters, *heterophily* is the degree to which two or more individuals who communicate are unalike. Attempts at communication between heterophilous individuals are less likely to be effective than when the two individuals are similar. Change agents frequently are professionals with a university degree in a technical field. This professional training often separates them from the people they hope to influence—their clients. Thus the change agent often resembles Robert Park's marginal man with a foot in both worlds.

If change agents are to be successful, they must empathize with the audience's perceptions. Most change agents, however, do not take the trouble to understand their audience's point of view. Even when they do, they are likely to reject indigenous knowledge, perhaps because it is not scientific. For example, almost every village in the Third World has a cadre of traditional birth attendants, mental health specialists (called *curanderos* in Spanish), massagers, shamans, and animal health curers (similar to veterinarians). University-educated change agents reject such traditional practitioners, often calling them quacks, despite the credibility with which they are regarded by the mass population.

In contrast, when development programs have collaborated with traditional practitioners, there have often been impressive results. National family planning programs in India, Mexico, Indonesia, and the Philippines carefully trained traditional birth attendants in family planning. The midwives then supported the health programs and encouraged women to adopt family planning, instead of spreading rumors about the innovations as they had done when they were not asked to participate. When the traditional birth attendants are given training in antiseptic procedures for delivering babies, infant mortality rates usually drop. Birth attendants are perceived by village women as trustworthy and expert. When government health and family planning programs oppose traditional practitioners instead of collaborating with them, development programs are usually less successful.

Case Illustration:
Introducing Water-Boiling in a Peruvian Village[1]

In the Peruvian village of Los Molinos, most villagers drink water from an irrigation ditch that is polluted. It is not feasible to install a sanitary water system, so the Public Health Service of Peru assigned Nelida, a public health nurse, to introduce the innovation of water-boiling to the 200 families living there. The seemingly simple act of water-boiling would greatly reduce the rate of illness and would decrease infant mortality. After two years of intensive efforts, Nelida was able to convince only 11 housewives (5 percent) to adopt this procedure. This failure was not due to a lack of interpersonal contact. Nelida made several visits to each family, and some families were contacted 25 times.

Why did Nelida's efforts fail? The primary reason was that she ignored the cultural beliefs of the villagers. In Los Molinos, all foods, liquids, medicines, and other objects are inherently hot or cold, regardless of their actual temperature. The hot-cold label relates more to prescribed behavior in terms of what to approach and what to avoid than to temperature. Extremes are to be avoided by sick individuals. Pork is classified as very cold; brandy is considered very hot. Both would be avoided by someone who is sick. Water in its natural state is classified as very cold. Changing it by boiling removes it from the extreme classification and makes it acceptable for the ill to consume. Thus illness is linked with boiled water. This hot-cold classification is found throughout Latin America, Africa, and Asia, although what is considered hot or cold may vary. The norms of Los Molinos prevented housewives from adopting water-boiling unless one were ill. Nelida ignored this hot-cold perception, which she regarded as just a traditional belief irrelevant to improving public health.

Nelida tried to persuade villagers to boil water on the basis of germ theory. She invited villagers to look at the polluted water through a microscope, but their perceptions did not match Nelida's. If germs were so tiny that they could not be seen without a special device, how could they harm a grown person? How could the germs survive in water that would drown a person? The housewives of Los Molinos had real problems to worry about, like hunger. Why would they reject the custom of their village and boil water when they were not sick because of something too small to be seen?

The relationship of sanitation to illness was not part of the culture of the villagers. Nelida's attempts to convince the villagers to add water-boiling to their daily activities would only be successful if she were a credible source of information or if trusted others in the village believed her. Nelida was perceived as a stranger sent from the outside to spy on the villagers, as a "dirt-snooper."

The handful of housewives whom Nelida persuaded to adopt the innovation did not help her credibility. One housewife was already sickly, so it was considered appropriate for her to boil water. Another was a recent migrant to Los Molinos. She was not bound by the norms of this village and was an outsider. She perceived Nelida as having higher status and sought her approval. But her opinion was unimportant, if not detrimental, in the eyes of the villagers. Nelida worked most closely with exactly the wrong housewives if she wanted the diffusion process for water-boiling to become self-sustaining.

Nelida was more innovation-oriented than client-oriented. She did not take the time to learn what was important to the villagers. She assumed that the value of knowing about sanitation and germ theory was self-evident and would be accepted. In ignoring village norms about hot and cold, she failed to connect with attitudes that she could have woven into her communication so that it was meaningful to the villagers.

In addition to being empathetic with the clients' attitudes and values, change agents can learn the identity of the people in a community who provide information and advice to others. While the change agent may be heterophilous, opinion leaders are homophilous with others in the system. The informal influence of opinion leaders is earned and maintained by their social accessibility and their conformity to the norms of the system (Rogers, 1995). If a system is open to change, the leaders will be innovative; if not, the leaders will reflect that attitude.

Opinion leaders model the behavior prescribed by the system; they would lose respect if they deviated too far from the norms. These people are at the center of interpersonal communication networks. The acceptance of an innovation is a social process which depends on the communication of information and on the interpersonal relationships in a system. If a change agent earns the respect of opinion leaders, acceptance of technological innovations is much more likely.

Sustainability of Development Programs

During the 1960s, the Comilla Academy for Rural Development in Bangladesh (then East Pakistan) was a noted success story in community development. The Comilla Academy was established with technical assistance and funding from the United States. One of the authors visited Comilla in 1965 and was impressed by the agricultural productivity, the incomes of villagers, and the steps toward gender equality taking place throughout Comilla District.

Six years later when he returned, the Comilla Academy was gone, as was all evidence that a local development program had once been strikingly successful among the several million people of Comilla District. This experience, and many others like it in various developing nations, marked the necessity for a new focal point for development communication. *Sustainability* is the degree to which a development project continues to be effective after the original development effort ends. Development agencies like the World Bank began to use future sustainability as a criterion for deciding whether or not to fund a development project. It would be futile to initiate a development project that would have no lasting impact.

In a broader sense, the growing concern with sustainability reflected a recognition that development was a long-term process. For a development project to have an important impact, it had to become self-sufficient. A project's continuing dependence on external funding, on expert personnel, or on sophisticated, imported technology usually meant a low degree of sustainability and a lack of long-term impact.

A key ingredient in sustainability is the communication relationship between the development project leaders and the people it is intended to help. To communicate a new idea effectively requires knowledge about a group's attitudes and cultural values. It is more meaningful to explain new ideas in language and with illustrations relevant to the people who will have to sustain the new ideas. A change agent must know what the group's traditional ways of conducting some activity means to that culture. Remember that culture is not simply a collection of beliefs, norms, and values; it is how these aspects work together to form a unique approach to the world.

Let us consider the introduction of a higher-yielding grain. Perhaps the traditional variety of grain, although less productive, was better synchronized with other elements of the culture. If a harvest ritual is linked with a religious celebration which is linked to a fertility rite and the new grain ripens two months before the old one did, it may be rejected because it does not fit the culture. Perhaps the new variety tastes unlike the old one. No amount of explaining about increased bushels of yield will settle the other questions raised. The people may thoroughly understand the benefits of the new grain itself and seem to accept it in the presence of the change agent. But it will not be sustained after the agent's departure unless the villagers have participated in the communication process concerning the new idea so that they have constructed a place for it in their culture.

Empowerment

The women's movement in the United States and other industrialized countries beginning in the late 1960s had repercussions in the developing nations of Latin America, Africa, and Asia. The World Conference on Women was held in Nairobi in 1985, which was followed by the Beijing Conference in 1995. Women in developing countries, particularly those living in villages and urban slums, were treated unequally to men. Some national governments (like India) created a ministry of women's affairs, and many countries launched special development programs to raise the status of women.

One measure of the impact of these programs, and other programs like them for ethnic minorities and for rural and urban poor, is *empower-*

ment—the degree to which an individual perceives that she or he controls her/his situation. An empowered person actively engages his/her environment, rather than passively reacts to events over which the individual feels that she/he has no control. During the past decade, the empowering dimension of development programs has been strongly emphasized. Such empowerment means that a development activity should be carried out through a process that increases control on the part of the individuals expected to gain from the development program.

The empowerment criterion of development interventions meant that these programs had to be carried out with the conscious participation of the intended audience. As Saul Alinsky (1972), the Chicago labor organizer, noted: Don't do for others what they can do for themselves. The concept of empowerment also has a foundation in Paulo Freire's (1968) *consciousness-raising*, the degree to which learners become aware of their oppression and are motivated to change their underdog situation. Instead of an adult literacy teacher showing a drawing of a farmer with a cow and asking that learners memorize the word "cow," Freire (1968) argued that the teacher should also show a drawing of a farmer with ten cows, and then ask the literacy class members why one farmer has only one cow while the other farmer has ten cows. The learners not only learn the word "cow" and its plural more easily, but they also begin to question their unempowered status. Perhaps they will then seek to become more empowered.

An illustration of the empowerment process is provided by the following exchange between a trainer and fifty village women in Rajasthan State in India.

Trainer: Who goes to bed last in your house?

Women: We do.

Trainer: Who gets up first?

Women: We do.

Trainer: Who works hardest?

Women: We do.

Trainer: Who feeds and cares for the milk animals?

Women: We do.

Trainer: Who hands over the milk to your husbands to collect the money?

Women: We do.

Trainer: Who are fools?

Women: We are!

The female trainer is an employee of the National Dairy Development Board (NDDB), a quasi-governmental organization in India that assists dairy farmers. Most of the seven million dairy farmers in India are women, although they mainly supply labor and seldom share in management decisions. The NDDB trains female dairy farmers to demand the right to own the family's milk cows, to sell their milk and keep the money received, and to play a leadership role in their dairy marketing cooperative. The NDDB women's program is probably the largest empowerment program for women in the world. Once the female dairy farmers in a village are empowered, they form a women's club. These women's clubs often organize to combat their husbands' alcohol consumption and to solve other social problems in their village. Such women's clubs, in India and in other nations, are informal schools for empowerment (Shefner-Rogers & others, 1998).

In very recent years many development programs have targeted audiences who are the poorest of the poor: women, the most remote villagers, and the most disadvantaged. Development programs are now being designed and implemented in ways that empower the participants. Development is thus being redefined not as programs targeted *at* people, but rather as programs which people help design and implement.

The Grameen (Rural) Bank in Bangladesh consists of two million poor village women who cannot otherwise obtain credit. The amounts needed are very small, often only a few dollars. Professor Yunis, a professor of economics at the University of Daka, created the idea of the Grameen Bank in 1977. Poor women could obtain loans from a cooperative bank if their local network of five friends would personally guarantee their loan. No collateral of the kind usually required by banks is necessary. The Grameen Bank spread rapidly through Bangladesh, achieving a repayment rate of 99 percent. The Ford Foundation sent a team of evaluators to Bangladesh in the late 1980s to determine the effectiveness of this development program. The U.S. evaluators returned with so much enthusiasm that they became champions for the idea, and there are now Grameen Banks in the Chicago slums, rural Arkansas, and in Native American villages in Alaska (Awal & Singhal, 1992; Papa & others, 1995, 1997). Further, the concept of Grameen Banks spread to Latin America and to the Southwestern United States (where they are called *Acción*). Elsewhere the idea is called micro-lending.

As you read the case below, note the intercultural communication between a Peace Corps volunteer, Bob, and the villagers. Do Bob's attitudes match the local development worker's? What are the prospects for sustainability in using the fertilizer to increase crop yields? Does Bob engage in empowerment strategies? What would you emphasize if you were attempting to persuade the villagers to adopt the new variety of rice?

Case Illustration:
Thrown Out on the Edge of Asia[2]

Bob started the day with a bottle of orange pop at a street stall in the village, as he did every morning. The wizened women who operated the stall offered him a plate of rice topped with smelly fish sauce. He refused politely. Bob was not accustomed to eating rice for breakfast. The fish sauce made him nauseous, and he doubted that the food was prepared in a very sanitary manner. He had diarrhea most of the time. One month earlier he was treated by Peace Corps doctors for amoebic dysentery. While he sipped on the soda, several school children stared at him. He guessed they were probably thinking, "What kind of grown man would drink orange pop for breakfast?"

A young soldier assigned to the Village Security Force loitered near the food stall. He asked Bob if he had seen any of the leftist guerrillas who visited the village at night. The soldier carried an automatic weapon and stood very close to Bob when he talked. He had fish sauce on his breath. The soldier referred to the guerrillas as "Communists," using the English word. Bob's responsibility as a Peace Corps volunteer was to promote agricultural development in the village and not to become involved in political conflicts. As he finished his drink, the soldier winked and said, "You and me together, Bop, we'll fight the Communists." Everyone in the village substituted a "p" for the final "b" in his name.

Bob usually understood about 10 percent of what people in the village said to him. He had supposedly reached fluency in the language during his predeparture Peace Corps training. But the villagers talked with a strong accent and usually spoke very rapidly, especially when they were nervous (as they usually were when they talked to him). Often, Bob tuned out of a conversation entirely, just guessing at what others meant from the context of the discussion. It did not seem to matter much, as the usual conversation consisted mainly of polite exchanges.

Bob nodded to several village women who were washing clothes at the village pump. It would be improper for him to talk to them when their husbands were not present. He suspected that the women were gossiping about him, perhaps about why he was not married at 23 years of age (the villagers typically married soon after reaching puberty). On the first day that Bob had arrived in the village, the village leader asked him his age. He also asked him his salary and his sexual preferences. Bob guessed that the village elder wondered why Bob had left a rich country like the United States to spend two years in this village, way out on the edge of Asia. Sometimes Bob wondered the same thing.

After breakfast at the street stall, Bob met his counterpart, a community development worker assigned to boost farm yields in the village. They bowed formally, pressed their right hand to their heart, and murmured the traditional morning greeting. His counterpart called Bob "uncle" out of polite respect, even though Bob was half his age. When they had begun working together, Bob insisted that they ask the villagers to identify their community problems (as he had been taught to do in his Peace Corps training). His counterpart pointed out that a needs survey was futile, as the villagers would all say that they needed more land on which to grow rice. One landlord owned 90 percent of the land in the village, including all of the land that was ideal for growing rice. Bob insisted on conducting the needs survey anyway. It showed that lack of rice land was the number-one problem in the village. Even the big landowner said that he needed more land!

Bob and his counterpart laid out a rice-growing demonstration plot on some land behind the village school. They planted a new rice variety that would almost double the yields if chemical fertilizer were applied. This morning, Bob and his counterpart inspected the rice seedlings for damage by brown leafhoppers. The rice plants were a dark, healthy green, due to the nitrogen fertilizer that they had applied to the plot. Chemical fertilizer was a new idea in the village, and most farmers were suspicious of the white powder that Bob told them would lead to higher rice yields. The villagers agreed that the plants appeared to be healthy and faster-growing than their own rice, but a rumor had spread, started by the landowner, that the nitrogen caused the rice plants in the demonstration plot to steal nutrients from neighboring fields. The villagers perceived the fertilizer as magic rather than as nutrients for plant growth (they did not share Bob's paradigm of plant growth).

Bob lavished attention on the demonstration plot, often visiting it four or five times a day to check on pests or other problems. When they had established the demonstration, Bob's counterpart insisted that they ask the village religious leader to bless their rice plot. The ceremony consisted of splashing some rice whiskey over a small statue of the goddess of fertility. Then a gourd of whiskey was handed around the gathering of local farmers and each gulped the fiery liquor. Bob remembered to reach for the flask with his right hand, as the left hand is considered unclean. He managed to avoid choking on the raw whiskey, which would be interpreted as a sign that he was not a real man.

Several farmers were assembled at the demonstration plot that morning. Bob told the small gathering that even if they could not expand the size of their rice acreage, they could increase their rice yields by planting the new seed variety and by applying chemical fertilizer. The farmers listened impassively. Bob realized that they were not convinced to adopt the new rice variety and the chemical fertilizer.

As the villagers drifted away from the demonstration plot, Bob spotted the arrogant young soldier at the back of the crowd. Bob clapped him on the shoulder, winked broadly, and said: "You and me together, Soldier, we'll bring about development." The soldier smiled and said, "Yes, development."

Mass Media and Development

The mass media of communication began to play a more important role in development in the 1960s. By 1970, radio sets were found in almost every village in most developing nations, and the mass media were perceived as a "magic multiplier" for development. An invisible college of communication scholars over the world conducted research on development communication, wrote books on this topic (for example, Schramm, 1963; Lerner, 1958; Rogers, 1976), and trained a cadre of students to expand this academic specialty.

The growing audiences for the mass media made it possible to use the media as a potential tool for development. After all, new information was at the heart of development. What better way to convey information to the many millions of poor people in a developing nation than via the media? It was realized, however, that the role of the media was mainly limited to creating awareness—knowledge of new ideas and perhaps stimulating interpersonal communication about a new idea. Both of these impacts increase the likelihood of changed behavior, but they are generally insufficient to effect a change without additional communication efforts.

The communication campaigns for Oral Rehydration Therapy (ORT) to prevent infant death from diarrhea were successful examples of the use of mass communication for development. A young Bangladeshi medical doctor developed a simple formula consisting of one part salt (for its electrolytic effects) and eight parts sugar, mixed in an empty Coke bottle filled with pure water. These ingredients are available in most villages in developing countries. Parents were highly motivated to use ORT. They understood that a baby sick with infectious diarrhea often died from dehydration within 24 hours. The ORT campaigns conducted in the 1980s throughout the developing world represented the successful dissemination of technical information. These campaigns were rather universally successful, saving large numbers of infant lives.[3]

Despite the success of some of these campaigns, many policy-makers continued to question the role that mass communication could play in development programs. Content analyses by communication researchers found that the mass media in developing nations were usually dominated by commercial programs and advertising content. When educational content was provided, the audiences paid little attention. They regarded the educational programs as dull, and they expected entertainment. When they turned to media such as television, they expected popular broadcasts (often imported from the United States, including *Bay Watch*) not education. Although the use of mass communication for development was largely underutilized in the 1970s and 1980s, its potential was recognized and efforts were made to explore new approaches, such as combining education and entertainment (Singal & Rogers, in press).

The Ethics of Changing Someone Else's Culture

Certain technological changes, when they are introduced, seem to provide unquestionable benefits to the people whose culture is being changed. An example is a development communication campaign for AIDS prevention in a country where the epidemic poses a grave threat to public health. But even in these cases, change agents have learned that they must carefully consider the potential hazards of changing someone else's culture. Introducing new ideas without considering what they replace or displace is an invitation to social upheaval. Remember the effect of uncertainty in interpersonal conversations with unalike others (Chapter 4). Magnify that uncertainty about being able to predict behavior to a cultural level. That gives an indication of the impacts when traditional patterns are overthrown.

Development programs are instances of planned change. Development workers have a responsibility to learn enough about a culture to assess the impacts of a change. However, all change has unforeseen consequences. For example, writing created a new way of thinking about the world. The movable printing press allowed people to record their views for history. But it also created a new class division: Literate versus illiterate. Knowledge was often the province of the privileged. Commoners could not own maps in the time of Columbus. Knowledge about geography could help win battles, and those in power wanted no competition.

Ethical issues today include an evaluation of the benefits versus the harmful consequences of a technological innovation. The ORT campaigns in developing nations saved the lives of infants, but this benefit led to higher unemployment in later years.

Ethical issues range from the interpersonal to the international. Take the example of a sojourner in Brazil. Most bureaucracies in that country can be frustrating if one is not willing to engage in private payments (bribery) to speed up a process. An informal occupational set of people, the *despachante*, charge a fee to work the system to get furniture through customs, to obtain an identification card, or to facilitate getting telephone service. A sojourner's personal value system may regard bribery as unethical and corrupt. These beliefs translate into months of waiting for some action. The media carry stories of ethnic killings—in Serbia, Azerbaijan, Rwanda, Iraq, and Cambodia. Do other countries have the right to intervene? Are they ethically obligated to intervene?

Rise of the Megacity

Throughout much of history, people lived primarily in rural settings, not in cities. As recently as 200 years ago, only a rather small percentage of the world's population lived in urban areas. The mid-19th century Industrial Revolution rapidly changed this residential pattern; by 1975, one-third of the world's population lived in a city. This change from village to city is an important factor in the study of intercultural communication. The culture of the village is quite different from the culture of the city. Villages are often monocultural; opposing beliefs, values, and ways of behaving do not exist. The occasional stranger can be ignored or sent away in order to preserve a single worldview. In contrast, cities are vast cultural cauldrons where people with different ideas and diverse customs are intermixed on a daily basis.

The importance of intercultural communication is magnified by the growth of cities. The world's population will expand from almost 6 billion in the year 2000 to 9 billion in 2030. About 250,000 years were required from the development of the first fully human being until the world's population reached 4.5 billion people in 1975. It will take only 55 years to double that number. We often think of the world's largest cities as being located in the industrialized countries of Europe, Japan, and the United States. Indeed, New York, London, and Tokyo are huge metropolitan cities. Less likely to come to mind are Sao Paulo, Rio de Janeiro, Mexico City, Bangkok, Calcutta, Bombay, Madras, and Cairo. These too are megacities, and they are growing much faster.

In the next few years, Mexico City will surpass Tokyo as the world's largest city. Over the next 30 years, 90 percent of all urban population growth (which is 80 percent of the growth of the entire world population) will take place in the cities of Latin America, Africa, and Asia, not in the industrialized West. Put in other terms, ten cities each the size of Bangkok (with six million people) will be added each year for the next 30 years. This population growth, representing 300 Bangkoks, will occur mainly in the suburbs of the existing megacities of Asia and Latin America.

What will these cities look like? Will they be modern luxury cities? What proportion of the residents in these cities will have piped water supplies? A sanitary sewer system?

Jakarta, the capital city of the third largest country in the world, provides a clue. That Indonesian city now has 17 million people. It has no sanitary sewer system and a minimal piped water supply. No budget is in place, or even planned, to increase either of these facilities. How will Jakarta accommodate twice the number of people (a population of 34 million is projected for the year 2030) when its infrastructure is inadequate today? Asian and Latin American nations will far outstrip the industrialized West in the number of megacities; the vast majority of the population in these cities will be the poor and the disenfranchised. Of the world's poor, 70 percent are women. How will these very large numbers make a living for themselves and their families? By 2010, half of the population of Southeast Asia will be under 15 years of age. Asian cities in which much of the world's population will live will be composed primarily of poor children.

Intercultural communication between the poor and the rich involves differences in power as well as differences in meanings. Communication between the rich and the poor involves far more than a rich traveler knowing how to ask for a bowl of noodles from an impoverished family at a soup stand in rural Cambodia. It involves more than white European Americans driving into a Black or Latino neighborhood in a U.S. city to purchase an ethnic meal or to listen to ethnic music. When economic differences become wide and are perceived as too inequitable by those who have little or nothing to lose, riots and revolutions often result.

Will cities of the future be marked by armed, walled enclaves to shut out the majority of the population? Architectural firms in the United States currently spend more money planning just one fortress-like structure than entire cities budget for planning for the needs of their entire population.

Earlier, we discussed development communication which can help to improve levels of living and begin to narrow the gap between the rich and the poor. We also discussed the ethics of making the decision to intervene in another person's culture. The process of intercultural communication involves communication between the powerful and the powerless, the rich and the poor, the young and the old, and between those whose belief systems differ. As the world's population increases, so does its diversity, especially in cities.

A factory in a suburb northwest of Chicago has been open for two and one-half years. It employs 1,200 people; the flags of 65 nations hang from its ceiling representing the countries of origin of employees. More than 20 languages are spoken. Twelve assembly lines produce computer modems around the clock. Asians with multiple college degrees work beside people newly arrived from Central American villages. Serbians work with Bosnians. One-third of the workers have no problem working on December 25, as they do not celebrate that particular date.

On one assembly line, ten workers are from India, several from the Philippines, three were born in the United States, one is from Iraq, one from Ecuador, one from Guatemala, and one from Serbia. The assembly line does not require interaction; instructions are clearly expressed in nonverbal symbols that can be interpreted regardless of language. The lunchroom, however, is segregated according to language spoken. The Illinois factory provides unlimited opportunity for interpersonal contact, but most employees lack the skills required for intercultural communication. Is this factory a scenario for the future of U.S. society? Will contact not be accompanied by understanding?

Case Illustration:
Los Angeles as a Cultural Mosaic

Perhaps more than any other large city in the United States, Los Angeles is an example of the cultural diversity in urban centers. LA has more Thais than any city but Bangkok, more Koreans than any city but Seoul, more El Salvadoreans than any city outside of San Salvador, and more Druze than anywhere but Beirut. In one sense, Los Angeles is the U.S. capital of the developing world. Its schools teach 82 different languages. Perhaps the city exemplifies what the world will look like in a few decades (London, 1996). Demographers at the University of Southern California published an atlas of ethnicity for Los Angeles, identifying each of the city's cultural islands in a different color. Appropriately, the report is entitled, A Human Mosaic *(Heer & Herman, 1990).*

One way to understand Los Angeles is through its main airport. Pico Iyer, an intellectual from India, recently lived for one week in LAX (Los Angeles International Airport) in order to better understand the multicultural nature of the city. Iyer (1995) claims that "LAX is a perfect metaphor for LA, a flat, spaced-out desert kind of place, highly automotive, not deeply hospitable, with little reading matter and no organizing principle." Like the city itself, LAX is a center of migration, with 30,000 international arrivals each day. A Traveler's AID desk in the Los Angeles airport can dispense help in 115 languages, including Khamu, Mien, Tigrinya, Tajiki, Pashto, Dari, Pangasinan, Waray-Waray, Twi, Bambara, and Bicolano. On arrival, Koreans can take the Seoul Shuttle direct to Koreatown, without feeling they ever left home. Newcomers from the Middle East can pile into the Sahara Shuttle, which is easy for them to identify, as the name is in Arabic script on the side of the van.

Most of the food service and janitorial staff in LAX, Iyer noted, have names like Hoa, Ephraim, Ignacio, Yovick, and Ingrid. "Many of the bright-eyed dreamers who arrive in LAX so full of hope never actually leave the place." Language and other intercultural communication problems abound in LAX. For example, a Vietnamese man who is lost tells an official that he has friends in Orange County who can help him. When the number is called, the people who answer say that they do not know anyone from Vietnam. A Nigerian woman disembarks, expecting to meet her husband in Monroe, Louisiana, only to learn that someone in Lagos had mistaken the "LA" (the state) on her itinerary for "LA," the city.

If you want to understand how diverse cultures mix in large U.S. cities, spend a week in LAX.

The Global Business Village of Today

Business activities were at one time almost entirely confined to the boundaries of a village or town. As nations grew, most business exchanges took place within a single country. Although trade between distant geographic locations has increased since the establishment of the Silk Road, it required a great deal of effort and resources and was thus limited to a very few. Not so today. Products can be shipped anywhere in the world to compete in the global marketplace. An example is semiconductor chips. A month's production from a large semiconductor plant can be loaded on a single forklift pallet and airfreighted to any location in the world. The shipping cost is an insignificant portion of the selling price.

Companies in many industries today operate in a global marketplace. They must design products to fit a wide diversity of cultures, advertise them in numerous languages, and meet the demands of very different consumers. The global marketplace means that these companies are vitally involved in intercultural communication. The introduction of a new shoe by Nike in 1997 provides an example of intercultural differences in the global market. The shoe had been tested extensively by Nike researchers and its squiggly symbol was found to have high impact on U.S. consumers. Unfortunately, the squiggle bore a close resemblance to the Arabic script for Allah (God). When the new shoe appeared in the marketplace, Muslims all over the world protested. Arabic nations threatened to boycott the new shoe, and certain countries demanded that Nike withdraw all of its business activities. The Nike Corporation immediately recalled the new shoe from all its sales outlets worldwide.

Many companies, formerly successful when operating only in their own nation, have failed in the global marketplace. Other companies have made regrettable errors due to their lack of intercultural awareness, as the Nike example illustrates. One nation whose businesses have been remarkably successful worldwide is Japan.

At the end of World War II, Japanese cities were devastated by U.S. bombing. More than a million of its citizens returned to the home islands from Japan's former overseas possessions. The economy was ruined, and factories had been reduced to piles of rubble. The mountainous land area contained few natural resources. Japanese products were widely regarded as shoddy. The prospects for Japan to become a world economic power appeared to be very slim.

The decades of the 1950s, 1960s, and 1970s proved that prediction completely inaccurate. By the 1980s, Japanese electronics products like radios, television sets, VCRs, computers, and other consumer products took over world markets. Japanese automobiles outsold those from the United States and established standards for quality. The United States had a huge trade deficit with Japan; more products were purchased from Japan than vice versa.

Perhaps the most amazing fact was that Japanese society had industrialized and modernized without becoming Westernized. The core values of traditional Japanese culture had not changed from those of centuries earlier when most Japanese people were living in rice-growing villages. Respect for elders, strong family unity, loyalty to the system (such as one's work organization, where most employees are guaranteed life-time employment), and a subservience of the individual to the collectivity continued as central features of Japanese culture.

Case Illustration:
Nemawashi: **Digging around the Roots**

One basis for classifying the multitude of cultures in the world is whether they are individualistic or collectivistic. As discussed in Chapter 3, an individualistic culture is one in which the individual's goals are valued over those of the collectivity. The United States is an individualistic culture. Achievement and initiative are prized over being a good team member. In contrast, a collectivistic culture is one in which the *collectivity's goals are valued over those of the individual. In a collectivistic culture like Japan, the individual is rewarded for sublimating his/her goals to those of the family, the community, or the work organization.*

The collectivistic nature of Japanese culture is exemplified by nemawashi, "digging around the roots." When an important decision is made in Japan, the decision process involves numerous stakeholders who discuss the matter until a high degree of consensus is eventually reached. The Japanese say that just as one would not suddenly yank a plant out of the ground in order to transplant it, "digging around the roots" should take place in order to prepare everyone who is involved in a crucial decision.

One of the authors asked Mr. Enomoto, chief engineer of the Toshiba Semiconductor Company, how his company had decided to begin producing a new semiconductor chip. Enomoto described how a proposal had been formulated by his staff, which was then discussed with company officials. Some of the deliberations took place in formal meetings, but the most important discussions occurred over drinks, on the golf course, and at coffee breaks and lunches. Eventually, over a period of several months, a general agreement began to emerge about producing the new semiconductor chip. Then a formal meeting was scheduled with the presidents of other corporations linked to Toshiba: a bank (that was asked to lend the $22 million to build a new plant); two companies (one an automobile company and the other a computer company) who agreed to purchase the new semiconductors; and a trading company that would market the new chip overseas. A document was then drawn up to summarize the agreement that was reached at the meeting, and this form was later circulated to the principal decision-makers for their stamped signatures. Some officials added amendments when they signed the agreement, and the document had to be circulated again to the previous signatories for their approval of the amendments. During this lengthy process, much further informal consultation took place among the participants in the decision process. Six months after initiation of the process—and as the result of extensive nemawashi—the decision was finalized. Work on the new semiconductor plant then began.

In Silicon Valley, a similar decision regarding a new semiconductor chip would be made in a two-hour meeting. When the author described this more rapid decision process to Mr. Enomoto, he remarked, "Yes, in America, you would make such a decision in a half day before lunch, but then it would require six months to implement it, while you coped with a host of unexpected problems. In Japan, we take six months to make the decision, so as to iron out anticipated problems, and then implement it quickly."

Many aspects of Japanese culture were viewed condescendingly by ethnocentric people in the United States. The cultures frequently collided when transacting business. Usually the Japanese had a better understanding of U.S. culture than vice versa, putting the Japanese at a considerable advantage. As U.S. businessmen increasingly found their companies defeated in the global marketplace by their Japanese counterparts, they demanded intercultural communication training for themselves and their employees. Dozens of training institutes arose in the 1980s and 1990s to provide training to U.S. businessmen on how to deal with the Japanese. This training was based, in part, on the proliferation of intercultural communication research conducted by scholars on U.S./Japan relationships.

Case Illustration:
Gift-Giving around the World

Mr. Smith, a well-intentioned U.S. business executive, flies to Tokyo to meet for the first time with officials of a Japanese company with which he wishes to sign an important agreement. Smith understands that Japan is a gift-giving culture, and so he purchases some expensive jewelry at Tiffany's to give to the wife of the Japanese company's president. Smith has the jewelry gift-wrapped because he knows that such wrapping is very important in Japan.

When Smith meets his Japanese counterpart, he presents his name card and bows. They both enjoy the getting-acquainted process, which Smith knows is necessary before getting down to business negotiations. Everything seems to be going smoothly. While meeting with the company president and his staff, Smith presents his gift to the Japanese official with a request that he give it to his wife. There is a slight pause in the conversation, and Smith realizes that he has violated a cultural norm. What did he do wrong?

First, Smith gave the gift in the presence of others. A gift should be presented when the giver is alone with the receiver unless there is a gift for everyone present. Considering that the two businessmen had just met, the expensive jewelry was a questionable gift, particularly since it was for the Japanese official's wife (rather than for him). A more modestly priced gift, like a pen with the logo of Smith's company on it, would have been more appropriate. Finally, the gift wrapping was black and white, colors often used in Japan for funerals.

The Japanese are the champion gift-givers of the world, perhaps because maintaining interpersonal relationships is considered so important in a collectivistic culture. But the custom of giving gifts is found throughout Asia, the Middle East, and Latin America. Many U.S. business people find it somewhat uncomfortable to give and receive gifts. In the extreme, they may misinterpret gift-giving as bribery and reject a gift, causing great discomfort to both parties. Often the message intended by a gift is not the one that is interpreted by the recipient. For example, a clock is the wrong gift in the People's Republic of China, as the word for clock sounds like the word for a visit to the dying. Thus the unsuspecting salesperson who gives a clock to a Chinese counterpart is unknowingly implying that their relationship will be terminated (Reardon, 1982).

Figure 9-2. A picture of Michael Jordan is esteemed at this traditional wedding ceremony in Torajaland in Sulawesi Province, Indonesia.

Source: Michael L. Abramson. Used with permission.

In the Arabic world, generosity is highly valued, so a gift should reflect this cultural value. However, there are many prohibitions which should be carefully studied before any exchanges. A gift of food or drink when invited to an Arab's home is insulting, as this act implies that the Arab is not a good host. A gift of liquor is inappropriate, for religious reasons. A gift to an Arab's wife or wives is also inappropriate. As the above examples imply, gift-giving (and receiving) can cause many problems for those who lack intercultural competence.

Toward a Global Culture

Despite the fundamental differences in worldviews between Japan and the United States, there are considerable similarities. Countries with sufficient resources have eliminated many of the constraints of geography. Air conditioning has eliminated the constraints of climate, availability of food and medicine are assumed. Large cities across the world resemble each other in terms of products sold, movies, television, traffic, hotels, airports, and fast food. McDonald's is everywhere, including New Delhi, Jakarta, and Beijing. This superficial shared experience implies the world's movement toward a global culture (McLuhan, 1964).

Those shared experiences, however, are far removed from the experiences in rural villages where much of the world's population still lives, struggling to coax an adequate harvest from a small plot of land with traditional tools. Nor is life in the megacities exempt from deprivation, squalor and misery. How can these rural and urban poor find a voice, so that their needs can be heard?

The end of the Cold War left only one superpower. In addition to its military dominance, the United States is the largest economic power. Its large domestic market with substantial disposable income allows U.S. businesses to be the leaders in creating new technologies, and its products are sold everywhere in the world. English has become the acknowledged universal second language of the world. U.S. media export news and programs with images of U.S. culture throughout the globe.

Developing nations see themselves as victims of a one-way flow of communication. They see these cultural influences as a continuation of the previous colonial system through a monopoly of information resources available only to wealthy nations. Now faced with the rapid growth of e-mail and the Internet, the nations of Latin America, Africa, and Asia wonder if this new communication technology will give them a voice, or whether their disadvantaged communication situation will be worsened.

We began this book with a picture of the history that has colored the perceptions of people from different cultures. Conflict and disagreement have accompanied intercultural relations throughout history. Misinformation and misunderstanding have been the hallmarks of cultural differences. Must this dismal past continue in the future? As Edward Hall (1981) said:

> The answer lies not in restricting human endeavors, but in evolving new alternatives, new possibilities, new dimensions, new options, and new avenues for creative uses of human beings based on the recognition of the multiple and unusual talents so manifest in the diversity of the human race. (p. 3)

Our goal in writing this book was to provide skills to break through the cultural boundaries separating us from others. We hope we have provided a framework for exploring beneath cultural surfaces, to find a common ground of shared understanding. Discovering the differences and similarities among cultures through communication is an enriching activity, one in which we hope you will participate.

Notes

[1] This case study is based on Wellin (1955).

[2] This case illustration takes its name and certain of its content from an autobiographical account written by a Peace Corps volunteer in the 1970s, but it is a composite based on numerous accounts by individuals serving in the Peace Corps.

[3] The first ORT campaigns in Honduras and The Gambia resulted in a few parents being confused about the ratios in the mixture. Some used eight parts *salt* and one part *sugar*. This crucial mistake could have lethal consequences. One solution was to premix the ingredients and distribute them in small foil packets. This change in the ORT campaign strategy made them somewhat more dependent on infrastructural facilities for their success, such as clinics and/or pharmacies that distributed the ORT packets.

Glossary

Acculturation is the process through which an individual is socialized into a new culture while retaining many elements of a previous culture.

Affect displays are kinesic behaviors that express emotions.

Ambiguity is the degree to which a communication message has many possible meanings to its receivers.

Assimilation is the degree to which an individual relinquishes an original culture for another.

Attitude is an emotional response to objects, ideas, and people.

Attribution is the process in which an individual explains the meaning of others' behaviors based on the individual's own experiences, values, and beliefs.

Beliefs are an individual's representations of the outside world.

Change agent is an individual who influences clients to adopt innovations.

Channel is the means by which a message is transmitted from its origin to its destination.

Code is a classification used by individuals to categorize their experience and to communicate them to others.

Code-switching is the process through which two or more individuals change from speaking one language to another during a conversation.

Collectivistic culture is one in which the collectivity's goals are valued over those of the individual.

Communication is the process through which participants create and share information with one another as they move toward reaching a mutual understanding.

Cosmopoliteness is the degree to which an individual has a relatively high degree of communication outside of the individual's local system.

Credibility is the degree to which a communication source is perceived as trustworthy and competent.

Culture is the total way of life of a people, composed of their learned and shared behavior patterns, values, norms, and material objects.

Cultural clash is the conflict that occurs between two or more cultures when they disagree about a certain value.

Cultural identification is the degree to which an individual considers himself/herself to be a representative of a particular culture.

Cultural relativism is the degree to which an individual judges another culture by its context (as opposed to ethnocentrism which judges others by the standards of one's own culture).

Culture shock is the traumatic experience that an individual may encounter when entering a different culture.

Decoding is the process by which a message is converted into an idea by the receiver.

Development is a widely participatory process of social change in a society intended to bring about both social and economic advancement for the majority of people through their gaining greater control over their environment.

Development communication is the exchange of information between two or more individuals in which one individual, a change agent, seeks to assist the other individual to achieve a higher socioeconomic status.

Discrimination is overt behavior that treats individuals unequally on the basis of their race, gender, or other characteristics.

Diversity is the degree to which a system is composed of a variety of individuals with different cultures.

Effects are the changes in an individual's knowledge, attitudes, and overt behavior due to exposure to a communication message.

Emblems are nonverbal behaviors that have a direct verbal counterpart and that are used intentionally to transmit messages.

Empowerment is the degree to which individuals perceive that they control a situation.

Encoding is the process by which an idea is converted into a message by the source.

Entertainment-education is the process of purposely creating a media message to both entertain and educate, in order to change audience members' behavior.

Ethnic group is a set of people who share a common culture that is usually based on a common nationality or language.

Ethnocentrism is the degree to which other cultures are judged as inferior to one's own culture.

Face is the public self-image that an individual wants to present in a particular social context.

Feedback is a message about the effects of a previous message on a receiver that is sent back to the source.

Heterophily is the degree to which two or more individuals who communicate are unalike.

High-context culture is one in which the meanings of a communication message are found in the situation and in the relationship of the communicators or are internalized in the individual's beliefs, values, and norms.

Homophily is the degree to which two or more individuals who communicate are alike.

Illustrators are a type of kinesic behavior that accompanies what is said verbally and cannot easily be translated into words.

Individualistic culture is one in which the individual's goals are valued over those of the collectivity.

Information is a difference in matter-energy that affects uncertainty in a situation where a choice exists among a set of alternatives.

Ingroup is a collectivity with which an individual identifies.

Innovation is an idea perceived as new by an individual.

Intercultural communication is the exchange of information between individuals who are unalike culturally.

Intercultural communication competence is the degree to which an individual is able to exchange information effectively and appropriately with individuals who belong to a different culture.

Interpersonal communication involves the face-to-face exchange of information between two or more people.

Intrapersonal communication is information exchange that occurs inside of one person.

Kinesics are nonverbal communication behaviors that involve body movement, including posture, gestures, gait, and facial expressions.

Linguistic relativity is the degree to which language influences human thought and meanings.

Low-context culture is one in which the meanings of a communication message are stated clearly and explicitly, without depending on the context of the communication situation.

Marginal man is an individual who lives in two different worlds, in both of which the individual is a stranger.

Mass communication is the exchange of information via a mass medium (like radio, television, newspapers, and so forth) from one or a few individuals to an audience of many.

Mediation is the process of finding peaceful solutions to a conflict through a neutral intervention.

Multiculturalism is the recognition that several different cultures can exist in the same environment and benefit each other.

Negotiation is the process of settling a conflict by facilitating understanding between the disputing parties.

Noise is anything that interferes with the communication process among participants.

Nonverbal communication is communication that does not involve the exchange of words.

Norms are the established behavior patterns for the members of a social system.

Outgroup is a collectivity with which an individual does not identify.

Paradigm is a conceptualization that provides explanations and ways of seeing and understanding to a community of individuals.

Paralanguage is the nonverbal aspects of voice other than verbal content, like loudness, speed of speaking, and grunts.

Perception is the way in which an individual gives meaning to an object.

Pluralism is the degree to which an individual is open to others' points of view.

Power is the degree to which one party controls resources valued by another party.

Prejudice is an unfounded attitude toward an outgroup based on a comparison with one's ingroup.

Proxemics is nonverbal communication that involves space.

Racism categorizes individuals on the basis of their external physical traits, such as skin color, hair, facial structure, and eye shape, leading to prejudice and discrimination.

Reacculturation is the process through which an individual readjusts to his/her passport culture after a sojourn in another culture (this concept is similar to reentry).

Reentry is the process that an individual goes through when returning to his/her passport culture.

Receiver is the individual who decodes the communication message by converting it into an idea.

Regulators are kinesic behaviors that control turn-taking and other procedural aspects of interpersonal communication.

Selective perception is the tendency for an individual to interpret communication messages in accordance with the individual's existing attitudes and beliefs.

Self-disclosure is the degree to which an individual reveals personal information about himself/herself to another person.

Sexism is the assignment of characteristics to individuals on the basis of their sex, so that the genders are treated unequally.

Social distance is the degree to which an individual perceives a lack of intimacy with individuals who are different in ethnicity, religion, occupation, or other characteristics.

Sojourner is an individual who visits another culture for a period of time but who retains his/her original culture.

Source is the individual who originates a communication act by encoding an idea into a message.

Stereotype is a generalization about some group of people that oversimplifies their culture.

Stranger is an individual who is different from oneself culturally.

Sustainability is the degree to which a development project continues to be effective after the original development effort ends.

Symbolic interactionism is the theory that individuals act toward objects on the basis of meanings and perceptions that are formed through communication with others.

Uncertainty is an individual's inability to predict or to understand some situation due to a lack of information about alternatives.

Values are what the people who share a culture regard strongly as good or bad.

References

Nathan Aaseng (1992), *Navajo Code Talkers*, New York, Wallace.

Cara Abeyta and Thomas Steinfatt (1989), "Intrapersonal Communication Processes in Intercultural Communication," in C. Roberts and K. Watson (eds.), *Intrapersonal Communication Processes*, New Orleans, Gorsuch and Scarisbrick and Spetre Associates, pp. 456–78.

Theodor W. Adorno, Else Frenkel-Brunswik, Daniel J. Levinson, and R. Nevitt Sanford (1950/1982), *The Authoritarian Personality*, New York, Harper and Brothers/New York, Norton.

Michael Agar (1994), *Language Shock: Understanding the Culture of Conversation*, New York, William Morrow.

Adalberto Aguirre, Jr. and Jonathan H. Turner (1995), *American Ethnicity: The Dynamics and Consequences of Discrimination*, New York, McGraw-Hill.

Saul D. Alinsky (1972), *Rules for Radicals: A Practical Primer for Realistic Radicals*, New York, Vintage Books.

Gordon W. Allport (1954/1979), *The Nature of Prejudice*, New York, Macmillan/Reading, MA, Addison-Wesley.

Molefi Kete Asante (1987), *The Afrocentric Idea*, Philadelphia, Temple University Press.

Mohammed A. Awal and Arvind Singhal (1992), "The Diffusion of Grameen Bank in Bangladesh: Lessons Learned about Poverty Alleviation," *Knowledge*, 14(1): 7–28.

Alan Axelrod (1993), *Chronicle of the Indian Wars: From Colonial Times to Wounded Knee*, New York, Prentice Hall.

Anna Banks and Stephen P. Banks (1995), "Cultural Identity, Resistance, and 'Good Theory': Implications for Intercultural Communication Theory from Gypsy Culture," *Howard Journal of Communication*, 6(3): 146–63.

Gregory Bateson (1972), *Steps to an Ecology of Mind: Collected Essays in Anthropology, Psychiatry, Evolution, and Epistemology*, New York, Ballentine.

Ruth Benedict (1946), *The Chrysanthemum and the Sword*, Boston, Houghton Mifflin.

271

Harumi Befu (1974), "An Ethnography of Dinner Entertainment in Japan," *Artic Anthropology*, 11:196–203.

Milton J. Bennett (1986), "A Developmental Approach to Training for Intercultural Sensitivity," *International Journal of Intercultural Relations*, 10:179–96.

Charles Berger and Richard J. Calabrese (1975), "Some Explorations in Initial Interactions and Beyond: Toward a Developmental Theory of Interpersonal Communication," *Human Communication Research*, 1:99–112.

David K. Berlo (1960), *The Process of Communication*, New York, Holt, Rinehart, and Winston.

Raymond L. Birdwhistell (1952), *Introduction to Kinesics*, Washington, DC, Foreign Service Institute.

Raymond L. Birdwhistell (1955), "Background to Kinesics," *ETC*, 13:10–18.

Raymond L. Birdwhistell (1970), *Kinesics and Context: Essays on Body Motion Communication*, Philadelphia, University of Pennsylvania Press.

Margaret T. Bixler (1992), *Winds of Freedom: The Story of the Navajo Code Talkers of World War II*, Darian, CT, Two Bytes.

Emory S. Bogardus (1929), "Measuring Social Distances," *Journal of Applied Sociology*, 13:110–17.

Emory S. Bogardus (1933), "A Social Distance Scale," *Sociology and Social Research*, 17:265–71.

Emory S. Bogardus (1959), *Social Distance*, Yellow Springs, OH, Antioch Press.

Paul Bohannan and Dirk van der Elst (1998), *Asking and Listening*, Prospect Heights, IL, Waveland Press.

S. Bradford (1960), "Over the River and into the Language Course," *Foreign Service Journal*, 37:24–25.

Rick Bragg (August 16, 1997), "The King Is Long Dead, But Long Live the King," *The New York Times*, p. 6.

Richard W. Brislin (1981), *Cross-Cultural Encounters: Face to Face Interaction*, New York, Pergamon.

Dee Alexander Brown (1971), *Bury My Heart at Wounded Knee: An Indian History of the American West*, New York, Holt, Rinehart, and Winston.

Judee K. Burgoon (1994), "Nonverbal Signals," in Mark L. Knapp and Gerald R. Miller (eds.), *Handbook of Interpersonal Communication*, Newbury Park, CA, Sage, pp. 229–85.

Judee K. Burgoon, David B. Buller, and W. Gill Woodall (1996), *Nonverbal Communication: The Unspoken Dialogue*, New York, McGraw-Hill.

Ric Burns, (1995), *The Way West* [videotape], Boston, WGBH Educational Foundation.

Richard Calvert, Jr. (1966), "The Returning Volunteer," *Annals of the American Academy of Political and Social Science*, 365:105.

Jim Carnes (1995), *Us and Them: A History of Intolerance in America*, Montgomery, AL, Southern Poverty Law Center.

John B. Carroll (ed.) (1940/1956), *Language, Thought, and Reality: Selected Writings of Benjamin Lee Whorf*, Cambridge MA, MIT Press.

Guo-Ming Chen and William J. Starosta (1998), *Foundations of Intercultural Communication*, Boston, Allyn and Bacon.

Lori Collins-Jarvis (1993), "Gender Representations in an Electronic City Hall: Female Adoption of Santa Monica's PEN System," *Journal of Broadcasting and Electronic Media*, 37(1): 49–65.

James S. Coleman, Elihu Katz, and Herbert Menzel (1966), *Medical Innovation: A Diffusion Study*, Indianapolis, Bobbs-Merrill.

Maurice Collis (1978), *Cortés and Montezuma*, New York, Discus Avon Books.

John C. Condon and Fathi Yousef (1975), *An Introduction to Intercultural Communication*, Indianapolis, Bobbs-Merrill.

Lewis A. Coser (1959), "Georg Simmel's Style of Work: A Contribution to the Sociology of the Sociologist," *American Journal of Sociology*, 63(6): 635–40.

Lewis A. Coser (1965), *Georg Simmel*, Englewood Cliffs, NJ, Prentice-Hall.

Lewis A. Coser (1977), *Masters of Sociological Thought: Ideas in Historical and Social Context*, New York, Harcourt Brace Jovanovich.

Jack L. Daniel and Geneva Smitherman (1990), "How I Got Over: Communication Dynamics in the Black Community," in Donal Carlbaugh (ed.), *Cultural Communication and Intercultural Contact*, Hillsdale, NJ, Lawrence Erlbaum Associates, pp. 27–40.

Charles Darwin (1872/1965), *Expression of the Emotions in Man and Animals*, London, John Murray/University of Chicago Press.

Rodolfo O. de la Garza, Louis DeSipio, F. Chris Garcia, John Garcia, and Angelo Falcon (1992), *Latino Voices: Mexican, Puerto Rican and Cuban Perspectives on American Politics*, Hartford, CT, Westview Press.

Edwin J. Dawson, William D. Crano, and Michael Burgoon (1996), "Refining the Meaning and Measurement of Acculturation: Revisiting a Novel Methodological Approach," *International Journal of Intercultural Relations*, 20(1): 91–114.

James W. Dearing and Everett M. Rogers (1996), *Agenda-Setting*, Newbury Park, CA, Sage.

James W. Dearing, Everett M. Rogers, Gary Meyer, Mary K. Casey, Nagesh Rao, Shelly Campo, and Geoffrey Henderson (1995), "Social Marketing and Diffusion-Based Strategies for Communicating with Unique Populations: HIV Prevention in San Francisco," *Journal of Health Communication*, 1:343–63.

Sue DeWine (1995), "A New Direction: Internationalizing Communication Programs," *Journal of the Association of Communication Administration*, 3:204–10.

Kathyrn Dindia, Mary Anne Fitzpatrick, and David A. Kenny (1997), "Self-Disclosure in Spouse and Stranger Interaction: A Social Relations Analysis," *Human Communication Research*, 23:388–412.

Robert A. Divine (ed.) (1960), *American Foreign Policy*, New York, Meridian Books.

Celia W. Dugger (December 28, 1996), "Tug of Taboos: African Genital Rites vs. U.S. Law," *The New York Times*, p. 1, 8.

Celia W. Dugger (January 19, 1997), "A Week of New York's Ethnic Media: A Glimpse of the World," *The New York Times*, p. 26.

Eric M. Eisenberg (1984), "Ambiguity as Strategy in Organizational Communication," *Communication Monographs*, 51:227–42.

Paul Ekman (1973), *Darwin and Facial Expression: A Century of Research in Review*, New York, Academic Press.

Paul Ekman (1985), *Telling Lies: Clues to Deceit in the Marketplace, Politics, and Marriage*, New York, Norton.

Paul Ekman and Wallace V. Friesen (1969), "Nonverbal Leakage and Clues to Deception," *Psychiatry*, 32:88–105.

Anne Fadiman (1997), *The Spirit Catches You and You Fall Down: A Hmong Child, Her American Doctors, and the Collision of Two Cultures*, New York, Farrar, Straus and Giroux.

Joe R. Feagin (1992), "The Continuing Significance of Racism: Discrimination against Black Students in White Colleges," *Journal of Black Studies*, 22 (4): 546–78.

Isabel Fonseca (1995), *Bury Me Standing: The Gypsies and Their Journey*, New York, Vintage.

Benson Fraser and William J. Brown (1997), "Identification with Celebrities and Role Modeling Values: A Case Study of Elvis Presley Impersonators," Paper presented at the World Communication Association, San Jose, Costa Rica.

Paulo Freire (1968), *Pedagogy of the Oppressed*, New York, Herder and Herder.

David Frisby (1984), *Georg Simmel*, London, Tavistock Publications.

David Frisby (1985), *Fragments of Modernity*, Cambridge, Polity.

Adrian Furnham (1987), "The Adjustment of Sojourners," in Young Yun Kim and William Gudykunst (eds.), *Cross-Cultural Adaptation: Current Approaches*, Newbury Park, CA, Sage, pp. 42–61.

Adrian Furnham and Stephen Bochner (1986), *Cultural Shock*, New York, Methuen.

Frank Gibney (1992), *The Pacific Century: America and Asia in a Changing World*, Tokyo, Kodansha International.

Todd Gitlin (1995), *The Twilight of Common Dreams: Why America is Wracked by Culture Wars*, New York, Henry Holt.

Erving Goffman (1959), *The Presentation of Self in Everyday Life*, Garden City, NJ, Doubleday Anchor Books.

William B. Gudykunst (1983), "Toward a Typology of Stranger-Host Relationships," *International Journal of Intercultural Relations*, 7:401–13.

William B. Gudykunst (1994), *Bridging Differences: Effective Intergroup Communication*, Second Edition, Newbury Park, CA, Sage.

William B. Gudykunst (1995), "Anxiety/Uncertainty Management (AUM) Theory: Current Status," in R. L. Wiseman (ed.), *Intercultural Communication Theory*, Newbury Park, CA, Sage.

William B. Gudykunst and Young Yun Kim (eds.) (1988), *Theories in Intercultural Communication*, Newbury Park, CA, Sage.

William B. Gudykunst and Young Yun Kim (1984/1993/1997), *Communicating with Strangers: An Approach to Intercultural Communication*, Third Edition, New York, McGraw-Hill.

William B. Gudykunst, Yuko Matsumoto, Stella Ting-Toomey, Tsukasa Nishida, Kwangsu Kim, and Sam Heyman (1996), "The Influence of Cultural Individualism-Collectivism, Self Construals, and Individual Values on Communication Styles across Cultures," *Human Communication Research*, 22(4): 510–43.

William B. Gudykunst, Tsukasa Nishida, and Karen L. Schmidt (1989), "The Influence of Cultural Relations and Personality Factors on Uncertainty Reduction Processes," *Western Journal of Speech Communication*, 53:13–29.

John T. Gullahorn and Jeanne E. Gullahorn (1963), "An Extension of the U-Curve Hypothesis," *Journal of Social Issues*, 14:33–47.

C. R. Hale, S. H. Jones, and H. Morton (1858), *Report of the Committee Appointed by the Philomathean Society of the University of Pennsylvania to Translate the Inscription on the Rosetta Stone*, Philadelphia, University of Pennsylvania.

Bradford J. Hall and Mutsumi Noguchi (1993), "Intercultural Conflict: A Case Study," *International Journal of Intercultural Relations*, 17(4): 399–413.

Edward T. Hall, Jr. (1947), "Racial Prejudice and Negro-White Relations in the Army," *American Journal of Sociology*, 52(5): 401.

Edward T. Hall, Jr. (1948), E. T. Hall Papers, Special Collections, University of Arizona Library.

Edward T. Hall, Jr. (1950), "Military Government on Truk," *Human Organization*, 9(2): 25–30.

Edward T. Hall (1955), "The Anthropology of Manners," *Scientific American*, 192:85–89.

Edward T. Hall, Jr. (1957), "Orientation and Training in Government for Work Overseas," *Human Organization*, 15(1): 4–10.

Edward T. Hall (1959a), *The Silent Language*, New York, Doubleday.

Edward T. Hall (1959b), "What Underdeveloped Countries Do Not Want," in Gove Hambridge (ed.), *Dynamics of Development: An International Development Reader*, New York, Praeger, pp. 369–72.

Edward T. Hall (1963), "Proxemics: The Study of Man's Spatial Relations," in Arden House Conference on Medicine and Anthropology (eds.), *Man's Image in Medicine and Anthropology*, New York, International Universities Press, pp. 442–45.

Edward T. Hall (1966), *The Hidden Dimension*, New York, Doubleday.

Edward T. Hall (1968), "Proxemics," *Current Anthropology*, 9:83–108.

Edward T. Hall (1969), "Listening Behavior: Some Cultural Differences," *Phi Delta Kappa*, 50:379–80.

Edward T. Hall (1976/1981), *Beyond Culture*, New York, Doubleday.

Edward T. Hall (1983), *The Dance of Life: The Other Dimension of Time*, New York, Doubleday/Anchor Books.

Edward T. Hall (1992), *An Anthropology of Everyday Life*, New York, Doubleday/Anchor Books.

Edward T. Hall and Mildred Reed Hall (1990), *Understanding Cultural Differences*, Yarmouth, ME, Intercultural Press.

Edward T. Hall and George L. Trager (1953), *The Analysis of Culture*, Washington, DC, Foreign Service Institute/American Council of Learned Societies.

Robin Hallett (1970), *Africa to 1875: A Modern History*, Ann Arbor, University of Michigan Press.

William Hart (1996a), "A Brief History of Intercultural Communication: A Paradigmatic Approach," Paper presented at the Speech Communication Association, San Diego.

William Hart (1996b), "A Citation Analysis of the *International Journal of Intercultural Relations*," Unpublished paper, Albuquerque, University of New Mexico, Department of Communication and Journalism.

William Hart (1997), "Intercultural Dialogues," Paper presented at the International Communication Association, Montreal.

Michael L. Hecht, Mary Jane Collier, and Sidney A. Ribeau (1993), *African American Communication: Ethnic Identity and Cultural Interpretation*, Newbury Park, CA, Sage.

Heini P. Hediger (1955), *Studies of the Psychology and Behavior of Captive Animals in Zoos and Circuses*, London, Butterworth.

David M. Heer and Pini Herman (1990), *A Human Mosaic: An Atlas of Ethnicity in Los Angeles County, 1980–1986*, Panorama City, CA, Western Economic Research Company, Report.

Philip H. Herbst (1997), *The Color of Words: An Encyclopedia Dictionary of Ethnic Bias in the United States*, Yarmouth, ME, Intercultural Press.

Melville J. Herskovits (1973), *Cultural Relativism*, New York, Random House.

Gert Hofstede (1990), *Culture's Consequences: International Differences in Work-Related Values*, Newbury Park, CA, Sage.

Alan Honour (1968), *The Man Who Could Read Stones: Chapollion and the Rosetta Stone*, Gloustershire, England, Kingswood.

Helen MacGill Hughes (1980), "Robert Ezra Park: The Philosopher-Newspaperman-Sociologist," in Robert K. Merton and Matilda White Riley (eds.), *Sociological Traditions from Generation to Generation: Glimpses of the American Experience*, Norwood, NJ, Ablex, pp. 67–79.

C. Harry Hui and Harry C. Triandis (1986), "Individualism-Collectivism: A Study of Cross-Cultural Researchers," *Journal of Cross-Cultural Psychology*, 17(2): 225–48.

I. P. (1987), *Eyewitness Accounts of Slavery in the Danish West Indies,* St. Thomas, USVI: Isador Paiewonsky.

Pico Iyer (August, 1995), "Where Worlds Collide: In Los Angeles International Airport, the Future Touches Down," *Harper's Magazine*, pp. 50–57.

Morris Janowitz and William Delany (1957), "The Bureaucrat and the Public: A Study of Informational Perspectives," *Administrative Science Quarterly*, 2:141–62.

Leo W. Jeffres (1997), *Mass Media Effects*, Second Edition, Prospect Heights, IL, Waveland Press.

E. E. Jones and Kenneth Davis (1965), "From Acts to Dispositions: The Attribution Process in Person Perception," in Leonard Berkowitz (ed.), *Advances in Experimental Social Psychology*, Volume II, New York, Academic Press.

Sidney M. Jourard (1971), *The Transparent Self*, New York, Van Nostrand Reinhold.

Kenji Kawano (1990), *Warriors: The Navajo Code Talkers*, Flagstaff, AZ, Northland.

Paul Kay and Willett Kempton (1984), "What Is the Sapir-Whorf Hypothesis?" *American Anthropologist*, 86:65–79.

Harold H. Kelly (1967), "Attribution Theory in Social Psychology," *Nebraska Symposium on Motivation*, Lincoln, University of Nebraska Press.

Harold H. Kelly (1973), "The Process of Causal Attribution," *American Psychologist*, 28:108.

Harold H. Kelly and J. Michela (1980), "Attribution Theory and Research," in M. Rosenweig and L. Porter (eds.), *Annual Review of Psychology*, 31.

Min-Sun Kim and William F. Sharkey (1995), "Independent and Interdependent Construals of Self: Explaining Cultural Patterns of Interpersonal Communication in Multi-Cultural Settings," *Communication Quarterly*, 43 (1): 20–38.

Young Yun Kim (1987), "Facilitating Immigrant Adaptation: The Role of Communication," in Terry Albrecht and Maria Adelman (eds.), *Communicating Social Support*, Newbury Park, CA, Sage.

Young Yun Kim (1988), *Communication and Cross-Cultural Adaptation: An Integrative Theory*, Clevedon, England, Multilingual Matters.

D. Lawrence Kincaid (ed.) (1987), *Communication Theory: Eastern and Western Perspectives*, San Diego, Academic Press.

Donald R. Kinder and Lynn M. Sanders (1996), *Divided by Color: Racial Politics and Democratic Ideals*, University of Chicago Press.

Mark L. Knapp and Judith A. Hall (1997), *Nonverbal Communication in Human Interaction*, Fourth Edition, New York, Harcourt Brace.

Thomas S. Kuhn (1962/1970), *The Structure of Scientific Revolutions*, University of Chicago Press.

Bernard Kutner, Carol Wilkins, and Penny Rechtman Yarrow (1952), "Verbal Attitudes and Overt Behavior Involving Racial Prejudice," *Journal of Abnormal and Social Psychology*, 47:649–52.

Jack Lambert (1992), *The Work Force Challenges of the 21st Century*, Washington, DC, National Association of Manufacturers, Report.

Susanne Langer (1957), *Philosophy in a New Key*, Cambridge, Harvard University Press.

Richard LaPiere (1934), "Attitudes and Actions," *Social Forces*, 13:230–37.

Paul F. Lazarsfeld and Robert K. Merton (1964), "Friendship as a Social Process: A Substantive and Methodological Analysis," in Monroe Berger, Theodore Abel, and Charles H. Page (eds.), *Freedom and Control in Modern Society*, New York, Octagon Books, pp. 18–66.

Eugene E. Leach (1986), "Mastering the Crowd: Collective Behavior and Mass Society in American Social Thought, 1917–1939," *American Studies*, 27 (1): 99–114.

William J. Lederer and Eugene Burdick (1958), *The Ugly American*, New York, Norton.

Penny Lee (1996), *The Whorf Theory Complex: A Critical Reconstruction, Studies in the History of Language Sciences, Vol. 81*, Philadelphia, John Benjamins.

Wendy Leeds-Hurwitz (1990), "Notes in the History of Intercultural Communication: The Foreign Service Institute and the Mandate for Intercultural Training," *Quarterly Journal of Speech*, 76:262–81.

Daniel Lerner (1958), *The Passing of Traditional Society: Modernizing the Middle East*, New York, Free Press.

Donald N. Levine, Elwood B. Carter, and Eleanor Miller Gorman (1976), "Simmel's Influence on American Sociology," *American Journal of Sociology*, 84 (4): 813–45, and 84 (5): 1112–32.

Robert A. LeVine and Donald T. Campbell (1972), *Ethnocentrism: Theories of Conflict, Ethnic Attitudes, and Group Behavior*, New York, Wiley.

Sheryl L. Lindsley and Charles A. Braithwaite (1996), "You Should 'Wear a Mask': Facework Norms in Cultural and Intercultural Conflict in Maquiladoras," *International Journal of Intercultural Relations*, 20 (2): 199–225.

Ralph Linton (1939), "One Hundred Per Cent American," *American Mercury*, 40:427–29.

Walter Lippmann (1922/1965), *Public Opinion*, New York, Harcourt Brace/New York, Free Press.

Scott London (January, 1996), "Global Villager: An Interview with Pico Iyer," *The Sun*, pp. 7–13.

John A. Lucy (1992), *Language Diversity and Thought: A Reformulation of the Linguistic Relativity Hypothesis*, New York, Cambridge University Press.

A. R. Luria (1968), *The Mind of a Mnemonist*, New York, Basic Books.

Myron W. Lustig and Jolene Koester (1996), *Intercultural Competence: Interpersonal Communication across Cultures*, New York, Harper Collins.

Hazel Rose Markus and Shinobu Kitayama (1991), "Culture and the Self: Implications for Cognition, Emotion, and Motivation," *Psychological Review*, 98(2): 224–53.

Judith N. Martin (1984), "The Intercultural Reentry: Conceptualization and Directions for Future Research," *International Journal of Intercultural Relations*, 8(2): 123–34.

Judith N. Martin (1986), "Communication in the Intercultural Reentry: Student Sojourners' Perceptions of Change in Reentry Relationship," *International Journal of Intercultural Relations*, 9(1): 14–21.

Judith N. Martin and Thomas K. Nakayama (1997), *Intercultural Communication in Contexts*, Mountain View, CA, Mayfield.

Don Martindale (1981), *The Nature and Types of Sociological Theory*, Prospect Heights, IL, Waveland Press.

Harriette Pipes McAdoo (1993), "Ethnic Families: Strengths that Are Found in Diversity," in Harriette Pipes McAdoo (ed.), *Family Ethnicity: Strength in Diversity*, Newbury Park, CA, Sage, pp. 3–14.

Sally McClain (1994), *Navajo Weapon*, Boulder, CO, Book Beyond Borders.

S. Dale McLemore (1970), "Simmel's 'Stranger': A Critique of the Concept," *Pacific Sociological Review*, 13:86–94.

Marshall McLuhan (1964), *Understanding Media: The Extensions of Man*, New York, McGraw-Hill.

George Herbert Mead (1934), *Mind, Self, and Society*, University of Chicago Press.

Mesia Report to Women (Spring, 1996), 24 (2): 8–10.

Albert Mehrabian and S. R. Ferris (1967), "Inference of Attitudes from Nonverbal Communication in Two Channels," *Journal of Counseling Psychology*, 31:248–52.

Albert Mehrabian and M. Wiener (1967), "Decoding Inconsistent Communications," *Journal of Personality and Social Psychology*, 6:109–14.

Robert K. Merton (1949), "Patterns of Influence: Local and Cosmopolitan Influentials," in Paul F. Lazarsfeld and Frank N. Stanton (eds.), *Communication Research, 1948–49*, New York, Duell, Sloan and Pearce, and New York, Harper; reprinted in Robert K. Merton (1968), *Social Theory and Social Structure*, New York, Free Press, pp. 441–24.

Robert K. Merton (1949/1957/1968), *Social Theory and Social Structure*, New York, Free Press.

David Humphreys Miller (1959), *Ghost Dance*. New York: Duell, Sloan and Pearce.

Desmond Morris, Peter Collett, Peter Marsh, and Marie O'Shaughnessy (1979), *Gestures*, New York, Stein and Day.

Madeleine Myers (ed.) (1994), *The Cherokee Nation: Life before Tears*, Lowell, MA, Discovery Enterprises.

Gunnar Myrdal (1944), *An American Dilemma: The Negro Problem and Democracy*, New York, Harper.

James W. Neuliep and James C. McCroskey (1998), *Ethnocentrism Trait Measurement: Intercultural Communication Research Instruments*. International and Intercultural Communication Conference, School of Communication, University of Miami.

Arthur Niehoff (1964), "Theravada Buddhism: A Vehicle for Technical Change," *Human Organization*, 23:108–12.

Kalervo Oberg (1960), "Cultural Shock: Adjustment to New Cultural Environments," *Practical Anthropology*, 7:177–82.

Suzanne Oboler (1995), *Ethnic Labels, Latino Lives: Identity and the Politics of (Re)Presentation in the United States*, Minneapolis, University of Minnesota Press.

John G. Oetzel and Keri Bolton-Oetzel (1997), "Exploring the Relationship between Self-Construal and Dimensions of Group Effectiveness," *Management Communication Quarterly*, 10 (3): 289–315.

Bolanle A. Olaniran and David E. Williams (1995), "Communication Distortion: An Intercultural Lesson from the Visa Application Process," *Communication Quarterly*, 43 (2): 225–40.

Mark P. Orbe (1997), *Constructing Co-Cultural Theory*, Newbury Park, CA, Sage.

Michael J. Papa, Mohammed A. Awal, and Arvind Singhal (1995), "Dialectic of Control and Emancipation in Organizing for Social Change: A Multi-Theoretic Study of the Grameen Bank," *Communication Theory*, 5 (3): 189–223.

Michael J. Papa, Mohammed A. Awal, and Arvind Singhal (1997), "Organizing for Social Change within Concertive Control Systems: Member Identification, Empowerment, and the Masking of Discipline," *Communication Monographs*, 64:1–31.

Michael J. Papa, Arvind Singhal, Sweety Law, Suruchi Sood, Everett M. Rogers, and Corinne L. Shefner-Rogers (1998), "Entertainment-Education and Social Change: An Analysis of Parasocial Interaction, Social Learning, and Paradoxical Communication," Paper presented at the International Communication Association, Jerusalem.

Robert E. Park (1922), *The Immigrant Press and Its Control*, New York, Harper.

Robert E. Park (1924), "The Concept of Social Distance," *Journal of Applied Sociology*, 8:339–44.

Robert E. Park (1928), "Human Migration and the Marginal Man," *American Journal of Sociology*, 33 (6): 881–93.

Robert E. Park (1950), *Race and Culture*, New York, Free Press.

Robert E. Park and Ernest W. Burgess (eds.) (1921), *Introduction to the Science of Sociology*, University of Chicago Press.

Sheila Parker, Mimi Nichter, Mark Nichter, Nancy Yuckovic, Collette Simms, and Cherly Rittenbergh (1995), "Body Image and Weight Concerns among African American and White Adolescent Females: Differences that Make a Difference," *Human Organization*, 54 (2): 103–14.

Doris A. Paul (1973), *The Navajo Code Talkers*, Bryn Mawr, PA, Dorrance.

Nathaniel Peffer (1970), *The Far East: A Modern History*, Ann Arbor, University of Michigan Press.

Mark Peffley and Jon Hurwitz (1993), "The Political Impact of Racial Stereotypes," Paper presented at the American Political Science Association, Washington, DC.

Arno Peters (1990), *Peters Atlas of the World*, New York, Harper and Row.

Spencer Phips (1745), *A Proclamation for Encouragement to Volunteers to Prosecute the War against the Indian Enemy*, Boston, John Draper, printer to His Excellency the Governour and Council.

Geoffrey K. Pullum (1991), *The Great Eskimo Vocabulary Hoax and Other Irreverent Essays on the Study of Language*, University of Chicago Press.

Kathleen K. Reardon (1982), "International Gift Giving: Why and How It Is Done," *Public Relations Journal*, 38 (6): 16–20.

Sherry Robinson (October, 1995), "Local Hero: Beyond Saddam: How Far Can Bill Richardson Go?" *Santa Fean*, 23 (9): 22–27.

América Rodriguez (1997), "Cultural Agendas: The Case of Latino-Oriented U.S. Media," in Maxwell McCombs, Donald L. Shaw, and David Weaver (eds.), *Communication and Democracy: Exploring the Intellectual Frontiers in Agenda-Setting Theory*, Mahwah, NJ, Lawrence Erlbaum Associates, pp. 183–94.

Everett M. Rogers (ed.) (1976), *Communication and Development: Critical Perspectives*, Newbury Park, CA, Sage.

Everett M. Rogers (1994), *A History of Communication Study: A Biographical Approach*, New York, Free Press.

Everett M, Rogers (1995), *Diffusion of Innovations*, Fourth Edition, New York, Free Press.

Everett M. Rogers and Marcel M. Allbritton (1997), "The Public Electronic Network: Interactive Communication and Interpersonal Distance," in Beverly Davenport Sypher (ed.), *Contemporary Case Studies in Organizational Communication*, New York, Guilford.

Everett M. Rogers, Shaheed N. Mohammed, Heidi A. Carr, Aya Matsushima, Karyn L. Scott, and Kathyrn Sorrells (1998), *Communication Workbook*, Dubuque, IA, Kendall/Hunt.

Everett M. Rogers, James W. Dearing, Nagesh Rao, Michelle L. Campo, Gary Meyer, Gary J. T. Betts, and Mary K. Casey (1995), "Communication and Community in a City under Siege: The AIDS Epidemic in San Francisco," *Communication Research*, 22 (6): 664–78.

Everett M. Rogers and William B. Hart II (1998), "Edward T. Hall and the Origins of Intercultural Communication," Paper presented at the National Communication Association, New York.

Everett M. Rogers, Lori Jarvis-Collins, and Joseph Schmitz (1994), "The PEN Project in Santa Monica: Interactive Communication and Political Action," *Journal of the American Society for Information Science*, 45 (6): 1–10.

Everett M. Rogers and Rekha Agarwala-Rogers (1976), *Communication in Organizations*, New York, Free Press.

Everett M. Rogers and Dilip Bhowmik (1970), "Homophily-Heterophily: Relational Concepts for Communication Research," *Public Opinion Quarterly*, 34 (4): 523–38.

Milton Rokeach (1960), *The Open and Closed Mind*, New York, Basic Books.

Milton Rokeach (1968), *Beliefs, Attitudes, and Values: A Theory of Organization and Change*, San Francisco, Jossey-Bass.

Morris Rosenberg (1979), *Conceiving the Self*, New York, Basic Books.

Clifford E. Rucker III and Thomas F. Cash (1992), "Body Images, Body-Size Perceptions, and Eating Behaviors among African-American and White College Women," *International Journal of Eating Disorders*, 12 (3): 291–99.

Bryce Ryan and Neal C. Gross (1943), "Diffusion of Hybrid Seed Corn in Two Iowa Communities," *Rural Sociology*, 8:15–24.

Mark K. Salzman (1986), *Iron and Silk*, New York, Vintage.

Larry A. Samovar and Jack Mills (1998), *Oral Communication: Speaking Across Cultures*, New York, McGraw-Hill.

Larry A. Samovar and Richard E. Porter (1972/1994), *Intercultural Communication: A Reader*, Belmont, CA, Wadsworth.

Edward Sapir (1935), "Communication," in *Encyclopedia of the Social Sciences*, Volume IV, New York, Macmillian, pp. 7–8.

Wilbur Schramm (1963), *Mass Media and National Development*, Stanford, Stanford University Press.

Joseph Schmitz, Everett M. Rogers, Ken Phillips, and Donald Paschal (1995), "The Public Electronic Network (PEN) and the Homeless in Santa Monica," *Journal of Applied Communication Research*, 23:26–43.

H. Ned Seelye and Alan Seelye-James (1995), *Culture Clash: Managing in a Multicultural World*, Lincolnwood, IL, NTC.

Corinne L. Shefner-Rogers, Nagesh Rao, Everett M. Rogers, and Arun Wayangankar (1998), "The Empowerment of Women Dairy Farmers in India," *Journal of Applied Communication Research* 26(3).

Nancy Shoemaker (1997), "How Indians Got to be Red," *American Historical Review*, 102(3): 625–44.

Lee Sigelman and Steven A. Tuch (1997), "Metastereotypes: Blacks' Perceptions of Whites' Stereotypes of Blacks," *Public Opinion Quarterly*, 61:87–101.

Georg Simmel (1900/1978), *The Philosophy of Money*, Translated by David P. Frisby and Thomas Bottomore, London, Routledge; originally published in German as *Philosophie des Geldes*, Leipzig, Duncker und Humblot.

Georg Simmel (1908), *Soziologie: Untersuchungen über die Formen der Vergesellschaftung* (Sociology: Studies in the Forms of Societalization), Leipzig, Duncker and Humblot.

Georg Simmel (1921), "The Social Significance of the 'Stranger'," in Robert E. Park and Ernest W. Burgess (eds.), *Introduction to the Science of Sociology*, University of Chicago Press, pp. 322–27.

Georg Simmel (1922/1955), *The Web of Group-Affiliations*, Translated by Reinhard Bendix, New York, Free Press.

Georg Simmel (1950), *The Sociology of Georg Simmel*, Translated by Kurt H. Wolff, New York, Free Press.

Arvind Singhal and Everett M. Rogers (in press), *Entertainment-Education*, Mahwah, NJ, Lawrence Erlbaum Associates.

Arvind Singhal and Kant Udornpim (1997), "Cultural Shareability, Archetypes and Television Soaps: 'Oshindrome' in Thailand," *Gazette*, 59 (3): 171–88.

Theodore M. Singelis and William J. Brown (1995), "Culture, Self, and Collectivistic Communication: Linking Culture to Individual Behavior," *Human Communication Review*, 21:354–89.

Paul C. P. Siu (1952), "The Sojourners," *American Journal of Sociology*, 58 (1): 34–44.

Alfred Smith (1960), *Communication and Culture*, New York, Holt, Rinehart, and Winston.

Tom W. Smith (1990), *Ethnic Images*, Chicago, National Opinion Research Center, GSS Topical Report 10.

Kathyrn Sorrells (1997), "Who Is the Stranger? Implications for Intercultural Communication," Paper presented at the National Communication Association, Chicago.

Gonzalo Soruco (1996), *Cubans in the Mass Media in South Florida*, Gainesville, University Press of Florida.

Nicholas J. Spykman (1925/1966), *The Social Theory of Georg Simmel*, New York, Russell/Atherton Press; University of Chicago Press.

Thomas M. Steinfatt (1988a), "Language and Intercultural Differences: Linguistic Relativity," Paper presented at the Speech Communication Association, New Orleans.

Thomas M. Steinfatt (1988b), "Levels of Meaning as a Model of Communication," paper presented to the International and Intercultural Communication Conference, University of Miami, Coral Gables.

Thomas M. Steinfatt (1989), "Linguistic Relativity: Toward a Broader View," in Stella Ting-Toomey and Felipe Korzenny (eds.), *International and Intercultural Communication Annual: Language, Communication, and Culture: Current Directions*, 13:35–75.

Thomas M. Steinfatt (1994), "Perceptions of Spanish and English Speakers of Code-Switching in Miami." Paper presented at the International and Intercultural Communication Conference, School of Communication, University of Miami.

Thomas M. Steinfatt and Diane M. Christophel (1996), "Intercultural Communication," in Michael B. Salwen and Don W. Stacks (eds.), *An Integrated Approach to Communication Theory and Research*, Mahwah, NJ, Lawrence Earlbaum Associates, pp. 317–34.

Robert L. Stevenson (1994), *Global Communication in the Twenty-First Century*, New York, Longman.

Everett V. Stonequist (1935), "The Problem of the Marginal Man," *American Journal of Sociology*, 51(1): 1–12.

Everett V. Stonequist (1937), *The Marginal Man: A Study in Personality and Culture Conflict*, New York, Charles Scribner's Sons.

Craig Storti (1994), *Cross-Cultural Dialogues*, New York, Oxford University Press.

Craig Storti (1997), *The Art of Coming Home*, Yarmouth, ME, Intercultural Press.

William Graham Sumner (1906/1940), *Folkways*, Boston, Ginn.

Ronald Takaki (1993), *A Different Mirror: A History of Multicultural America*, Boston, Little, Brown.

Gabriel Tarde (1903), *The Laws of Imitation*, Translated by Elsie Clews Parsons, New York, Holt.

Hugh Thomas (1993), *Conquest: Montezuma, Cortés, and the Fall of Old Mexico*, New York, Touchstone.

Hugh Thomas (1997), *The Slave Trade: The Story of the Atlantic Slave Trade, 1440–1870*, New York, Simon and Schuster.

William I. Thomas and Florian Znaniecki (1927/1984), *The Polish Peasant in Europe and America*, New York, Knopf; Urbana, University of Illinois Press.

James D. Thompson (1967), *Organizations in Action*, New York, McGraw-Hill.

Ferdinand Toennies (1940), *Fundamental Concepts of Sociology*, New York, American Book Company.

Alvin Toffler (1970), *Future Shock*, New York, Bantam Books.

Amy S. Tolbert and Gary N. McLean (1995), "Venezuelan Culture Assimilator for Training United States Professionals Conducting Business in Venezuela," *International Journal of Intercultural Communication*, 19 (1): 111–25.

Harry C. Triandis (1986), "Collectivism vs. Individualism: A Reconceptualization of a Basic Concept in Cross-Cultural Psychology," in C. Bagley and G. Verma (eds.), *Personality, Cognition, and Values*, New York, Macmillan, pp. 57–89.

Harry C. Triandis (1990), "Cross-Cultural Studies of Individualism and Collectivism," in J. Berry, J. Dragums, and M. Cole (eds.), *Cross-Cultural Perspectives*, Lincoln, University of Nebraska.

Harry C. Triandis (1994), *Culture and Social Behavior*, New York, McGraw-Hill.

Harry C. Triandis (1995), *Individualism and Collectivism: New Directions in Social Psychology*, Boulder, CO, Westview Press.

Stewart L. Tubbs and Sylvia Moss (1994), *Human Communication*, Seventh Edition, New York, McGraw-Hill.

John Useem, Ruth Useem, and John Donoghue (1963), "Men in the Middle of the Third Culture: The Roles of American and Non-Western People in Cross-Cultural Administration," *Human Organization*, 22:169–79.

Neil Vidmar and Milton Rokeach (1974), "Archie Bunker's Bigotry: A Study in Selective Perception and Exposure," *Journal of Communication*, 24 (1): 36–47.

Heinrich Vedder (1932), *South West Africa in Early Times*, London, Cass.

James Diego Vigil (1998), *From Indians to Chicanos*, Prospect Heights, IL, Waveland Press.

L. S. Vytgosky (1962), *Thought and Language*, Cambridge, MA, MIT Press.

Amanda Vogt (1998), "Courage Like a Wild Horse," *Chicago Tribune*, February 24, Section 5, p. 4.

Paul Watzlawick, Janet Beavin, and Donald Jackson (1967), *The Pragmatics of Human Communication*, New York, Norton.

Bruce Watson (August, 1993), *"Jaysho, Moasi, Dibeh, Ayeshi, Hasclishnih, Beshlo, Shush, Gini,"* *Smithsonian*, pp. 34–43.

Edward Wellin (1955), "Water Boiling in a Peruvian Town," in Benjamin D. Paul (ed.), *Health, Culture and Community*, New York, Russell Sage Foundation.

Robert Whiting (1989), *You Gotta Have Wa*, New York, Collier Macmillan.

Benjamin Lee Whorf (1940), "Science and Linguistics," *Technology Review*, 42 (6): 229–31, 247–48.

Benjamin Lee Whorf (1940/1956), *Language, Thought, and Reality: Selected Writings of Benjamin Lee Whorf*, Edited by John B. Carroll, Cambridge, MA, MIT Press.

D. Lawrence Wieder and Steven Pratt (1990), "On Being a Recognizable Indian among Indians," in Donal Carbaugh (ed.), *Cultural Communication and Intercultural Contact*, Hillsdale, NJ, Lawrence Erlbaum Associates, pp. 45–64.

Gregory Howard Williams (1995), *Life on the Color Line: The True Story of a White Boy Who Discovered He Was Black*, New York, Penguin/Plume.

Jeanne Williams (1992), *Trails of Tears: American Indians Driven from Their Lands*, Dallas, TX, Hendrick-Long.

Clint C. Wilson II and Félix Gutiérrez (1995), *Race, Multiculturalism, and the Media: From Mass to Class Communication*, Second Edition, Newbury Park, CA, Sage.

Kurt H. Wolff (1950), "Introduction," in Georg Simmel, *The Sociology of Georg Simmel*, New York, Free Press.

Denis Wood (1992), *The Power of Maps*, New York, Guilford.

Author Index

Subject Index

Acción, 251
acculturation, 190, 219
active listening, 158
affect displays, 175–176, 185, 188
African Americans, 151–152, 196, 198, 199,
    204, 209, 230–233
AIDS prevention, 99–100
ambiguity, 129, 154
American dilemma, 231
anthropology, 62–69
appearance, 185
Archie Bunker effect, 147–148
artifacts, 184–185
Asian Americans, 155, 196, 198, 199, 204
assimilation, 189–211, 219
    continuum to cultural maintenance,
        191–194
    definition, 190
attitude, 56, 81, 84–85,
attribution, 131–134
authoritarian personality, 58–59

beliefs, 81–82, 111
body weight, 145–147

change agent, 244
    heterophily with clients, 246–248
channel, 115, 133
Chicago School, 39–40, 48, 148
Chicanos, 192–193, 196, 201, 209
Christianity, 28–29, 197

chronemics, 170, 181–182, 185
Civil Rights, 199, 232–233, 235
clitorectomy, 98
co-culture, 80, 209
code, 114, 117, 133, 228
code-switching, 148–149, 158
code-talkers, 117–120
collective cultural consciousness, 3–4
collectivistic culture, 86–90, 111, 155, 259–260
Columbus, 31–32
colonialism, 21–23
color of words, 209
communication, 133–134, 155
    definition, 113
    interpersonal, 125–133, 135
    intrapersonal, 125–133, 135
    model of, 114–116
    nonverbal, 67–68, 107, 161–188
    participants in, 116
    verbal, 135–159
conflict, overcoming, 237–238
consciousness-raising, 250–251
contact theory of prejudice, 58, 223
content, and communication relationships,
    153–154
continuum of intercultural differences,
    105–107, 111
Cortés, 22
cosmopoliteness, 46–47, 76, 77,
credibility, 46

289